Technical English 2

English

Teacher's Book

Celia Bingham

With additional material by David Bonamy

Pearson Education Limited

Edinburgh Gate
Harlow
Essex CM20 2JE
England

and Associated Companies throughout the world.

www.pearsonELT.com

First published 2008
Fifth impression 2013

ISBN: 978-14058-4559-5 (book)

ISBN: 978-14058-8145-6 (book for pack)

Set in Adobe Type Library fonts

Printed in Malaysia (CTP-PJB)

Acknowledgements

We would like to dedicate this book to the memory of David Riley, whose tireless professionalism contributed so much to its creation and success.

The author would like to thank Ben Greshon (Senior Editor) and Carol Osbourne (Editor).

The publishers and author would like to thank the following for their invaluable feedback, comments and suggestions, all of which played an important part in the development of the course: Eleanor Kenny (College of the North Atlantic, Qatar), Julian Collinson, Daniel Zeytoun Millie and Terry Sutcliffe (all from the Higher Colleges of Technology, UAE), Dr Saleh Al-Busaidi (Sultan Qaboos University, Oman), Francis McNeice, (IFOROP, France), Michaela Müller (Germany), Małgorzata Ossowska-Neumann (Gdynia Maritime University, Poland), Gordon Kite (British Council, Italy), Wolfgang Ridder (VHS der Stadt Bielefeld, Germany), Stella Jehanno (Centre d'Etude des Langues/ Centre de Formation Supérieure d'Apprentis, Chambre de Commerce et d'Industrie de l'Indre, France) and Nick Jones (Germany).

Illustrated by Mark Duffin, Peter Harper and HL Studios

Cover image: *Front*: iStock Photo: Kristian Stensoenes

All other images © Pearson Education

Every effort has been made to trace the copyright holders and we apologise in advance for any unintentional omissions. We would be pleased to insert the appropriate acknowledgement in any subsequent edition of this publication.

Designed by HL Studios, Long Hanborough

Cover design by Designers Collective

Project managed by David Riley

Contents

Introduction

Technical English is a two-level course for students in technical or vocational education, and for company employees in training at work. It covers the core language and skills that students need to communicate successfully in all technical and industrial specialisations. *Level 1* is for students with a basic knowledge of general English who require an elementary course in English for specific purposes. This is benchmarked against CEF level A1. *Level 2* is for students who have completed Level 1, or have an elementary knowledge of general English, and now require a pre-intermediate course in English for specific purposes. This is benchmarked against CEF level A2.

The course uses a multi-thread syllabus consisting mainly of communicative functions, notions, grammar, vocabulary and skills. The work-specific communicative functions (eg *giving instructions, making recommendations*) and technology-specific notions or concepts (eg *causation, resistance*) are selected on the basis of relevance to the needs of students in technical training and work contexts. Exponents of functions and notions are selected on the basis of frequency and relevance to needs. In Level 1 the grammar is sequenced; in Level 2 a more cyclical approach is taken, in which functions and notions re-appear with more complex grammatical exponents.

The vocabulary of the course is a selection of common-core lexical items that have a high frequency of use across a range of technical and industrial contexts. Many of these items can be found in general contexts, but have a greater frequency and often a more specific meaning in technical contexts. Many of them are the kind of words which a specialist in one field might use to explain technical concepts and specialised terms to the general public, or to specialists in other fields. (There are supplementary materials for students who need exposure to a more specialist industry-specific vocabulary: see *Additional Support* at the end of this introduction).

The methodology is transparent and straightforward, with a practical task-based approach. Activities are firmly rooted in shared meanings and clear contexts. The approach recognises that the students may have differing motivations towards learning English, but assumes that they have a knowledge of, and interest in, technology and wish to develop their careers and technical skills. The topics and texts reflect current and future developments in technology, and are designed to stimulate students' interest and motivation to find out more about them. From the beginning of the course, students are encouraged to use their technical knowledge and problem-solving skills.

Course Book 2

The Course Book contains twelve core units and six review units. Each core unit is divided into three sections. Each section (corresponding approximately to a 60 – 90 minute lesson) is contained on two facing pages, unified by a single theme, which may be a function, a concept or a topic. There is a four-page review unit after every two core units.

Core units

Start here

This is a warm-up activity which begins each double-page section. It is often a question (such as *How do you think this works?*) based on a photograph or diagram, which pairs or groups discuss before they begin a reading or listening activity. The warmer is intended to activate students' existing knowledge about the topic of the unit and stimulate their interest in finding out more.

Listening

Listening skills are developed through a variety of activities using audio texts set in both work and training contexts. The listening activity requires students to carry out a practical task during or after listening, such as completing a specification chart, filling in a form, or labelling a spidergram. Audio texts set in work contexts include instructions, IT hotlines, customer service, brainstorming sessions, travel directions, phone calls, interviews and announcements. Audio texts set in a training context include extended passages in monologue form such as lectures, presentations and technical demonstrations. Students are guided towards extracting key information and listening for discourse markers which structure the talk. Typical tasks here are to complete the notes on a talk, or arrange notes into the correct order.

Speaking

Speaking is an important skill, whether the user is talking to colleagues at work, dealing effectively with customers seeking advice or technical support, or in interactive training contexts such as tutorials or technical demonstrations. Speaking tasks in Course Book 2 reflect real-world situations, such as reporting to a client, giving instructions, checking and reporting on progress, reporting damaged goods, checking information, comparing products, giving technical support, making recommendations, giving warnings, and giving directions. At this level, students are guided towards preparing and giving short talks and presentations based on notes and diagrams. They describe and compare products, explain how devices and systems work and report back on the decisions made by their groups. Speaking activities are conducted in pairs, small groups or individually to the class. In addition, there are speaking activities in the *Task* section (see below).

Reading

Reading is a key skill needed by technologists both in the training context and at work. The texts they have to process in real life can vary enormously in length, complexity and genre. Readers' purposes vary from in-depth understanding to following instructions or searching for statistics. The reading texts in Course Book 2 reflect real-life texts and purposes, and are all based on authentic sources. These sources include websites, FAQs, manuals, technical magazine articles, CVs, textbooks, troubleshooting guides, customer service guides, e-mails, catalogues, adverts, user guides, posters, textbooks, reports and specification charts. Labelled diagrams and photographs are liberally provided to aid comprehension of technical data, and students are always given some background information or asked to think about a topic (often in the *Start here* activity) before they start reading, so that they are using the texts actively. For example they may be asked to look at a diagram of a device and discuss how it might work using their own knowledge *before* reading about how the device works. The texts use carefully controlled language and are accompanied by simple and practical tasks such as checking information, labelling a diagram, correcting details or completing a specification chart. Activities which develop an awareness of cohesive devices and discourse markers are developed at this level.

Scanning

Course Book 2 develops the skill of scanning at speed for information. In several units there is a scanning activity which consists of questions asking for short, factual information. Students find this information in a timed activity by scanning quickly through a number of texts on the *Speed Search* pages (see below) at the back of the book. In these activities it is important to set the questions and start the timer (for example the stopwatch function of a mobile phone) *before* the students open the book at the Speed Search pages.

Writing

Writing skills are developed through a variety of tasks in realistic contexts, reflecting the range of text types which students might have to produce in a work context or as part of their technical training. Writing activities in a work context include short reports, product comparison, instructions and procedures and e-mails to colleagues and customers. Activities in a training or educational context include describing devices and explaining how systems work. Some peer-correction of written work is encouraged at this level, as well as collaborative group work leading to individual writing. Where such writing tasks are set as homework, it is important to allow time in class for the group work to be completed. Some writing activities encourage personalisation, for example where students write a set of safety rules for their own workplace or college.

Task

The *Task* feature provides students with opportunities to combine and use their language, skills and technical knowledge to communicate in contexts that reflect real-life work or training situations. Tasks require different combinations of skill, knowledge and procedure. Some are in fact problem-solving or cognitive exercises designed to activate their background knowledge to help them in a reading, writing, listening or speaking activity. Others (normally coming at the end of a section) combine one or more skills, for example completing a flow chart about a process they know about, and then explaining it to the class. Some tasks can be done individually, but most are done using pair work, group discussion, brainstorming and collaborative problem-solving leading to a joint output, for instance when groups have a meeting to decide on the best 4x4 car to buy for their oil rig, and then write their joint conclusions and recommendations. Such tasks also involve some jigsaw reading, where group members study different data in the *Extra material* section (see below) and then meet to exchange ideas.

Language

The language box draws students' attention to the key grammar of a lesson. The grammar is presented in a simple, straightforward manner and gives only the basic minimum of information necessary. The box is intended for reference or study only, and normally follows a reading or listening activity in which the student has understood the grammar point in context. Where necessary, the language box is accompanied by a short language practice exercise. If students need more information about grammar, or for revision, they can refer to the *Language summary* at the back of the course book.

Vocabulary

Vocabulary activities develop students' knowledge and use of common-core technical or sub-technical vocabulary. Many activities use visuals to clarify the meanings of core technical terms such as *rotary*. Others deal with lexical sets (eg shapes and physical properties) and word families and affixes (eg *compress, compress, compressor*). Some pronunciation work on syllable stress (eg _engine, engin_eer) is covered here. Students are made aware of words used across several specialisms and everyday words that take on special meanings in technical contexts. Everyday words are presented alongside their more technical Graeco-Latin synonyms (eg *send/ transmit, take out/ extract*). Generic terms such as device, instrument and system are introduced at this level.

Reference

Grammar summary

This gives more information about all the language points dealt with in the core units. It can be used as a reference during a lesson, or for revision.

Reference section

This section at the back of the book includes useful reference material for the student, for example units of measurement and their abbreviations, how to say mathematical symbols and operations, how to say internet symbols, fractions and British and American English.

Extra material

This contains the materials needed by one side of a pair of students, or members of a group, to enable them to carry out the communication activities in the Task sections.

Audio script

This is a complete transcript of all the listening material in the Course Book. This can be used in different ways according to the levels and needs of your students. Students can use it to check their answers after they have completed a listening task.

Speed search

This is a double-page spread which contains a number of reading texts of different styles, topics and formats. The texts do not show any reference to the pages or units they are related to. Students are given a short time to scan quickly through the two pages to find the specified information. (See *Scanning* above)

Review units

Each Review Unit revises and practices material from the preceding two core units. In addition it contains a *Project* section, which gives the students opportunities to do some simple further research into topics linked to the topics of the core units. They are encouraged to use the internet or a library to carry out the research and present the results to the class either individually or as group tasks.

Teacher's Book 2

Unit summary

Each core unit in the Teacher's Book has a summary of the language, vocabulary and activities to be found in the core units of the Course Book.

Briefing

Each core unit in the Teacher's Book has a briefing which gives background information about the technical topics in the core units, and highlights any features of the language which need special attention in the unit. It also lists some Web sites which give more in-depth information about the topics.

Teaching notes

Each double facing page in the teaching notes corresponds to a double facing page section in the Course Book. Each main unit of the Teacher's Book contains procedural notes for each activity in the Course Book, ideas for extra activities if appropriate, answer keys and audio scripts. Every review unit contains answer keys for the review units in the Course Book plus a photocopiable *Quick Test* of the preceding two main units, to test lexis, grammar, functions, reading and writing.

Word list

This is at the end of the Teacher's Book. It contains all the key words used in the Course Book. It is sorted into alphabetical order with references to the unit where each word appears.

TestMaster CD-ROM

This contains entry and exit tests, progress tests and individual unit tests which can be downloaded and edited as required. Test can be customised for specific purposes and institutions. The TestMaster CD-ROM is enclosed with the Workbook.

Additional support

Course Book CD This contains all the recordings for the listening exercises in the Course Book.

Workbook with Audio CD This provides additional material based on the Course Book, which can be set as class revision or homework. It also contains a unit-by-unit word list.

Companion Website The Companion Website contains supplementary teaching activities and industry-specific material to support the Course Book and the Workbook.

David Bonamy

1 Action

Contents

Briefing

This unit looks at instructions, progress reports and methods of doing things.

Section 1 deals with the actions of teams of mechanics in a **pit-stop**, when a racing driver brings the car temporarily out of the race into the **pit-stop lane** to have it serviced. Usually all four wheels are taken off and replaced with new ones, and the tank is refilled with fuel. The whole operation takes about ten seconds so that no time is lost in the race. Each task is carried out by its own **team** or **crew**. Four teams of mechanics work on the wheels, and one team works on the fuel. As soon as the car stops, the *wheel-gun team* of four mechanics run forward and loosen the **wheel nuts** using **wheel guns** (electrically-powered wrenches). The *wheel-jack* teams raise and lower the car. The *wheel-off* and *wheel-on* teams run forwards and backwards quickly, taking the old wheels off and replacing them with new wheels. The new tyres are already at the correct **air pressure**, and are kept warm with electric blankets so that the pressure will not change when the tyres are moving. While this is going on, the fuel team continue pumping the fuel in.

Section 2 continues the topic of car servicing. To **strip off** old paint is to scrape it off with a sharp instrument. To *take* something *apart* is to *dismantle* (or *disassemble*) it: the opposite is to *put* it *together* again (that is, to *assemble* or *reassemble* it). The Task features three car service jobs. In *changing a wheel*, wheel nuts should be loosened a little before the car is raised on the jack. To *check the oil level* in a car engine, you first pull out the **dipstick** to see if the level is right. If the oil level is low, you take off the **oil filler cap** and pour in some oil. Then you check the dipstick again to check the level again. To *clean a spark plug*, you take off the cover then unscrew the spark plug using a **spark plug wrench**. You measure the **gap** in the spark plug, and if it is too small because it is caked in carbon, you clean it with a wire brush. Then you screw the plug back in the socket and put the cover back on.

Section 3 begins by looking at ways of **activating** or starting a device. Many ticket machines are activated by touching the **screen**. The **outboard motor** of a motor boat is started by pulling a **cord** or cable, which turns the engine. Some motorbikes can be started by pushing a **kick-start lever** sharply downwards. The burglar activates a **burglar alarm** by breaking the **laser beam** and opening an electrical circuit. The robotic cyclist in the reading text stays upright on its bicycle by means of **sensors** which **detect** changes in the robot's position and its surroundings. A **gyro sensor** prevents it from falling: its rotating axis (like a child's spinning top) automatically stays vertical, and can detect when the robot moves away from the vertical. The computer (away from the robot) transmits the correct route wirelessly to the robot and adjusts the direction of the bicycle if it moves away from this route.

Pit-stop servicing: http://comunidades.msn.es/McLaren/yourwebpage5.msnw

Car servicing jobs: http://www.motester.co.uk/cog.html

Car parts and servicing: http://www.rac.co.uk/web/knowhow/

The cycling robot: http://www.murataboy.com/en/about/mtc.html

Teacher's notes

1 | Teamwork

Start here

1 Introduce the lesson by focussing students' attention on the photo. Ask students if they have ever been to a motor racing event or if they watch Formula One Grand Prix races on the television, and to tell the class why they are interested in these races and who their favourite drivers are. Then ask students to tell you what is happening in the photo and pre-teach some vocabulary that they will be using in this lesson (*pit stop*, *pit-stop crew*, *mechanics*, *tyres*, *air pressure*, *fuel*, *fuel hose*, *nozzle*, *jack*, etc.).

Ask students to answer the questions in pairs. Get feedback from the class but don't confirm answers at this stage as they will be checking them in the next exercise. Finally, ask them how long it normally takes a pit-stop crew to replace the tyres and refuel a car in a Formula One race.

Reading

2 Tell students that they're going to read an interview with the head of a pit-stop crew. Ask students what the time strip which runs down the left-hand side of the text shows. (It shows the time it takes for the pit-stop crew to replace the tyres and refuel the car in the pit stop). Then ask students to read the interview and underline all the jobs that the mechanics do.

When they've finished, elicit the names of the different crews and write them on the board (*the wheel-gun team*, *the wheel-jack team*, *the fuel team*, *the wheel-off team* and *the wheel-on team*). Then ask students to write the jobs they underlined in the text under these categories. They can compare their answers with a partner before you check the answers with the class.

The text includes a number of phrasal verbs, for example, *take away*, *take off*, etc. Don't focus on this yet as they will be studying this in the next lesson.

c) about 20
Important jobs:

Chief Mechanic/Crew Leader gives orders to the pit stop crew and signals to the driver what to do.

The wheel-on team bring out the new wheels, adjust the air pressure in the tyres, put new wheels on the car and clean the driver's visor.

The wheel-gun team loosen and tighten the nuts on the wheel with their wheel gun.

The wheel-jack team place the jacks under the car, raise the car off the ground. They also lower the car to the ground and take the jacks away.

The fuel team carry the fuel nozzle and hose to the car, push the nozzle into the fuel socket and switch on the fuel pump. They hold the nozzle in place until all the fuel is in the car, and clean spilled fuel off the car.

The wheel-off mechanics take the old wheels off the car and take them away.

3 Ask students to look at the picture of the racing car. Tell them to work on their own and label the parts with the words in the box. They can then check their answers with a partner before you check with the class.

> **1** wheel gun
> **2** jack
> **3** hose
> **4** nozzle
> **5** flap
> **6** socket

4 This exercise revises the imperative form. Tell students to imagine that they're a member of a pit-stop crew. Focus their attention on the checklist and read out the second and third instruction for Team 1: *Raise the car off the ground* and *WAIT*. Remind students that you use the imperative structure for instructions and point out that imperatives use the infinitive without *to*.

Tell students to complete the instructions in the checklist and to refer back to the interview to help them. They could do this activity in pairs. Then check the answers in class by asking five different students to read out the instructions for each team.

> TEAM 1: WHEEL-JACK
> **1** Place the jacks under the front and rear of the car.
> **4** Lower the car to the ground.
> **5** Take the jacks away.
> TEAM 2: WHEEL-GUN
> **4** Raise a hand to signal that everything is OK.
> TEAM 3: WHEEL-OFF
> **2** Take the wheels away.
> TEAM 4: WHEEL-ON
> **2** Adjust the air pressure in the tyres.
> **4** Take the covers off the new wheels.
> **5** Put the new wheels on the car.
> TEAM 5: FUEL
> **1** Push the nozzle into the fuel socket on the car.
> **2** Pump the fuel into the car.
> **3** Pull out the fuel nozzle.
> **4** Clean spilled fuel off the car.

Extra activity

To finish off this lesson, ask students to work in pairs. Tell them to write five instructions for their partner to follow. They can either be classroom instructions, e.g. *Open your book on page 5. Look at the picture*, etc., or instructions for a stretching exercise, e.g. *Stand up. Raise your left hand*, etc. Students then give their partner the instructions for them to follow.

---

2 Training

Start here

1 ▶ 💿 02

This lesson continues the theme of working for a pit-stop crew. Ask students to imagine that they're a new member of the pit-stop crew and that a trainer is giving them instructions on how to do their job. Focus their attention on the list of instructions in the table. Tell students that the instructions are in the wrong order and to list them in the correct order from 1 (the first instruction) to 10 (the last instruction). They could do this in pairs.

Play the recording for students to check their answers. Allow students to compare their answers. Then go through the correct answers with the class.

Tighten the wheel nuts.	8	Adjust the air pressure in the tyre.	2
Raise the car with the jack.	5	Bring the new wheel out.	1
Loosen the wheel nuts.	3	Put the new wheel on.	7
Take the old wheel off.	6	Put the jack under the car.	4
Take the old wheel away.	10	Lower the car and take the jack away.	9

▶ 💿 02

A: OK, the first thing you gotta do is bring the new wheel right up to the car. OK?

B: Yeah. I'll get it now.

A: Good. Now, the air pressure in the tyre is probably wrong, so you need to adjust it. OK? Check the pressure, then either let some air out or pump some more air in.

B: Got it. Right, I've done it.

A: Good. Now before you start lifting up the car, you must loosen the wheel nuts a bit, so get your wheel gun and loosen the nuts. … Done that?

B: Yeah, done it.

A: Right, now you're going to use the jack, so first of all put the jack under the front of the car. OK?

B: Yeah.

A: And then raise the front of the car carefully. Have you done that?

B: Yeah.

A: Right, so now take the wheel off and put it down next to you on the ground.

B: Yeah. I've done that.

A: Good. Now get the new wheel, pick it up and put it on the car. Have you done that?

B: Yes.

A: Right. Now pick up your wheel gun again and tighten up the wheel nuts. …

B: Aha. That's done.

A: Good. Now lower the car … and take the jack away.

B: Done it.

A: And of course finish off by taking the old wheel away. Just roll it away and put it over there.

B: OK.

Vocabulary

2 Ask students to look at the pictures of the actions. Students match the pictures with the phrasal verbs in the box. They can then compare their answers with a partner before you check with the class.

Language

Present continuous and present perfect

Go through the Language box with the students. Students won't have difficulty with the meaning of the phrasal verbs in 2. However, they will need practice with the word order. Point out that these phrasal verbs are made up of two parts: a verb (e.g. *take*) and adverb (e.g. *off*). Tell them that all the phrasal verbs in this lesson are 'separable', i.e. the object can separate the verb and the adverb (**take the tyres off**). The object can also come after the adverb (**take off the tyres**). However, when the object is a pronoun (*them*), it must always come between the verb and the adverb (**take them off** not ~~take off them~~).

Tell students that they'll find more information about phrasal verbs in the Grammar summary on page 104, and more information showing all forms of the present continuous and the present perfect in the Grammar summary on page 100.

1 put down	**5** take away
2 pick up	**6** push in
3 take off	**7** lift up
4 put on	**8** pull out

3 ▶ 💿 03

In this exercise, students revise the present continuous and present perfect. Tell them that they're going to listen to a trainer giving instructions to a new member of the pit-stop crew. Go through the example first and make sure students know what to do. Say the instruction: *Bring out the new tyres*, and make sure they respond with: *Right. I'm bringing them out now. OK, I've brought them out.*

Play the recording. Pause after each instruction for students to confirm it. You could then play the recording again, pausing it for individual students to confirm each of the instructions.

▶ 💿 03

1 Bring out the new tyres.
2 Lift up the front of the car.
3 Take off the two wheels.
4 Put on the new wheels.
5 Take away the old wheels.
6 Pump in the petrol.
7 Switch off all the electrical systems.
8 Turn on the emergency power source.

Speaking

4 Focus students' attention on the checklist. Explain that each of the sections 1–6 are different jobs the trainee mechanics have to do and that there are three instructions for each job. The trainee has to say which ones he/she has done, is still doing and hasn't done yet. Read through the example with the class, taking the part of the supervisor and asking a confident student to take the part of the trainee.

Put students into pairs to continue the exercise. Tell students that they'll find a list of irregular past participles in the verb list on page 105 to help them. Go round monitoring the class, taking note of any difficulties they may have with the tenses, which you can deal with in a feedback session.

1

Supervisor:	*How are you getting on?*
Trainee:	I've put the new tyres on. I'm still tightening the wheel nuts. It's almost done.
Supervisor:	*OK, good. Have you adjusted the air pressure yet?*
Trainee:	No, I haven't done that yet. I'll do it next.

2

Supervisor:	*How are you getting on?*
Trainee:	I've taken the cover off. I'm still repairing the computer. It's almost done.
Supervisor:	*OK, good. Have you taken out the damaged chip yet?*
Trainee:	No, I haven't done that yet. I'll do it next.

3

Supervisor:	*How are you getting on?*
Trainee:	I've replaced the burnt wire. I'm switching on the power. It's almost done.
Supervisor:	*OK, good. Have you checked the other wires yet?*
Trainee:	No, I haven't done that yet. I'll do it next.

4

Supervisor:	*How are you getting on?*
Trainee:	I've switched off the electricity. I'm still testing all the circuits. It's almost done.
Supervisor:	*OK, good. Have you found any faults yet?*
Trainee:	No, I haven't yet.

5

Supervisor:	*How are you getting on?*
Trainee:	I've stripped off the old paint. I'm still plastering the holes in the walls. It's almost done.
Supervisor:	*OK, good. Have you bought the new paint yet?*
Trainee:	No, I haven't yet. I'll do it next.

6

Supervisor:	*How are you getting on?*
Trainee:	I've taken apart the telephone. I'm still putting it together again. It's almost done.
Supervisor:	*OK, good. Have you tested it yet?*
Trainee:	No, I haven't done that yet. I'll do it next.

Language

Yet

Go through the Language box with students. Explain that *yet* is used with the present perfect and refers to time before now. You use it in questions when you are asking about something that you expected or hoped to have happened before now, e.g. *Have you finished the job yet?*, and in the negative when you expected something to have happened, but it hasn't, e.g. *No. Sorry, I haven't finished it yet.*

Task

5 Ask students to look at the photos. Tell them that they show different jobs you do on cars.

Put students into three small groups. In large classes, put them into six groups. If there are three groups in the class, make sure that they each choose a different job. If there are six groups, there should be two groups for each job. Tell the groups to agree a set of instructions for the job in their groups and write these down. Ask them to make sure that they've included everything and that the instructions are in the correct order.

6 Tell students to turn to page 111. Here they'll find instructions for the three jobs. However, the instructions are all mixed up. Tell them to find the instructions for their job, check them against their list and add any missing instruction to their list. If necessary, they should rewrite their list of instructions.

7 Tell students to work with someone from another group, who has chosen a different job. Go through the instructions with students first, and tell them to put away their list of instructions and not to look at it while they're doing the roleplay. Go round monitoring and giving help.

3 Method

Start here

1 Ask students to look at the photos and to tell you what the devices are (a touch-screen ticket machine; a cordless phone, an outboard motor on a boat, a kick start on a motorbike, a laser beam burglar alarm). Then ask them to explain how they think you activate each of the devices. Accept all ideas, but do not confirm at this stage, as they will be checking their answers in 2.

2 Read the example sentence to the class and tell them that when you want to explain how you do something, you use *by* followed by verb + *ing*. Ask students to complete the sentences with the words in the box and to check their ideas in 1.

> **1** touching
> **2** picking up, pressing
> **3** pulling
> **4** switching on, kicking
> **5** breaking

Speaking

3 Go through the example question and answer with the class first. Ask students to look back at the photo of the touch-screen ticket machine in 1 and ask a student the question. Point out the alternative reply: *He does it …,* and tell them that you can use *does* to avoid repeating the verb *activate*.

Then put students in pairs to ask and answer questions about the other photos in 1.

> **1** A: How does the passenger activate the ticket machine?
> B: He activates it/He does it by touching the screen.
> **2** A: How do you switch on the phone?
> B: You switch it on/You do it by picking up the handset and pressing the green button.
> **3** A: How does the user start the outboard motor?
> B: He starts it/He does it by pulling the handle of the cord.
> **4** A: How does the rider start the engine?
> B: He starts it/He does it by switching on the battery and kicking the lever downwards.
> **5** A: How does the burglar activate the alarm?
> B: He activates it/He does it by breaking the lower beam.

Language

Method

Go through the Language box with the class which explains one way to talk or write about method, i.e. how you do something. The examples shown here refer to when the method is an action.

Tell students that they'll find more information about method in the Language box on page 9 and in the Grammar summary on page 106.

4 Put students in pairs to match the devices with the methods to start or activate them. You could set this up as a competition and ask students to raise their hands when they've finished the exercise.

> **1** c   **2** f   **3** a   **4** e   **5** b   **6** d

Speaking

5 Students work in pairs to ask and answer questions using the devices and methods from 4.

> **1** A: How do you activate the accelerator on a motorbike?
> B: By rotating the handle.
> **2** A: How do you activate a voice-operated computer?
> B: By speaking to it.
> **3** A: How do you activate a solar battery?
> B: By putting it under an electric lamp.
> **4** A: How do you activate the emergency stop in a train?
> B: By pulling the lever.
> **5** A: How do you activate a shop door alarm?
> B: By stepping on a sensor in the door mat.
> **6** A: How do you start a car engine?
> B: By inserting the key and turning it.

Writing

6 Ask students to work on their own and write sentences explaining how the people in the list activate the devices in 4. They can then compare their sentences with a partner before you check with the class.

> **1** You activate (the driver activates) the accelerator on a motorbike by rotating the handle.
>
> **2** You activate (or the user/the passenger activates) the voice-operated computer by speaking to it.
>
> **3** You activate (or the user activates) the solar battery by putting it under an electric lamp.
>
> **4** You activate (or the passenger activates) the emergency stop in a train by pulling the lever.
>
> **5** You activate (or the customer activates) the shop door alarm by stepping on a sensor in the door mat.
>
> **6** You start (the driver starts) the car engine by inserting the key and turning it.

Reading

7 Ask students to close their books and to think about all the things a robot can do. Then brainstorm the things robots can do with the class.

Put students into pairs. Ask them to cover the article and look at the photo of the robot and discuss with their partner what they think this robot can do, then to say how they think it works. Go round monitoring. Get feedback from students. Allow any ideas but do not confirm their ideas at this stage as they'll be checking their ideas in the article in the following exercise.

8 Tell students that they're going to read an article about the robot. Focus their attention on the table below the article which explains what Murata Boy can do. Ask them to read the article and complete the table, writing in the name of the device which allows the robot to do these things and where the device is located. Students can then check their answers with a partner before you check them with the class.

	device	location
1	sensor	body
2	wireless receiver	box on its back
3	sensor	frame of the bike
4	camera	head
5	sensor	chest

Language

Go through the Language box with students which shows another way to talk or write about method, when the method is a device.

Speaking

9 Tell students to imagine that they are journalists at a robot show, and that they are going to interview the inventor of Murata Boy. Tell them to read the replies to the interview and then write the questions.

Check the answers with the class. Then ask individual students to read out one of the interview questions in any order and another student gives the reply.

> **1** What can the robot do?
>
> **2** How does it work?
>
> **3** How can it detect changes in the surface of the road?
>
> **4** How can it detect walls and move away from them?
>
> **5** How can it look ahead and move straight forward?

> **Extra activity**
>
> Ask students to write some brief notes about a device that they're interested in. When they've finished, they work with a partner and explain how it works. Their partner should ask follow-up questions about the device to clarify anything they don't understand about it.

2 Work

Contents

1 Routines

Listen to conversation between two offshore oil workers and complete a duty roster about days on and off.

Listen again and fill in gaps in conversation with present simple or present continuous.

Language: present simple (routine) vs present continuous (present actions/ future plans)

Speaking: changes to a work routine: *What does he usually do? What's he doing today.*

Word list: *attend (meeting), check, conduct (drill), fly, go, inspect, meet, oil rig/platform, on leave, on/off duty, onshore/offshore, operate, supervise repair, train, travel*

Listen to oil workers talking about who they report to and supervise. Tasks: (1) locate them on organisation charts; (2) complete job descriptions with third person present simple.

Language: present simple in job descriptions.

Speaking: asking and answering questions about job descriptions and who one works for and supervises. First about oil workers, then about themselves.

Word list: *assistant, crane, crew, deck, drill, department, electrician, engineer, maintenance, operator, report to, sub-sea, supervise, supervisor*

2 Plans

Listening: phone call arranging a meeting. Tasks: (1) decide on the purpose of the call; (2) make notes about details of the call (day/ time/ participants/ agenda of meeting); (3) complete phone conversation, focussing on verb forms

Language: present continuous; *going to*; *want/ plan/ hope/ intend + to.*

Speaking: questions and answers about plans, based on diary entries.

Word list: *agenda, arrange, discuss, give (a talk), hold (a meeting), inspect, meeting, o'clock, order, participant, prevention, run (fire drill), site*

Task: make a plan with times for student's own tasks, and present them to the class.

Writing: (a) rewrite an email substituting equivalent phrases; (b) write email based on scenario (c) reply to partner's email

Language functions in email: thanking, referring to topic, reminding of background, giving new information, requesting action

Word list: *concerning, confirm, inform, (un)fortunately, with regard to, with reference to*

3 New job

Starter: discussing what goes into a CV.

Reading: a completed CV.

Task: answer questions about the CV.

Scanning task: scan range of job ads to meet specified criteria.

Complete past tenses in spoken description of CV. Then listen to the description and check answers.

Word list: *audio, Curriculum Vitae, CV, digital, diploma, education, employer, employment, full-time, media, occupation, qualification, technician, training, work experience,*

Vocabulary: word families: *mechanic, mechanics, mechanism, mechanical*: meaning and syllable stress changes.

Match questions to items on CV.

Interview each other using provided CV.

Write short version of own CV and roleplay job interviews with additional questions.

Word list: *as above, plus electrician/ electricity/ electrical, electronics/ electronic, technician/ technical, technology/ technologist*

Briefing

This unit deals with aspects of work such as routines, job descriptions, work plans, and the use of e-mails. It also looks at CVs, job advertisements and job interviews.

Section 1 deals with typical job descriptions and work routines on an offshore oil rig (or oil platform) where oil is drilled from beneath the sea bed. Because the platforms are out at sea, offshore oil workers cannot simply go home each evening after work, so they live on the platform and work intensively for some weeks before taking longer periods of leave. People working on a platform closer to their home country might work two weeks on two weeks off ('fortnight on fortnight off', or 'two and two'), or 'three on, three off', while those working further from their home might be 'month on, month off.'

Some of the most important crews or teams on an oil platform are mentioned in this section. The drill crew look after the derrick (the tall structure supporting the drilling equipment) and the drilling and pumping operations. As the drill bit cuts into rock, fluid is pumped through the well to remove the debris. In the drill crew, a team of roughnecks assist the driller, derrick man and pump man. The deck crew look after the equipment on the deck of the oil rig, especially the cranes which do the heavy lifting of equipment. A roustabout assists the crane operators by guiding the crane around the deck. The sub-sea crew are engineers and skilled scuba divers: they maintain the underwater pipes and the blowout preventer, a valve that seals off the well if a fire or explosion occurs below it. There is also an electrical department and a mechanical department that maintain all the equipment on the platform.

Section 2 deals with the work of a safety officer on the offshore oil platform. The oil industry is very safety-conscious. When new oil workers arrive on a rig for the first time they are given a tour of the installation, detailing all safety aspects including fire extinguishers, emergency muster stations (places to meet in an emergency), lifeboat stations and emergency procedures. Everyone attends weekly safety meetings, where all safety issues on the rig are discussed. A fire and boat drill is often held on the same day, which involves a mock fire and a mock 'abandon rig' exercise.

Section 3 deals with a job-seeker's CV or curriculum vitae, using the Europass CV format produced by the Council of Europe. The example given in this section is a short extract: a full CV would contain more personal details (such as nationality, date of birth, phone number, gender) and a section on mother tongue and language competencies (skills). It would also include a section on other competencies such as technical, organisational and computer skills. An example of a completed CV, the instructions for using the template and useful advice for completing an effective CV can be found in the web sites listed below. For example, one useful piece of advice to students from the website is this: 'if your work experience is still limited (because you have just left school or university), describe your education and training first; highlight work placements during training.' The heading *type of business or sector* refers to the general category of industry the applicant has worked in. Other examples of sectors are engineering, construction, IT, and petroleum. The heading *occupation or position held* (in Anna's CV) is sometimes also called *job title;* the heading *main activities and responsibilities* can also be called *job description*. The heading *title of qualification awarded* can also appear simply as *qualification; principal subjects/occupational skills covered* refers to the individual subjects studied in the course leading to the qualification. The heading *desired employment* is the job which Anna is actually applying for.

Offshore oil rigs: http://en.wikipedia.org/wiki/Oil_platform

Details of jobs in offshore oil industry: http://www.rigjobs.co.uk/jobs/deck.shtml

Europass CV: http://europass.cedefop.europa.eu/europass/home/hornav/Downloads/navigate.action

Europass CV advice and instructions: http://europass.cedefop.europa.eu

Teacher's notes

1 Routines

Start here

1 Tell students to look at the photo of the helicopter landing on an offshore platform and ask them to imagine working on an offshore oil platform. Allow them some time to think about what kind of jobs they would have to do on the platform. Tell them to consider the type of conditions that they would have to work in. For example, would they be working in the North Sea or in the Gulf? Put students into pairs to discuss whether they'd like to work on an offshore oil platform and to give reasons for their answers.

Listening

2 ▶ 🄲 **04**

Tell students that they're going to listen to a phone conversation between two friends, Tore and Ken, who work on different offshore oil platforms.They are discussing holidays. Focus their attention on the duty roster and explain that *On duty* means the period of time when you're expected to be at work and *On leave* means a period of time when you're on holiday. Ask students to listen to the recording and complete the duty roster for Tore and Ken.

> Tore – On duty: 2 weeks. On leave: 2 weeks.
> Ken – On duty: 3 weeks. On leave: 3 weeks.

▶ 🄲 **04**

[T = Tore; K = Ken]

T: Hi, Ken, How are things on your rig?

K: Hi, Tore. Well, we're working very hard at the moment. But I'm going on leave tomorrow.

T: That's great. Where are you going? Back home?

K: I usually go home to Nigeria. But this time I'm flying to France for a holiday.

T: Ah, fantastic. Do you work two weeks on, two weeks off?

K: No, I do three on and three off. How about you?

T: I work two two.

K: When's your next leave?

T: I'm on the helicopter right now! I'm flying to Norway!

3 Play the recording again for students to complete the conversation. Alternatively, ask students to complete the conversation first, and then check it with the recording. They could then practise the conversation in pairs.

Language

Present simple and present continuous

Go through the Language box with the class, which contrasts the uses of the present simple tense and the present continuous.

Tell students that they'll find more information about the present simple and the present continuous in the Grammar summary on page 100.

1 're working (things happening temporarily around now)

2 'm going (plans in the near future)

3 are you going (plans in the near future)

4 go (regular or routine events)

5 'm flying (plans in the near future)

6 Do you work (regular or routine events)

7 do (regular or routine events)

8 work (regular or routine events)

9 'm flying (things happening now)

Extra activity

Ask students to look back at their answers in the conversation. Tell them to circle all the examples of the present simple tense and underline the present continuous tense. Then ask them to identify the different uses of the present simple and present continuous tense. (See answers in brackets above.)

Speaking

4 Focus students' attention on the duty roster showing the work routine for Bill, Tore and Adel. Point out that some of the usual routine jobs have been crossed out and new routine jobs added for these three people because of staff illness. Go through the example dialogue with the class. You could take the part of A and ask the questions and get a confident student to take the part of B and give the replies.

Students then work in pairs and ask each other about the changes in the work routine. Go round monitoring and take note of any problems.

5 ▶ 🎧 05

Tell students that they're going to hear Tore, Ken, Bill and Adel talking about their jobs. Focus their attention on the organisation charts and go through the names of the jobs with them. Find out if any of students do any of these jobs or know of anyone who does.

Play the recording. Students tick the correct jobs for each worker in the organisation charts.

> 1 Bill – Assistant Sub-Sea Engineer
> 2 Tore – Assistant Crane Operator
> 3 Ken – Assistant Driller
> 4 Adel – Chief Electrician

▶ 🎧 05

1 Hi, my name's Bill, and I work in the Sub-sea crew. I'm an Assistant Sub-Sea Engineer. Basically, I repair and maintain the platform and the pipes under the sea. I report to Mike, the Sub-Sea Engineer.

2 Good morning. My name is Tore, and I'm from Norway. My job title is Assistant Crane Operator. I operate and maintain the cranes on the main deck. I report to the Crane Operator.

3 Hello, I'm Ken. I'm an Assistant Driller, and I operate the drilling equipment. I supervise the Derrick Man and the Pump Man. I report to the Driller. He's the boss.

4 Hi, my name's Adel and I'm the Chief Electrician on the rig. I maintain and repair all the electrical equipment on the rig. I supervise a team of three electricians, and I report to the Maintenance Supervisor.

6 Tell students to read the first sentence and ask them which tense they need to use to complete the sentence and why. (They need to use the present simple because they're talking about a regular or routine event.) Then ask students to work on their own to complete the job descriptions with the correct form of the verbs in the box.

> 1 repairs, maintains, reports
> 2 operates, maintains, reports
> 3 operates, supervises, reports
> 4 maintains, repairs, supervises, reports

Speaking

7 Put students into pairs. Tell them that they are oil rig workers and they are going to find out about each other's jobs. Go through the questions with the class. Ask them if they can think of any other questions they might like to ask, and write these on the board.

While students are asking each other about their jobs, go round monitoring and make notes of any problems they might have which you can deal with later in a feedback session.

8 Ask students to write down their job title and a short description of their job. If you have students in your class who do not have a job, ask them to write the title of a job they would like to do in the future and a short description for it.

9 Put students into pairs. They ask and answer questions about their jobs. Tell them not to look at the job description they wrote in 8.

When they've finished talking about their jobs, they could look at each other's descriptions from 8 and correct or revise them as necessary.

> **Extra activity**
>
> Brainstorm a list of jobs on the board. Ask students to choose two jobs, which must not be the same as the ones they discussed in 9. Tell them to write short descriptions for them, but not to write the name of the job. Then ask them to exchange their descriptions with a partner who guesses what the job is.

2 Plans

Start here

1 Ask students to look at the photo and explain that this man is a safety officer on an offshore platform. Ask them to think of the jobs that he does and to discuss these with a partner.

Listening

2 ▶ 🔵 06

Tell students that they're going to listen to the Safety Officer making a phone call. This is a gist listening exercise, so tell them that all they have to do is to find out the reason for his phone call. Go through the three options with the class, then play the recording for students to choose the correct reason.

> **c)** to arrange a meeting

▶ 🔵 06

1

[T = Tore; B = Ben]

T: Hello, Deck Crew. Tore speaking.

B: Oh, hi Tore. This is Ben. How's it going?

T: Not bad. But this strong wind is a problem for the cranes. Anyway, what can I do for you?

B: I want to hold a meeting for the deck crew sometime soon.

T: OK. What's the meeting going to be about?

B: I'm going to tell them about the new safety rules for crane operators.

T: OK, that's fine. When are you having the meeting?

B: How about three o'clock next Thursday?

T: Yeah, that's great. Three o'clock next Thursday. See you then. Bye.

B: Cheers. Bye.

3 Focus students' attention on the headings for the notes. Go through them with the students so that they know what information they need to listen out for. Play the recording again for students to complete the notes.

> Day: Thursday
> Time: 3.00 pm.
> Participants: Deck crew
> Agenda: New safety rules for crane operators

4 Ask students to read through the conversation first and fill in the gaps if they can. Students now listen to the recording one more time and check their answers.

> **1** want to   **3** 'm going to
> **2** going to   **4** are you having

Language

Present continuous and *going to*

Go through the Language box with the class, which shows various ways of talking about the future in English. Explain that you use *going to* + verb when you're talking in general about something you've already decided to do in the future, whereas you use the present continuous for things you've planned to do in the future, particularly in relation to a business appointment or social arrangement. Point out the verbs *want*, *intend* and *hope* to express the future are followed by *to*-form.

Tell students that they'll find more information about the different ways of expressing the future in the Grammar summary on page 100.

Speaking

5 Tell students that they are Ben, the Safety Officer. Refer them to the diary notes and tell them that they're going to take it in turns to explain their plans to a partner. Go through the example with the class first. Go round monitoring, and check that they're using the present continuous and *going to* future correctly. Make notes of any common problems that you can deal with later in a feedback session.

> **1** On Monday at 9.30, I'm meeting the Safety Manager. We're going to discuss the safety report.
> **2** On Monday at two o'clock, I'm taking a helicopter to the HQ. I'm going to meet the Company Manager.
> **3** On Tuesday at twelve o'clock, I'm writing the new safety rules for the cranes.
> **4** On Wednesday at eight o'clock, I'm inspecting the fire exits.
> **5** On Wednesday at ten o'clock, I'm running a fire drill.
> **6** On Wednesday at two o'clock, I'm visiting the Nord Platform. I'm going to discuss the new safety rules with the manager.
> **7** On Thursday, I'm having a day off.
> **8** On Friday at 9.30, I'm writing the report about my visit to Nord Platform.
> **9** On Friday at two o'clock, I'm inspecting the sub-sea safety equipment.

6 Students work in the same pairs and make questions to ask Ben about his plans in his diary. Go through the example with the class and make sure that they understand that they should use the present continuous with plans and *going to* future with something that they intend to do. Again go round monitoring and taking notes of any common problems.

> **1** When are you meeting the Safety Manager? What are you going to discuss?
> **2** When are you taking a helicopter to the HQ? Who are you going to meet?
> **3** When are you writing the new safety rules for the cranes?
> **4** When are you inspecting the fire exits?
> **5** When are you running the fire drill?
> **6** When are you visiting the Nord platform? What are you going to discuss?
> **7** When are you having a day off?
> **8** When are you writing the report about the visit to the Nord Platform?
> **9** When are you inspecting the sub-sea safety equipment?

Task

7 Go through the instructions with the class and make sure that they understand what to do. Allow them time to make their lists and work out their timetables for doing them. Students then present their plans to the class. You could encourage other students to ask them questions about their plans and encourage them to talk about their plans in more detail.

Writing

8 Tell students to close their books as you write the headings in bold from the right-hand box on the board in random order. Then ask students to open their books. Focus their attention on the email and ask them to cover the right-hand box. Ask them to read the email and match the headings to the paragraphs. Tell them that this email shows the typical style for organising paragraphs in emails. Ask them if the organisation of paragraphs is the same in their country.

Ask who has sent the email and how well he/she knows the person he/she has sent the email to. Then explain that business emails in English generally have a neutral style, but business letters are more formal. Then ask students to uncover the right-hand box and point out the phrases in italics and their equivalents. Students work on their own to replace the phrases in italics with alternatives from the box. Students could then compare their emails with a partner. The students will have different versions of the email, so check their emails by asking a few students to read out theirs to the class.

Sample answer:

9 Go through the situation and instructions with the class. Students then work on their own to write the email. Tell them to refer to the email and the alternative phrases in the box in 8 to help them. Allow them plenty of time to write their emails and encourage them to check their work for errors when they have finished.

10 Students exchange their emails with a partner. Tell them that they are now Ben, and that they must reply to the email they've been given. Go through the points that need to be included in their reply with the students.

If you are short of time in class, you could give students this for homework.

3 New job

Start here

1 Tell students to close their books and ask them what a CV is (a list of all your personal information, qualifications, work experience and other details for applying for a job). Ask them what the abbreviation stands for (*Curriculum Vitae*) and if they know the American English term for it (*Résumé*). Find out how many of the students have written one and how often they update it. Then elicit from them the type of information that goes into it.

Reading

2 Students now check their answers to 1 by looking at the CV for Anna Petersons. Tell them not to worry about the numbers on the right for now. Ask them how different Anna's CV is from the one they described in 1, for example, in the organisation of the information. This CV is an example of a chronological format, listing the applicant's employment starting from the most recent and gives information on the applicant's educational background. It is based on the Europass format of the Council of Europe. If students are interested, they can key the word *Europass* into a search engine to see the full format. Another format is a functional CV which focuses on the skills of the applicants, and is more commonly used if the applicant wants to change career.

Ask students to read the CV and answer the questions about it. Refer students to the box and encourage them to look at the Council of Europe website to see the full formatted version.

> 1 Petersons
> 2 Senior Audio Maintenance Technician
> 3 Omega Studios, Riga, Latvia
> 4 Maintains digital audio equipment, makes recordings, does troubleshooting and repairs, buys new equipment
> 5 Comet Electronics, Riga, Latvia
> 6 Repaired video and DVD equipment
> 7 Diploma in Audio Technology
> 8 Thames Valley University, London, UK

Scanning

3 This scanning activity is a feature of *Technical English 2*. It provides students with a speed reading exercise in which they can practise the skill of scanning for information. It is set up as a competition to encourage students to read the material as quickly as possible in order to find the information to complete the task and to ignore information that is not relevant.

Go through the instructions for the task with the students. Then ask them to turn to pages 118–119 and find the advert which is most appropriate for Anna. Ask students to put up their hand when they've finished, so that you know who is the winner.

> Experienced AUDIO TECHNICIAN at Tower Recording Studios

Listening

4 Ask students to read the text about Anna's CV and fill in the gaps. They could do this exercise with a partner. In this exercise, students revise the past simple tense. Tell them that they'll find a list of irregular past simple verbs on page 105 if they need help.

Do not confirm answers at this stage as they will be checking their answers in 5.

> 1 worked
> 2 left
> 3 became
> 4 studied
> 5 received
> 6 started

5 ▶ 💿 07

Play the recording of Anna talking about her CV. Students listen and check their answers to 4. Ask individual students to read out the answers and check their pronunciation of regular *ed* verbs.

If they need to revise this pronunciation, write /d/, /t/ and /ɪd/ on the board and ask them to put the regular verbs: *worked*, *studied*, *received* and *started* into the correct columns. Remind them that you can pronounce the *ed* endings on regular verbs with a /t/, /d/ or an /ɪd/ sound. When a verb ends in *t* or *d*, such as *need* or *want*, you pronounce *ed* as /ɪd/. With unvoiced sounds /f/, /k/, /p/, /s/, etc, the *ed* ending is pronounced /t/ and with voiced sounds /g/, /n/, /v/, etc. the *ed* ending is pronounced /d/. Make sure that they don't pronounce verbs ending with *t* and *d* with two syllables, e.g. /~~worked~~/ for *worked* /wɜ:kt/.

▶ 💿 07

From 2003 until 2005, I worked at Comet Electronics as a technician. I left Comet in 2005 and became a full-time student at Thames Valley University in September 2005. From 2005 to 2006, I studied audio electronics at Thames Valley. In 2006, I received my Diploma in Audio Technology. Then in September 2006, I started work as an audio maintenance technician at Omega Studios.

Vocabulary

6 Focus students' attention on the table. Tell them to add the headings to the coloured boxes for each of the columns in the table.

	Noun				Adjective
	person	**equipment**	**college subject**	**scientific concept**	
1	en gin <u>eer</u>	<u>en</u> gine	en gin <u>eer</u> ing		
2	el ec <u>tri</u> cian			el ec <u>tri</u> ci ty	el <u>ec</u> tric al
3		el ec <u>tron</u> ics	el ec <u>tron</u> ics	el <u>ec</u> tron	el ec <u>tron</u> ic
4	mech <u>an</u> ic	<u>mech</u> an is m	mech <u>an</u> ics		mech <u>an</u> ic al
5	tech <u>ni</u> cian				<u>tech</u> ni cal
6	tech <u>no</u> log ist		tech <u>no</u> lo gy		

7 Refer students back to the table and tell them to underline the stressed syllables in each of the words in the white boxes. Point out that the first row has been done for them. Do not confirm answers at this stage.

8 ▶ 🔊 08

Students listen to the recording and check their answers to 7. Ask them what happens to the word stress. Then play the recording, pausing after each group of words for students to repeat.

Tell students that when they make a note of any new vocabulary they should mark the stress of the word. They can check the stress by looking in their dictionaries.

(See answers in 6.)

▶ 🔊 08

1 engineer   engine   engineering
2 electrician   electricity   electrical
3 electronics   electron   electronic
4 mechanic   mechanism   mechanics   mechanical
5 technician   technical
6 technologist   technology

9 Students choose the correct words in the brackets to complete the sentences. Check answers by asking individual students to read them out. Make sure that they are putting the stress on the correct syllable of the words in brackets.

1 engineer, engine
2 mechanic, mechanical
3 technician, technical
4 electrician, electrical

Reading

10 Refer students back to the CV on page 14. Point out the numbers on the right of the CV which refers to each section. Ask them to read the questions and find the section it refers to in the CV and then write the correct section number next to the question.

a 6   **b** 5   **c** 3   **d** 2   **e** 13   **f** 15   **g** 10

Speaking

11 Put students into A and B pairs and ask them to read the instructions for their role. Tell them to refer to Anna's CV. Student B then interviews Anna, asking her questions about her CV. When they have finished, they then swap roles. While they are doing the activity, go round the class, monitoring students. Then go through any common errors with the class at the end of the activity.

Task

12 Ask students to write a short version of their CV, using Anna's CV as a model.

13 Tell students that they're going to prepare for a job interview. Tell them to think about a job they would like to apply for and make brief notes in answer to the questions.

14 Students now work in small groups. Each student takes it in turns to pass round their CV. They should tell the other members in the group what job they are applying for. The other students in the group then interview them, referring to their CV and asking questions about their qualifications and experience for the job. Tell students being interviewed that they can refer back to the notes they made in 13 if necessary.

The interviewers can make a note of whether they think the interviewee should get the job. When they've finished, find out which students have been offered a new job.

Answer key

1

1	Take it away.	9	Put it on.
2	Switch it on.	10	Take them out.
3	Take it off.	11	Put them down.
4	Pick them up.	12	Pour it out.
5	Switch it off.	13	Push it in.
6	Push them down.	14	Push it forward.
7	Pull it back.	15	Put it in.
8	Pull it out.	16	Pour it in.

2
1 switched off, switching it off
2 brought out, bringing it out
3 taken off, taking them off
4 put on, putting them on
5 taken away, taking them away
6 put back, putting them back

3

1	checked	8	unblocked
2	found	9	stripped
3	replaced	10	cleaned
4	adjusted	11	repaired
5	put	12	repainted
6	examined	13	pumped
7	took	14	did

4
1 shields, looking
2 brings, carrying
3 raise, putting
4 keep, covering
5 protect, wearing
6 opens, pressing

5 *Sample answer:*
The Crane Operator supervises the Assistant Crane Operator.
He reports to the Operation Manager.
The Electrician and the Mechanic report to the Maintenance Manager.
The Part-time Repair Man reports to the Mechanic.
The Senior Technician supervises the Junior Technician.
He reports to the IT Manager.
The Operation Manager, the Maintenance Manager and the IT Manager report to the Chief Engineer.

6

1	repairs	6	orders
2	maintains	7	works
3	checks	8	reports
4	makes	9	supervises
5	inspects	10	has

8 Students can choose from any of the options below:
One thing you should do before your interview:
• find out about the company and the job
• read the job advert carefully and think how your CV matches what they want
• prepare a list of the questions you think the interviewer will ask you
• prepare a list of questions you would like to ask the interviewer
One thing you should do during your interview:
• answer every question fully
• be positive and honest about yourself
• ask questions about the job
• show your knowledge about the company
• show you are interested in the job
• talk about your ambitions
One thing you should not do during your interview:
• dress untidily
• be late for the interview
• be rude or impolite
• talk negatively about your previous employer
• answer only *Yes* or *No*

9

1	do you work	6	did you leave
2	have you been	7	I wanted
3	I've been	8	Have you finished
4	did you work	9	did you complete
5	I was		

10
1 ticket machine
2 burglar alarm
3 outboard motor
4 accelerator

11
1 ~~mechanism~~ mechanic, ~~mechanical~~ mechanics, ~~technique~~ technical
2 ~~electricity~~ electrician, ~~electrician~~ electrical
3 ~~technical~~ technician
4 ~~electronic~~ electronics, ~~electron~~ electronic(s)

12 With reference to our phone call this morning, this is to let you know that I have now written the report. I'd be grateful if you would let me know how many copies you need.
Best wishes
Marcia

Project

13 & 14 At the end of every Review Unit is a project. Students can research their projects on the internet, or in the library.

Tip: Key the name of your industry into a search engine. Add other key words such as *technician*, *job*, *career*.

Example: Construction Industry: structural engineer, quantity surveyor, site manager, architectural technician, etc.

Quick test answer key

Part 1: Vocabulary & grammar

1
1 raise	**4** supervise
2 tighten	**5** maintains
3 pull	

2 **1** b **2** d **3** a **4** e **5** c

3
1 engineering	**4** technical
2 electrician	**5** technologist
3 mechanism	

4
Chief Electrician
Maintenance Supervisor
Assistant Sub-Sea Engineer
Crane Operator

5
1 's the robot doing	**4** Has he hit
2 's riding	**5** hasn't fallen off
3 's moving	

6
4 Has he hit any objects <u>yet</u>?
5 ... he hasn't fallen off the bike <u>yet</u>.

7
1 I'm taking them off the car.
2 He's switched it off.
3 They're bringing them out.
4 I've put it under the table.

8
1 works; is visiting	**4** hope to/are going to discuss
2 are planning; have	
3 operate; am training	**5** want to; to finish

9
1 studied	**4** worked
2 received	**5** returned
3 went	

Part 2: Reading and writing

Reading

1 Nobody. The robot car drives itself.
2 They can travel around city streets without crashing into vehicles, trees and other objects.
3 By using a kill-switch.
4 By means of sensors in the robot car.
5 By using a Lidar scanner.

Writing

1 Thanks for
2 concerning
3 This is to inform you that
4 I would appreciate it if you could
5 I am attaching

Review Unit A Quick test

Total _____/50

Part 1: Vocabulary and grammar

1 **Underline the correct word in each sentence.**

1 The wheel-jack mechanics **lower/raise** the car off the ground.

2 They put the new wheel on the car and **tighten/loosen** the nuts.

3 You **pull/press** the cord to start the motor.

4 I **report to/supervise** a team of five technicians.

5 John **operates/maintains** the machines and checks them daily for any problems.

(5 marks)

2 **Match the beginning of the sentences with their endings.**

1	take off	a	the fuel hose
2	switch off	b	the wheel
3	pull out	c	the spanner from the ground
4	push down	d	the engine
5	pick up	e	the pedal

(5 marks)

3 **Complete the table.**

Noun			adjective
person	equipment	college subject	
engineer	engine	1 _____	
2 _____			electrical
mechanic	3 _____	mechanics	mechanical
technician			4 _____
5 _____		technology	

(5 marks)

4 **Put these job titles in order of rank.**

Assistant Sub-Sea Engineer   Maintenance Supervisor
Chief Electrician   Crane operator

1 _____
2 _____
3 _____
4 _____

(4 marks)

5 **Complete the phone conversation about the robot, using the present continuous or the present perfect.**

A: What (1) _____ (the robot/do) now?

B: He (2) _____ the bike (ride).
He (3) _____ in a straight line. (move)

A: (4) _____ (he/hit) any objects?

B: No, he hasn't.

A: Is the road flat?

B: No, it isn't, but he (5) _____ (not fall off) the bike.

(5 marks)

6 **You can put *yet* in two places in exercise 5. Write *yet* in the dialogue where appropriate.**

(2 marks)

7 **Rewrite the sentences, using the words in brackets.**

1 I'm taking the tyres off the car. (them)

_____

2 He's switched off the electricity supply. (it)

_____

3 They're bringing the new wheels out. (them)

_____

4 I've put the box under the table. (it)

_____

(4 marks)

8 **Underline the correct words in the sentences.**

1 Frank Neumann **is working/works** for a car manufacturing company in Frankfurt. He **is visiting/visits** a factory in Berlin this week.

2 They **are planning/plan** to go to Egypt this year. They **are having/have** their annual holiday in August every summer.

3 I normally **am operating/operate** the drilling equipment, but I **am training/train** a new pump man at the moment.

4 I **am/hope to** meet the chief mechanic next week. We **are discussing/are going to discuss** the new pit stop procedures.

5 They **want to make/making** a new robot. They hope **to finish/finishing** it by next year.

(5 marks)

9 Complete the sentences.

receive	return	study	went	work

I (1) _____ engineering at Edinburgh University.
In 2005, I (2) _____ a Masters degree in
Petroleum Engineering. I then (3) _____ to Dubai, and
I (4) _____ for Agip for three years. I (5) _____
to the UK in March this year, and I'm now looking for a
new job.

(5 marks)

Part 2: Reading and writing

Reading

Read the text and answer the questions.

Automotive manufacturers in America are developing
cars that can drive themselves. They can travel around
city streets without crashing into vehicles, trees or other
obstacles. One of the cars named 'Boss' can travel 85 km
with no driver at the controls.

A driver follows behind the robot car in a support car.
The driver can stop the robot car immediately by using a
kill-switch when the car is in danger of crashing.

The driver knows that the robot car is in danger of hitting
things by means of sensors. These sensors are mounted
on the roof of the robot car, one on each of its four
corners, and in the bumpers. By using an algorithm to
read the data from the radar sensors and cameras, the
driver knows where fixed and moving objects are. 'Boss'
has a Lidar scanner. This scanner has 64 individual
lasers. By rotating at about 10 times a second, the
scanner can take about a million measurements. These
measurements warn the driver in the support car about
any objects that are near the robot car and the exact
distance these objects are from the car.

1 Who drives the robot cars?

_____

2 What can the robot cars do?

_____

3 How does the driver in the follow-up car stop the
robot car?

_____

4 How does the driver know that the robot car is in
danger of hitting things?

_____

5 How does the driver know how far objects are from
'Boss'?

_____

(5 marks)

Writing

**Complete the letter, using five of the phrases in the box.
Use the correct punctuation.**

	as you may be aware	
I would appreciate it if you could		
concerning	please do not hesitate to call me	
do let me know	Thanks for	
I am attaching	This is to inform you that	
	unfortunately	

Dear Mr Morgan

(1) _____ your letter, dated 11th October,

(2) _____ the job as Maintenance
Supervisor. (3) _____ I am available for
an interview on Tuesday 21st October. (4) _____
_____ send me a full copy of the job
description. (5) _____ the contact
details of my previous employers as reference.

Kind regards
Adam Davies

(5 marks)

3   Comparison

Contents

1   Limits

Starter: give meaning of road signs which state limits.

Listen to phone conversation between customer and ferry company. Tasks (1) label minivan with dimensions; (2) complete conversation focussing on comparative adjectives.

Read ferry web page describing dimension limits on vehicles. Task: say which vehicles (diagram) can board ferry.

Word list: *car ferry, dimension, including, limit, luggage, maximum, measure, passenger, roof rack, standard, trailer, type (of vehicle), weight, within (limits)*

Language: *-er than; more/ less* + adj; *too wide for; not wide enough for*

Explain problem from given dimensions: *The lorry is too high for the bridge.*

Task: compare a road-ready plane with (a) a car (b) a plane. Then write a report in reply to an email.

Word list: *airfield, destination, hangar, land (vb), mode, runway, strength, weakness, wingspan*

2   Products

Listen to six phone calls to customer service.

Information tasks: (1) match the calls with six explanations of purpose of call; (2) complete customer call form with details.

Complete phrases heard in calls, focussing on modals *would, could, shall* etc.

Match phrases with functions: (1) saying what you want; (2) offering to do something; (3) asking someone to do something; (4) checking information.

Roleplay the conversations.

Word list: *address book, assistance, catalogue, complain, fault, information, mobile phone, place/ cancel an order, recharging time, request, screen size, service, storage capacity, talking time*

Specification charts comparing two mobile phones. Tasks: (1) complete a phone conversation with comparative adjectives; (2) practise a similar conversation using more data from the charts.

Language: use of *one* and *with/without*: *Which one would you like? The black one with/without the cover.* Identify where *one* is missing in a text.

Speaking: practise specifying which one (of a pair) is required.

Word list: *capacity/ storage, diagonal, dimensions, playback, rechargeable, storage*

3   Equipment

Starter question: discuss world records.

Read email correspondence to determine purpose, background, new information, requested action, promise of action.

Scanning specifications to find required data and answer questions using superlatives.

Word list: *expensive, fuel consumption, heavy, light, noisy, propeller, power, powerful, rapid, shaft, tender (formal offer)*

Language: superlative *the –est (of), most/ least*

Speaking: make comparisons between lists of three items. Then students make up their own lists and compare them.

Problem-solving task: simulate a meeting to decide on the best 4x4 vehicle for use in an oil rig in the desert. Specs of four vehicles are at the back of the book.

Write a report of the meeting.

Word list: *cab, diesel, (driver's) petrol, ground clearance, LPG (liquid petroleum gas), towing power, wheelbase*

Briefing

This unit deals with making comparisons, and specifying dimension and weight limits.

Section 1 begins by looking at road signs expressing maximum dimensions and weights of vehicles. The weight limit on lorries on the weak bridge is 17 T (tonnes) **mgw (maximum gross weight)**. The **gross** weight is the full weight of the lorry including its contents, while the tare weight is the weight of the empty lorry. (In other contexts, the opposite of gross is **net**, or **nett**, as in gross pay and net pay (after tax and other deductions). The reading text deals with the maximum dimensions of vehicles on a ferry. A **standard** (or normal) car has a different dimension limit and price from a *large* car, *high* car and so on. A **roof rack** is a set of bars fixed to the roof of a car so that other items, such as bicycles, can be attached to them. A **trailer** is a wheeled container pulled or towed by a motor vehicle. The Task describes a **road-ready plane**, a small aeroplane which can drive straight off the airport runway and onto a road, where it moves like a car. When the vehicle is in **flying mode** (that is, when it functions as a plane), the wings are down, while in **car mode** the wings fold upwards out of the way. The **wingspan** is the distance from one **wingtip** (the end of one wing) to the other. In car mode, it can reach a normal car's **cruising speed**: this is a steady speed with no braking or acceleration.

Section 2 begins with various features of a mobile phone. **Talking time** means how long you can talk before the batteries run down; video time or music time would use up battery power at a different rate from talking. If you keep the phone switched on without making any calls it will use less battery power. **Storage capacity** (or simply **capacity**) refers to the size of the memory for storing photos, music, addresses, etc., measured in megabytes or **gigabytes** (**GB**). An **organised address book** would allow the user to store addresses under categories or in folders as on a computer. The **charging time** of a battery is the length of time it takes to recharge it from the mains electricity. The batteries in a mobile phone are **rechargeable**. The **screen size** on a TV, computer monitor, mobile phone display and so on is normally measured *diagonally* from one corner to its opposite corner.

Section 3 begins with discussing world records. The record for the world's smallest transistor may already have been broken because of rapid developments in this field. **Carbon nanotubes** are extremely thin fibres, measured in nanometres: the prefix **nano-** means *divided by one thousand million*. In the reading text a company wants to purchase new **outboard motors** for its fleet of boats. The purchaser publishes the required **specifications**, and invites more than one supplier to submit a competitive **tender**: this is a formal **quotation** stating price and service offered. In this example, the purchaser has requested tenders from five suppliers, and now wants to test the five motors against each other. **Fuel consumption** is distance per unit of fuel, for example *25 miles per gallon* (**mpg**). **Acceleration** is measured as the time it takes to reach a speed after starting the engine: for example *0 – 40 km/h in 10 seconds*. In the Task, engineers have to choose the best vehicle for their work. In **four-wheel drive** (**4x4**) vehicles, engine power is applied to all four wheels.

The **wheelbase** of a car is the length from front axle to rear axle; **clearance** is the distance from the axles to the ground – this will depend on the size of the wheels. The **cab** (in cranes, tractors, etc.) is where the driver sits.

UK road signs: http://www.direct.gov.uk/en/TravelAndTransport/Highwaycode/index.htm

Sample ferry regulations on dimensions: http://www.speedferries.com/speedVehicle.php

Road-ready plane: http://www.terrafugia.com/index.html

Outboard motors: http://www.popularmechanics.com/outdoors/boating/1276841.html?page=1

Sample 4x4 specifications: http://www.toyota.com/landcruiser/specs.html

18-nanometre transistors: http://technology.newscientist.com/article/dn9217

Teacher's notes

1 | Limits

Start here

1 Ask students to look at the road signs and try to explain what each of them means. Write *weight*, *height*, *length* and *width* on the board and ask students to write the adjectives for the nouns.

Ask students where they would see these signs.

> **1** weight limit for a lorry
> **2** height limit
> **3** width limit
> **4** length limit for a lorry
> **5** safe height limit below an electrical cable
> **6** weight limit for weak bridge

Listening

2 ▶ 🎵 09

Tell students that they're going to listen to a phone conversation. Explain the situation: a customer is phoning a car ferry company to check if it's possible to take her van onto their car ferry. Refer students to the specification chart in the margin. Tell students to listen to the phone conversation and complete the chart with the three dimensions of the van. Point out that these dimensions are approximate, not exact.

> **1** 3.2 m
> **2** 7 m
> **3** 1.9 m

▶ 🎵 09

[S = Salesperson; C = Customer]
S: How wide is your van?
C: It's just under 1.9 metres wide.
S: OK, that's fine. The vehicle must not be wider than 2 metres.
C: Great.
S: How long is it?
C: It's exactly 7 metres long.
S: Please measure it again carefully. It must not be longer than 7 metres.
C: OK, I'll do that and get back to you.
S: How high is it?
C: It's just over 3.2 metres high, including the bicycles.
S: Mm. That's too high. The vehicle must not be higher than 2.9 metres.
C: OK, I'll take the bikes off.

3 Ask students to listen to the recording again and complete the phone conversation. They can then compare their answers with a partner before you check with the class. Point out that the question word *How* is used with adjectives. Ask a few follow-up questions, e.g. *Can the vehicle be 3 metres wide? Can the vehicle be 6.5 metres long? And can the vehicle be 3.5 metres high?*

> **1** wide is your van
> **2** 1.9
> **3** wider than
> **4** How long is it?
> **5** 7
> **6** longer than
> **7** How high is it?
> **8** 3.2
> **9** higher than

Reading

4 Ask students to look at the illustrations of the vehicles and to tell you which car is the 'high car', the 'standard car', the 'car with the trailer' and the 'large car'. Then ask them to read the web page from the car ferry company SuperFerries and answer the two questions.

> • The top car and the bottom two cars can board the ferry. The vehicle types are, from top to bottom:
> • high car, car and trailer, large car, standard car.

Language

Comparatives

Go through the rules in the Language box about the comparative form carefully with the class. The main problem students will have with the comparative is spelling and when to use *-er* or *more*, e.g. they may say ~~more cheap~~ instead of *cheaper* and ~~expensiver~~ rather than *more expensive*. Students may also use *that* instead of *than*, e.g. *The car is wider ~~that~~ the bridge*. So, provide students with plenty of extra practice. Point out that *more* is only used with adjectives of more than one syllable, but you can use *less* with adjectives of one syllable and above.

Tell students that they'll find more information about the comparative form in the Grammar summary on page 104.

> **Extra activity**
>
> Ask students to compare the dimensions of some objects in the classroom.

5 Go through the instructions with the class and make sure that they understand what to do. Go through the example and explain that you use *too* and *not enough* when something is the wrong dimension. You use *too* + adjective, e.g. *The lorry is **too high** for the bridge* when something is more than appropriate, and *not* + adjective + *enough* when something is less than appropriate: *The bridge is**n't** high **enough** for the lorry*. Students also confuse *too* with *very*. *Very* is used before adjectives to emphasise the adjective, i.e. make it stronger. It doesn't mean that it is a problem. For example, *The lorry is very big*.

Elicit the answer to the other problems from students:

> 1 The bridge is 2.7 metres high, but the lorry is 2.9 metres high. The lorry is too high for the bridge. / The bridge isn't high enough for the lorry.
> 2 The ship is 12.2 metres wide, but the canal is 11.5 metres wide. The ship is too wide for the canal. / The canal isn't wide enough for the ship.
> 3 The plane is 19.3 metres long, but the hangar is 18.8 metres long. The plane is too long for the hangar. / The hangar isn't long enough for the plane.
> 4 The CD is 12.2 centimetres in diameter, but the box is 11.3 centimetres wide. The CD is too wide for the box. / The box isn't wide enough for the CD.
> 5 The coin is 3 millimetres thick, but the slot is 2.88 millimetres wide. The coin is too thick for the slot. / The slot isn't wide enough for the coin.
> 6 The screw is 5.5 centimetres long, but the hole is 4.35 centimetres long. The screw is too long for the hole. / The hole isn't long enough for the screw.

Task

6 Put students in pairs. Ask them to look at the pictures and read the information about the Terrafugia road-ready plane. When they've finished ask them to discuss the questions and make notes. Check if they know the meaning of *wingspan*. Get them to guess from the context. (It means the total width of the plane from the tip or end of one wing to the tip of the other.)

Writing

7 Ask students to read the email. Then ask them to tell you what information they need to include in the reply to the company director. Tell students that they should organise their email in paragraphs, using the same order as the points 1–7. Students then work on their own and write a reply to the email.

When they've finished, they could exchange their emails with their partner from 6 and compare them.

Students could write the email for homework if you are short of time.

2 Products

Start here

1 Ask students to look at their mobile phones and think about which features are most important to them. Tell them to write down a list of the features in order of importance and then compare their list with a partner.

Listening

2 ▶ 🔊 10

Tell students that they're going to listen to six phone calls to a customer service operator at Delta Electronics. Ask them to look at the customer call record and read the purpose of each call. Then play the recording for students to complete the call record.

CALL NO.	NAME	PURPOSE OF CALL
6	Gray	complained about fault in ephone
3	Walters	cancelled order for classic ephone
5	Brandt	requested service assistance
1	Willard	requested ephone catalogue
4	Martinez	requested information about ephones
2	Jensen	placed an order for classic ephone

▶ 🔊 10

[J = Julia; MW = Mr Willard; MJ = Ms Jensen; MW = Mr Walters; MW = Ms Martinez; MB = Mr Brandt; MG = Ms Gray]

Phone call 1

J: Delta Electronics. This is Customer Service, Julia speaking. How can I help you?
MW: Oh, hello. Do you sell ePhones?
J: Yes, we do. Would you like a catalogue?
MW: Yes, I would. Thanks.
J: Fine. I'll send you one right away. What's your name?
MW: Willard.
J: Sorry, could you repeat that, please?
MW: Willard.
J: How do you spell that?
MW: W-I-L-L-A-R-D.
J: And could I have your phone number, please?
MW: 0133 48655

Phone call 2

J: Delta Electronics. This is Customer Service, Julia speaking. How can I help you?
MJ: Hello. I'd like to order an ePhone, please.
J: Certainly. Which model would you like to order?
MJ: The classic one, please. The 12 GB model.
J: Fine. Could I have your name, please?
MJ: Jensen.
J: Did you say Johnson?
MJ: No, Jensen. J-E-N-S-E-N.
J: And could you give me your phone number, please?
MJ: 0288 34500

Phone call 3

J: Delta Electronics. This is Customer Service, Julia speaking. How can I help you?
MW: Hello. I'd like to cancel an order, please.
J: I see. Do you think you could tell me the model number, please?
MW: It was a classic ePhone, 12 GB. I ordered it by phone yesterday.
J: Right. So, do you want me to cancel it?
MW: Yes, please.
J: OK. And what's your name, please?
MW: It's Walters.
J: Could you repeat that, please?
MW: Walters.
J: Thank you. And would you mind giving me your phone number, please?
MW: It's 0987 38206

Phone call 4

J: Delta Electronics. This is Customer Service, Julia speaking. How can I help you?
MM: Er, hello. I'd like some information about the ePhone, please.
J: Certainly. What would you like to know?
MM: Well, first of all, what's the screen size?
J: Let's see. Yes, it's 88.9 millimetres.
MM: Oh, right. It's quite large.
J: Yes. Would you like me to send you a specification table?
MM: Yes, I would. Thanks.
J: Could I have your name, please?
MM: Yes, my name is Martinez.
J: Sorry, did you say Martins?
MM: No, Martinez.
J: And could I have your phone number, please?
MM: Yes, it's 9604 33887.

Phone call 5

J: Delta Electronics. This is Customer Service, Julia speaking. How can I help you?
MB: Oh, hello. Yes, I bought a classic ePhone last week, and it doesn't work.
J: Oh, I'm sorry to hear that. What is the problem, exactly?
MB: I can't hear any sound.
J: Right. Shall I put you through to the service department?
MB: Yes, please.
J: OK, hold on. Could you give me your name, please?
MB: It's Brandt.
J: Could you say that again, please?
MB: Brandt.
J: Thanks. And would you mind giving me your phone number, please?
MB: Sure. It's 9977 00885

Phone call 6

J: Delta Electronics. This is Customer Service, Julia speaking. How can I help you?
MF: Good morning. I wish to complain about a phone I bought from you.
J: Certainly. Would you mind telling me what the problem is?
MF: The phone doesn't work. I can't make any phone calls.
J: I'm sorry to hear that. Could you give me your name, please?

MF: Yes, my name is Gray.
J: Is that AY or EY?
MF: It's GRAY.
J: And could you tell me your phone number, please?
MF: Yes, it's 3022 11816.

3 Play the recording again for students to complete the sentences.

1	could
2	Could
3	'd
4	Do, could
5	'd
6	Would, to
7	Shall
8	Would, telling

4 Ask students to read through the different functions first. Then tell them to look back at the sentences in 3 and match each one to one of the functions listed.

a)	3, 5
b)	6, 7
c)	2, 4, 8
d)	1

Speaking

5 Ask students to read through the phone conversations in the audio script on page 121. Then put students in pairs. Ask them to roleplay the phone conversations in 4, taking it in turns to be the customer and the service staff.

6 Ask students to look at the chart. Explain that it's a product comparison chart about two ePhones. Allow them a few minutes to look through the categories and their comparisons between the phones. Then ask them to complete the phone conversation. Ask individual students to write the answers on the board and check their spellings.

1	thinner
2	lighter
3	smaller
4	bigger

7 Ask students to practise the phone conversation with a partner. When they've finished, ask them to practise the phone conversation again, this time asking and answering questions about the other information in the comparison chart.

8 Ask students to read through the dialogue quickly and identify which word *one* refers to. Tell them they'll find the answer by reading the sentence that comes immediately before the first time *one* is said.

MP3 player

Language

The pronoun *one*

Go through the Language box with the class. Point out that *one* is a word and that can be used instead of repeating an object. Provide students with plenty of practice and encouragement as this will improve their fluency in speaking and writing.

Tell students that they'll find more information about some common combinations using *one* in the Grammar summary on page 101.

Speaking

9 Ask students to read the dialogue and add the missing *one* to four places. Do not confirm answers at this stage.

▶ 🎧 **11**

Play the recording for students to listen and check their answers.

10

(see underlined answers in audio script below.)

▶ 🎧 **11**

A: Hello, I'd like to buy a portable radio, please.
B: Certainly. We have two colours, red or black. And there are two models. There's <u>one</u> with rechargeable batteries, and there's <u>one</u> with normal batteries. Which <u>one</u> would you like?
A: I'd like the red <u>one</u> with the rechargeable batteries, please.

Put students in pairs. Ask them to practise the corrected dialogue in 9 with their partner.

11

> **Extra activity**
>
> Ask students to practise similar conversations to the one in 9. Write the following on the board:
>
> **Mobile phone**
> Model: with or without external antenna
> Colour: silver or blue
>
> **Sports car**
> Model: with or without steel rim wheels
> Colour: white, black, red or dark blue
>
> **Speed boat**
> Model: with 3-blade or 4-blade propeller
> Engine: 2-stroke or 4-stroke
>
> Go round the class, monitoring students as they're having their conversations.

3 Equipment

Start here

1 Put students into small groups and ask them to discuss the questions. After five minutes, feedback with the class If they disagree with the record, ask them what the new record is and how long they think that the record will last.

> **Extra activity**
> For homework, you could ask students to find out some more records on the internet and write sentences as in 1 to test the rest of the class.

Reading

2 Tell students that they're going to read emails from two men who work for a company that hires motorboats to tourists. Ask them to read the emails. Then tell them to read the questions and underline the answers to them in the email. Then check answers with the class.

Point out that *Cheers* is an informal way of saying thanks.

1 a) To tell Jeff (the Chief Engineer) to test five engines from different suppliers.
   b) To tell Bob (the Manager) that they've finished the test and that he'll send a report in a couple of days.
2 a) He reminds Jeff about replacing the outboard engines.
   b) He wants Jeff to let him know which of the engines he tests is the cheapest and which performs the best.
3 a) He tells Bob that they've finished the tests.
   b) Jeff promises to send a full report in a couple of days.

Scanning

3 Go through the instructions for the task with students. Ask them to read the list of specifications and test results for the five engines. Then ask them to turn to pages 118–119 and find the information about the engines. Remind them to find the information as quickly as they can, and not to look at every word in the text. They then underline the correct answers from the list. Ask students to put up their hand when they've finished, so that you know who the winner of the Speed search competition is.

Specifications
1 longer
2 B
3 cheapest
4 as powerful as
Test results
1 fastest
2 most rapid
3 quietest
4 A

3 Comparison

Language

Superlatives

Go through the Language box with the class about changing the comparative into the superlative form. Do another couple of examples with the class to check they understand, e.g. *smaller – smallest, cheaper – cheapest, more interesting – most interesting*, etc.

> **Extra activity**
>
> To help students remember the comparative and superlative forms of adjectives, get them to make word lists under the headings *adjective, comparative* and *superlative* and add to this list whenever they come across a new adjective. You could start off with examples from this lesson.

Speaking

4 Ask students to make comparisons between each group. They should think of as many differences as possible. For example, *Zinedine Zidane is the oldest football player. Zinedine Zidane speaks more languages than Wayne Rooney.*

Go round the class, checking that they're using the superlative form correctly. When they've finished, you could ask some students to tell the class about their comparisons and see if they agree with them.

5 Put students into pairs. Tell them to write down three items or products that they both know about. Then ask them to compare the items or products and make notes. Then ask students to read out their comparisons to the class.

Task

6 Put students into groups of four. Allow them to decide who will be Student A, B, C and D. Then ask them to read the situation and allow them to ask you any questions about it. Tell them to underline any important information in the text. Then ask students to look at the following features that are required for the car.

Ask students to read the information about their 4x4 at the back of the book on the pages listed. Give them a few minutes to digest the information and plan how they are going to persuade the rest of the team to buy their vehicle.

In their group, they then try to persuade the rest of the team to buy their car. In a feedback session, find out which is the best choice of vehicle.

Writing

7 Students work on their own and write a short report on their meeting. Refer students to the example at the bottom of the page and tell them that they should organise their report into paragraphs using these headings. Remind them that in the third paragraph they should mention their group's decision and the reason for their choice of vehicle. Refer students back to the email on page 21 which will help them to organise their email.

Students could write the email for homework if you are short of time.

Contents

Briefing

This unit looks at engineering, manufacturing and telecommunications **processes**.

Section 1 deals with **tunnel digging**, an engineering process. This is a key component of many **infrastructure** projects, such as road, rail and airport building, basic utilities such as water, electricity, gas and sewage, and oil and gas pipelines. The **tunnel drill** featured in this section is one of the largest in the world. It is currently being used to dig a 6.5 mile-long tunnel beneath the Niagara River in Canada that will divert 132,000 gallons of river water per second to a hydroelectric plant. At the front of the drill is the **cutter face**, a circular steel plate that rotates against the rock face. Arranged on this face are 85 large rolling steel disc **cutters**, or teeth. They spin freely as the cutter face rotates, carving concentric circles in the rock and producing more than 1,600 tons of **rubble** (waste pieces of rock) an hour. The cutter face contains a small door through which workers crawl to replace cutters when they wear out. As the rubble falls to the ground, **scoops** (like giant spoons) in the side of the head collect and deposit it into **chutes**. As the head rotates upward, the rubble slides down the shoots onto a **conveyor belt**, which carries it to the rear of the machine. **Hydraulic cylinders** attached to the drill's spine propel it forward like an inchworm. To stabilise the machine as it crawls, steel shoes push outward, gripping the tunnel walls, while two retractable legs lift it off the floor. As the machine excavates, two drills just behind the cutters bore into the unsupported roof. Workers fill the holes with bolts and **grout** (or **cement**), turning the rock into a protective canopy.

Section 2 deals with **car assembly**, a manufacturing process. The assembly **plant** (or **factory**) is the final phase in the process of manufacturing a car. Thousands of components are brought together here to be fitted together in **assembly lines**, in which the product moves along a line in stages to be assembled by robots and human workers. In the **chassis line**, parts are fitted to the **chassis** (pronounced *shassy*). This is the *lower* base frame of the car, which supports the **engine**, **suspension**, **exhaust**, **axles**, **transmission** (gear system) and **drive shaft**. Meanwhile, in the **body shop**, panels are welded to a frame to form the **body**. This is the *upper* part of the car (where the driver and passengers sit). The completed body moves from the body shop to the **paint shop** (where it is painted) and the **trim line** (where parts such as the **windscreen** are added to the body). Finally, the body and chassis lines come together: the completed body and chassis are fitted together (or **mated**) in the **final assembly line**.

Section 3 deals with the process of transmitting **TV programmes** via a **satellite** to a computer on Earth. **Communications satellites** can receive TV and radio signals from one region of the world and transmit them to other regions. These satellites stay in a **geostationary orbit**, moving above the equator at the same speed as the Earth spins. A **transmit dish** at an **Earth station** sends signals to the **receive dish** on the satellite, which then transmits signals to hundreds of thousands of TV **satellite dishes** mounted on buildings on Earth. A dish consists of a parabolic **reflector**, a **horn** and **cables**. The horn (also called a low-**noise block** or **LNB**) converts the signal to the correct **frequency** and sends it via cables to the **DTV** (**digital television**) **card** in the computer. The DTV card processes the signal and plays the video and audio on the computer monitor. A **setup** (or **set-up**) is a way of connecting together items of equipment so that they work together correctly.

The Robbins MB471-316 tunnel drill: http://www.robbinstbm.com/_inc/pdf/TBMs_11_2_06.pdf

Glossary of tunnel drilling terms: http://www.robbinstbm.com/news/glossary.shtml

Parts of a car: http://peugeot.mainspot.net/glossary/index.shtml

Car assembly: http://www.madehow.com/Volume-1/Automobile.html

Satellite TV: http://electronics.howstuffworks.com/satellite-tv.htm/printable

Digital TV receiver set-up: http://www.digitalnow.com.au/dvb_setup.html

Teacher's notes

1 Infrastructure

Start here

1 Put students in pairs. Ask them to look at the picture and discuss the questions with a partner. Then ask the class for their ideas. Accept all answers, but do not confirm what the drill does or how it works as they will read about this in exercise 3.

> It's a tunnel drill.

Listening

2 ▶ 🔘 12

Ask students to look at the specification chart. Tell them that they're going to listen to someone talking about a tunnel drill and that they have to complete the information in the chart. Play the recording once. Students listen and complete the chart. They can compare their answers with a partner. Play the recording once again if necessary. Then check answers with the class.

MB471-316 Tunnel Drill Specifications	
Length	24.4 metres
Diameter	14.3 metres
Speed	3 metres per hour
Manpower needed	230 workers
Cost	$31 million

▶ 🔘 12

This monster is one of the biggest tunnel drills in the world. It's the MB471/316 Tunnel Drill, and it costs more than thirty-one million dollars. It's twenty-four point four metres long and measures about fourteen point three metres in diameter across the cutter face. It weighs two thousand tons and moves at a massive speed of three metres per hour. It needs at least two hundred and thirty workers to operate and maintain it.

Reading

3 Tell students that they're going to read an article from a technical magazine about the tunnel drill from the Listening. The headings are missing from the article. Ask them to read the article once through to get the general meaning of the text and to compare the text with their ideas in 1.

Next ask students to read the headings and then go through the text again. Tell them to underline any words that are similar to those in the headings. This will help them to match the headings to the paragraphs.

Ask students how each of the headings start (with a verb ending in -ing, e.g. Collecting, Cutting, etc.). Explain that verbs ending in -ing at the beginning of sentences are used as a noun, and that it's common to start headings for procedures n this way.

> 1 Cutting the rock surface
> 2 Collecting the rocks
> 3 Moving the cutter
> 4 Supplying the electricity
> 5 Strengthening the roof
> 6 Controlling the movement

Vocabulary

4 Tell students that there are lots of names of parts of the body and clothing which refer to parts of the tunnel drill in the article. Ask them to look through the article again quickly and make a list of all the body parts and clothing that they can find.

> a) face, teeth, tooth, body, legs, arms, heart
> b) belts, shoes

5 Students could work in pairs to do this exercise. For each of the words they listed in 4, they should write down other technical contexts in which these items could be used. Tell them to use a dictionary if necessary.

> *Possible answers:*
> 'Teeth' are also found on gears.
> 'Belts' are used with car engines, to drive fans, compressors and camshafts.
> 'Shoes' are used with electric trains, to connect the train to the rail and draw its power.
> 'Face' is used with tools. It's the most important or working side of the tool.
> 'Body' is used with vehicles, e.g. the fuselage of planes, or the outer structure of a car.
> 'Legs' are used with pylons to carry the weight of bridges.
> 'Arms' are used with cranes. The crane moves objects by lifting them with a hook attached to a long arm.
> 'Heart' is used with ships, to mean the central or innermost part of it.

Language

Present simple passive

Go through the Language box with the class. Here students are presented with the present simple passive for describing a process. Point out that you form passive sentences with the verb *be* + past participle. Tell students that you use the agent when you want to name the person or thing doing the action, but that it's often not necessary to include the agent because it's unimportant who or what does the action.

Explain that the passive is often used in technical language for two main reasons: it makes the writing clearer when describing a process and it helps the reader to focus on what happens to things rather than on the person or thing that does the action.

Tell students that they'll find more information about the passive used in technical writing in the Grammar summary on page 102.

6 Ask students to read through the set of instructions first. Then tell them they have to change the instructions into a description of a process, using the passive. Go through the example with the class. They then work on their own to write the description. They could then compare their descriptions in pairs before you check with the class.

Sample answer:
First, the engine is run for a few minutes. Then it is switched off. Now the oil drain plug is taken off. Next the old oil is emptied into a container. Now the old drain plug is put on. Then the oil filler cap is taken off. Now the new oil is poured in. Finally, the oil filler cap is put back on.

7 Ask students to think about a process that they're familiar with. Tell them that they should first write a set of instructions for this process, like the one in 6. Then they should rewrite the instructions as a description of the process, using the passive. If students can't think of a process, point out the examples given.

8 Students could work with a partner to complete the sentences with the correct form (in the active or passive) of the verbs in brackets.

1 make, are filled
2 pushes, is driven
3 flows, is cooled
4 is monitored, controls
5 are brought, are cleaned, is removed, are painted, are taken

9 Refer students back to the headings in 3. Tell them that they are going to write headings like this for the main stages of a process that they know about. Tell them that they can use the same process that they wrote about in 7, or they can think of a new one to write about. As in 3, all the headings should begin with a verb ending in *-ing*.

10 Allow students a few minutes to prepare for their talk and make a few brief notes under each of their headings, if they wish. Remind them that they should use the passive structure in their presentation.

They then take it in turns to give a short talk to the class explaining their process. When they have finished, allow students to ask the speakers follow-up questions about the process.

2 Manufacturing

Start here

1 To introduce this section, revise words for parts of a car. Draw a simple diagram of a car on the board and ask students to copy it. Make sure you include the following features: *bonnet; aerial; windscreen; rear side window; wing mirror; bumper; boot; tyre*. Ask students to work in pairs and mark these parts of a car in their drawing. Then check answers with the class, and ask them if they can name any other parts of a car.

Put students into pairs and ask them to discuss the questions. Make sure that they understand what a *chassis*, *drive shaft* and *transmission* are in a car. (A *chassis* is the base frame that supports the engine and body of a car; a *drive shaft* is the rotating shaft that transmits the power from the engine to the wheels; *transmission* is the system by which power is transmitted from the engine of the car to the axle.)

Write the headings *body*, *chassis*, *drive shaft*, *axle* and *transmission* on the board and feedback from the class. Choose a pair of students to tell the class all they know about the location and function of the body of a car, and then ask other students to add any other information. Then choose another pair to talk about the next part of the car, and so on.

2 Pre-teach some key vocabulary. Tell students to close their books and ask them what an *assembly plant* is. (A *plant* is another name for a *factory*, and an *assembly plant* is a factory where the parts of a product are put together.) Then ask students what an *assembly line* is. (It's where the product moves along and is assembled in stages.) Finally, ask them who assembles cars in an assembly plant. (The cars are assembled by human workers and robots.)

Then ask students to open their books and focus their attention on the pictures. Tell them that they show the main stages in assembling a car. Point out that the stages are in the wrong order.

Draw students' attention to the flow chart under the pictures. Tell students that they should work with a partner and discuss the correct order of the pictures for the stages in assembling a car. Tell them that they should write the figure number of the pictures in the correct box in the flow chart. Do not confirm answers at this stage as this will be done in 4 on the next page.

3 Ask students to make captions for the pictures in 2 using the verbs and nouns in the box. Remind them of the headings they wrote for the main stages of a process in Lesson 1 and tell them that as with these headings, all the captions should begin with a verb ending in *-ing*.

Students can then compare their answers with a partner. Again, do not confirm answers as this will be done in 4 on the next page.

Reading

4 Ask students to read the car company website to check their answers to 2 and 3.

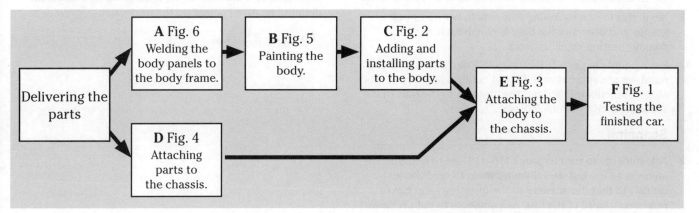

Delivering the parts → **A** Fig. 6 Welding the body panels to the body frame. → **B** Fig. 5 Painting the body. → **C** Fig. 2 Adding and installing parts to the body. → **E** Fig. 3 Attaching the body to the chassis. → **F** Fig. 1 Testing the finished car.

Delivering the parts → **D** Fig. 4 Attaching parts to the chassis. → **E** Fig. 3

Extra activity

Write the following words on the board:

finally, first, lastly, meanwhile, next, now, simultaneously, then

Ask students to look back at the text in 4 and underline these words. Then write the following headings on the board and ask students to put the words they underlined in the text into the correct columns.

at the beginning	after this	at the same time	at the end
first	then, next	meanwhile, simultaneously	finally, lastly

Language

Aim, purpose or objective

Go through the Language box with the class. Point out the two answers to the question and explain that by not repeating the object in the reply to the question, as in the first one, it will make them sound more fluent.

Tell students that they'll find more information about the purpose of an action in the Grammar summary on page 106.

Speaking

5 Refer students back to the website text in 4 once more. Ask them to work on their own and match the actions in the car assembly plant with the purpose of the actions. You could do the first one with the class as an example.

> **1** b **2** e **3** d **4** f **5** a **6** c

6 Put students in pairs. They take it in turns to ask and answer the questions in 5. Point out that they should use the passive form in the question. Go through the example with the class. Go round the class monitoring, and taking notes of any problems with forming questions in the passive which you can deal with later in a feedback session.

> **1** Why are thin metal sheets welded to a frame?
> To make the car body.
> **2** Why is the chassis turned upside down?
> To install the fuel system easily.
> **3** Why are special clothes worn by the robots?
> To protect the wet paint from dust.
> **4** Why is the chassis turned the rightside up?
> To lower the engine into it.
> **5** Why is the finished car put on rollers?
> To check the movement of the wheels.
> **6** Why is the car body checked by hand?
> To inspect it for faults in the paint.

7 Tell students to look back at 4 and find the answer in the text first. They then write the question for the answer.

> **1** How are the parts delivered?
> **2** Where are the panels welded to the frame?
> **3** How are the parts carried around the plant?
> **4** Why is the body checked?
> **5** Who is the body checked by?
> **6** How is the windscreen inserted?

Extra activity

Ask students to think of a process that they know about. If possible, choose a process that has two parallel processes happening at the same time, like the chassis line and the body shop line in car assembly plant. Here are some examples: making concrete, pitching a tent, sailing a dinghy from a pier, baking bread, processing milk.

Then tell students to draw a flow chart like the one in 2, giving five or six important stages in the process. Students can then explain the process to the class.

3 Communications

Start here

1 Begin this lesson by asking students to work in small groups and discuss what they know about how communication satellites work.

Put students in pairs to do the quiz. Point out that all the numbers are approximate. Do not confirm answers at this stage. Students will find out the answers to the quiz in the Scanning activity which follows.

Scanning

2 Ask students to turn to pages 118–119 and to find the answers to the quiz in 1. Remind them to read the text quickly to find the answers to the questions and not to read every word of the text. Ask students to put up their hand when they've finished so that you know who the winner of the Speed search competition is. Then ask that student to read out the correct answers and find out from the class how many students got all the answers correct in the quiz.

1 c **2** b **3** a **4** b

> **Extra activity**
>
> You could then ask students to read the text again and answer these follow-up questions:
>
> How often does the satellite revolve around Earth? (once every 24 hours)
>
> Why do you only need to direct your dish at the satellite once? (the satellite always appears in the same location – the satellite and Earth rotate at the same time)
>
> What is the feed horn used for? (to convert high-frequency signals to low-frequency ones)

Reading

3 Focus students' attention on the diagram. Ask them to read the instruction leaflet and label the diagram with the words in the box. They can compare their answers with a partner before you check with the class.

1 satellite
2 TV station
3 feed horn
4 dish
5 DTV card
6 TV
7 computer

4 Ask students to look back at the text in 3 and decide what thing *which* refers to in each case. Check their answers and point out that *which* refers to the noun that immediately comes before it. Then go on to study non-defining relative clauses on the next page.

1 b **2** a **3** b **4** a

Language

Non-defining relative clause

Go through the example in the Language box with the class. Explain that in the second example the two sentences are joined together by using a relative clause. Tell students that you can join two sentences in this way when the object at the end of the first sentence becomes the subject of the second sentence. This avoids repeating the name of the object.

Tell students that relative clauses in this lesson are non-defining relative clauses. They provide extra information about the sentence; this information is not necessary for the sentence to make sense. Point out that you put a relative clause immediately after the noun you are describing, and that in non-defining relative clauses you always begin with a relative pronoun such as *which* (for things) or *who* (for people). Also point out that a comma is used before relative pronouns in non-defining relative clauses.

Tell students that they'll find more information about non-defining relative clauses in the Grammar summary on page 103.

5 Go through the example with the class first. Remind students that you use *who* for people and *which* for things. Then ask students to work on their own to do this exercise.

> 1 My computer has a DTV card, which is connected by cable to my satellite dish.
> 2 If your DTV card doesn't work, contact our technician, who will repair it.
> 3 The dish reflects the signal to the feed horn, which converts the signal to a lower frequency.
> 4 Please send any complaints to our customer service manager, who will then contact you.
> 5 The radio station sends signals to the satellite, which then transmits the signals to my dish.
> 6 My DTV card extracts the audio and video, which are then displayed on my PC monitor.

Vocabulary

6 Ask students to match the words in the left-hand box with a word that has a similar meaning in the right-hand box. Allow students to do the exercise in pairs if they wish.

> transmit – send
> receive – get
> convert – change
> extract – take out
> display – show
> operate – work

7 Go through the first example with students to show them how to make compound adjectives. Point out that they need to use a hyphen to join the two words to make the adjectives. In item 3, point out that the plural changes to the singular (13 amps to 13-amp).

> 1 high-frequency
> 2 high-pressure
> 3 13-amp
> 4 13,800-volt
> 5 1.8 metre-wide

Speaking

8 Ask students to draw a simple diagram about a setup that they know about. They then make notes about it. If they can't think of a setup, they can use the diagram for the satellite dish from 3 and make notes about it.

9 Students take it in turns to describe their setup and explain how it works to the class, using their diagram to help them.

Answer key

3

1	more common	8	less combustible
2	faster	9	least harmful
3	less noisy	10	smallest
4	noisier	11	cleanest
5	heavier	12	quietest
6	better	13	least expensive
7	safer	14	more durable

4

1 f   2 c   3 e   4 d   5 a   6 b

5

1	I'd	4	Shall	7	do
2	Would	5	could	8	I'll
3	could	6	did		

6

○ … There's <u>one</u> with a cable, and there's a wireless <u>one</u>. … There's <u>one</u> with a USB connection, and there's <u>one</u> with FireWire connection. Which <u>one</u> would you like?

● I'd like the <u>one</u> with the USB cable connection, please.

7

1 d   2 a   3 f   4 b   5 c   6 e

8

Sample answer:
First of all, the spark plug cover is taken off. Then the spark plug is loosened with a special wrench. Next it is removed from the socket. Then it is cleaned using a wire brush. Next the spark plug is replaced in the socket. Then it is tightened using the wrench. Finally, the cover is put back on the spark plug.

9

1 Hammer the rod into the ground.
2 Strip the insulation off the end of the 3-metre wire.
3 Twist the wire around the rod ten times to make a good connection. This is the earth wire.
4 Attach the detector to the other end of the earth wire.
5 Take the 6-metre wire, and connect one end to the other end of the detector. (This wire is your antenna.)
6 Hang the antenna from a tree, (make sure that the bare end does not touch the earth).
7 Connect the two wires from the earphones to each end of the detector.
8 Put the earphones on. You can hear the radio station (if you are very close to the transmitter!).

10

1 Launching the communications satellite
2 Transmitting programmes to the satellite
3 Receiving digital signals from the satellite
4 Installing your satellite dish and digital receiver
5 Connecting your dish to the digital TV receiver
6 Converting high-frequency signals to low-frequency ones
7 Extracting the video and audio from the digital signal
8 Playing the video and audio via the monitor and speakers

11

1	road-ready	3	3-blade	5	voice-activated
2	4-stroke	4	6-metre	6	touch-screen

12

1 a) How are the car parts delivered? They're delivered by truck or rail.
  b) Where are they delivered? To the delivery area.
2 a) Where are the parts carried? To different parts of the plant.
  b) How are they carried? By forklift trucks or conveyor belts.
3 a) Where are the panels welded to the frame? At the body shop.
  b) Who welds the panels to the frame? 400 robots.
  c) Why are they welded to the frame? To make the body of the car.
4 a) When is the car body checked? It's checked after painting.
  b) Who checks it? It's checked by human workers.
  c) Why is it checked? To look for faults in the paint.
5 a) Where is the windscreen inserted? It's inserted in the front of the car body.
  b) Who inserts it? It's inserted by robots.
  c) How is it inserted? Using laser guides.
6 a) Where are the chassis and body moved to? They're moved to the final assembly line.
  b) Why are they moved there? To attach the body to the chassis.

13

1 The car parts are delivered to the delivery area by truck or rail.
2 The parts are carried to different parts of the plant by forklift trucks or conveyor belts.
3 The panels are welded to the frame at the body shop by 400 robots to make the body of the car.
4 The car body is checked after painting by human workers to look for faults in the paint.
5 The windscreen is inserted in the front of the car body by robots using laser guides.
6 The chassis and body are moved simultaneously to the final assembly line to attach the body to the chassis.

14 *Sample answer:*

First, the bonnet of the car is opened and the battery is located. Then the battery cables are loosened using a wrench. Next the battery cables are removed from the posts. The negative (or earth) is removed first then the positive. Then the detached ends of the cables are carefully laid to one side. Next the corrosion from the top of the battery is wiped away, using baking soda and water. If corrosion is very heavy, it is cleaned from the posts using a wire brush. Now petroleum jelly is applied to the inside of the terminals and the posts. Finally, the cables are reattached and the car bonnet is closed.

Project

15 At the end of every Review Unit is a project. Students can research their projects on the internet, or in the library.

Quick test answer key

Part 1: Vocabulary and grammar

1

1 order	3 cancel	5 complain
2 catalogue	4 fault	

2

1 noisy (the other words are to do with speed), or rapid (you use -*er* and -*est* to make the comparative and superlative for the *slow*, *fast* and *noisy*. But for *rapid*, you say *more rapid* and the *most rapid*.)
2 conveyor belt (the other words cut rock. The conveyor belt carries rock.)
3 propeller (the other words are parts of a car. You find propellers on planes or hovercraft.)
4 spark plug (the other words are to do with telecommunication. Spark plug is part of a car.)
5 paint (the other words mean to connect one thing to another thing. Paint means to put colour on something.)

3

1 operate	3 receive	5 extracting
2 transmits	4 convert	

4

1 weight	3 diameter	5 thickness
2 height	4 width	

5

1 The height of the van is 3.2 metres.
2 The drill is 23.5 metres long.
3 The weight is 5.8 kilos.
4 The cable is 7.5 mm thick.
5 The width of the computer table is 600 millimetres.

6

1 heavier	3 highest	5 not big enough
2 thinner	4 the least expensive	

7

1 I ~~shall~~ 'd like …
2 Sorry, could you ~~spelling~~ spell your surname?
3 ~~Would I~~ Shall I/Would you like me to send you …
4 Would you mind ~~to give~~ giving me your name …
5 Would you like me to put you on our emailing list?

8

1 Every Monday, the maintenance supervisor checks the equipment to make sure that nothing is broken.
2 Marta phoned up the shop to cancel her order.
3 You must measure the length of the car to check that it isn't longer than five metres.
4 The builders must wear hard hats at all times to protect their heads.
5 They use a tunnel drill to cut holes into the surface of rocks.

9

1 The cars are driven around the track to test the brakes.
2 All phone calls are answered by a voice-activated machine.
3 Customers are given a refund on faulty goods.
4 The speed and direction of the drill is controlled by the machine operator.
5 The planes are flown for 740 km on a single tank of fuel.

10

1 I'm having a meeting with John, who knows about the problem with the drill.
2 It's a device on our new model, which helps to prevent road accidents.
3 This company has made robots for 20 years, which are sold all over the world.
4 Sara is the project manager, who will answer all your questions.
5 I like the Toyota Land Cruiser, which is the most expensive car.

Part 2: Reading and writing

Reading

1 T   2 F   3 T   4 F   5 F

Writing

First, the bonnet is opened and the brake master cylinder is located. It's at the back of the engine. Next/Then, the top of the cap is cleaned to stop any dirt from entering the cylinder. Then/Next the cap is pulled off and the fluid level is checked. Now the brake fluid is added up to the line marked 'full'.

Finally, the cap is put back on, it's tightened and the bonnet is closed.

Review Unit B Quick test

Part 1: Vocabulary and grammar

1 Complete the dialogue with the correct word from the box.

cancel   catalogue   complain   fault   order

1 My _____ number for the ePhone is 49216.

2 Do you have a _____ with your new models?

3 Sorry, Can I _____ my credit card. I don't need it now.

4 There's a _____ with this MP3 player. I can't hear anything.

5 I'd like to _____ about my broadband connection.

(5 marks)

2 ~~Cross out~~ the odd word in each list.

1 slow, fast, noisy, rapid

2 conveyor belt, drill, teeth, cutter

3 axle, body, chassis, propeller

4 dish, frequency, spark plug, feed horn

5 add, attach, paint, weld

(5 marks)

3 Replace the words in italics with a word from the box in the correct form.

convert   extract   operate   receive   transmit

1 How do you *work* this machine? _____

2 The satellite *sends* signals to the receiving dish. _____

3 They didn't *get* any complaints. _____

4 Can you *change* metres into feet? _____

5 The most common way to get fuel is by *taking* oil *out* from oil wells in oil fields. _____

(5 marks)

4 Complete these sentences with the words in the box.

diameter   height   thickness   weight   width

1 You measure the _____ of a person or thing in kilos.

2 You measure the _____ or a person or thing in metres.

3 You measure the _____ of a circle from one side through the centre to the other side.

4 You can measure the _____ of a river with a waterproof tape measure.

5 You can measure the _____ of the wall with this gauge.

(5 marks)

5 Write a second sentence to mean the same as the first sentence.

1 The van is 3.2 metres high.

_____

2 The length of the drill is 23.5 metres.

_____

3 It weighs 5.8 kilos.

_____

4 The thickness of this cable is 7.5 mm.

_____

5 The computer table is 600 millimetres wide.

_____.

(5 marks)

6 Underline the correct word.

1 This bag is **heavyer/heavier** than 10 kg. I'm sorry, you can't take it on the plane.

2 I need a **thiner/thinner** wire than this one. It's too thick.

3 The **highest/most high** building in Taiwan is Taipei 101.

4 Let's buy **the less expensive/the least expensive** phone.

5 The car is **not enough big/not big enough** to carry all the equipment.

(5 marks)

7 Find the mistake in each sentence and correct it.

1 I shall like some information, please.

2 Sorry, could you spelling your surname?

3 Would I send you our latest catalogue?

4 Would you mind to give me your name and address, please.

5 Would you like me put you on our emailing list?

(5 marks)

B Quick test   PHOTOCOPIABLE

8 Rewrite each sentence by joining the sentences with the infinitive of purpose (*to* + verb).

1 Every Monday, the maintenance supervisor checks the equipment. He makes sure that nothing is broken.

_____

2 Marta phoned up the shop. She cancelled her order.

_____

3 You must measure the length of the car. You need to check that it isn't longer than five metres.

_____

4 The builders must wear hard hats at all times. They must protect their heads.

_____

5 They use a tunnel drill. It cuts holes into the surface of the rock.

_____

(5 marks)

9 Change these sentences from the active to the passive. Write the agent only if necessary.

1 The mechanics drive the cars around the track to test the brakes.

_____

_____

2 A voice-activated machine answers all phone calls.

_____

_____

3 Our company gives customers a refund on faulty goods.

_____

_____

4 The machine operator controls the speed and direction of the drill.

_____

_____

5 The pilots fly the planes for 740 km on a single tank of fuel.

_____

_____

(5 marks)

10 Add *which* or *who* and a comma in the correct place in each sentence.

1 I'm having a meeting with John knows about the problem with the drill.

2 It's a device on our new model helps to prevent road accidents.

3 This company has made robots for 20 years are sold all over the world.

4 Sara is the project manager will answer all your questions.

5 I like the Toyota Land Cruiser is the most expensive car.

(5 marks)

Part 2: Reading and writing

Reading

Read the text. Are the sentences true (T) or false (F)?

> The A380 'superjumbo' airliner is the biggest plane in the world. The plane is designed to help with the rise in the number of airline passengers, and the increasing amount of air traffic at airports, which aren't large enough for the number of planes that take off and land.
>
> The plane is nearly 25 metres tall, 73 metres long and has a wingspan almost as big as a football pitch; it's 80 metres from wing-tip to wing-tip. It has an upper and lower deck and two aisles. The aisles are wider than on other passenger planes to allow passengers to get on and off the plane quickly.
>
> Singapore Airlines, which flew the first superjumbo in October 2007, has a total of 555 seats, 416 more seats than on a Boeing 747 passenger plane. The passenger seating is arranged into economy, business class and first class. However, the plane is built to carry over 800 economy class passengers. By converting all the seats to economy ones, the plane is more economical to fly and better for the environment than other passenger jets.

1 Airports are becoming too small for the numbers of passenger planes.

2 It's difficult for passengers to get on and off superjumbos.

3 Singapore Airlines has three classes of passengers.

4 You can't have more than 800 passengers on a A380 airliner.

5 All of the superjumbos are cheaper and more environmentally-friendly than other passenger planes.

(5 marks)

Writing

In your notebooks, explain this process using the passive and the words/phrases in the box.

finally   first   next   now   then

How to check and add brake fluid in a car

1 Open the bonnet and locate the brake master cylinder. It's at the back of the engine.

2 Clean the top of the cap to stop any dirt from entering the cylinder.

3 Pull off the cap and check fluid level.

4 Add brake fluid up to the line marked 'full'.

5 Put the cap back on, tighten it and close the bonnet.

(5 marks)

5   Descriptions

Contents

1   Uses

Starter: discuss uses of tools.

Read descriptions of unusual tools and machines. Task: match these with photos.

Listen to descriptions of uses and match them to the photos.

Listen again and complete the dialogues with phrases that describe use, e.g. *it's (used) for finding lost objects*; *it's designed to …*

Word list: *beeping sound, emit, instrument, jump leads, produce, re-start, roadside assistance, socket, tag, underwater, vehicle, wrench*

Language: *for + -ing*; *to + infin*; *(acts) as + noun*; *you can use it/ it can be used for/to/as*

Speaking practice using above structures: *What's this device used for? It's used for finding lost objects.*

Discuss the uses of unusual devices.

Vocabulary: verb/ agent nouns (e.g. *calculate/calculator*)

Task: brainstorm unusual uses for everyday objects.

Word list: *calculate/calculator, conduct/conductor, contain/ container, generate/generator, propel/propeller, stabilise/ stabiliser, receive/receiver, transmit/transmitter*

2   Appearance

Pre-reading starter: describe photos of unusually shaped buildings.

Speaking: describe the buildings for partner to identify photos.

Read descriptions of the buildings and match to the photos.

Language: *it looks like/is shaped like/is in the shape of/is triangular in shape*; *it's L-shaped/in the shape of an L.*

Word list: *bridge (on ship), chain, chisel, cylinder, deck, dome, H-shaped, hull, link, L-shaped, ocean liner, sail, shaped, skewer, skyscraper, tripod, upside-down, wedge-surfboard*

Vocabulary: (a) nouns/ adjectives of shape: *triangle/ triangular*, etc. (b) prounuciation: syllable-stress change: *triangle/ triangular*; (c) select correct word (adj or noun) in sentences.

Vocabulary: *A-frame, U-bend*, etc.

Task: 20 questions game practising various questions including shape and use

Word list: *circle/circular, cone/conical, cube/cubic, cylinder/cylindrical, hemisphere/hemispherical, rectangle/ rectangular, semi-circle/semi-circular, sphere/spherical, square/square, triangle/triangular*

3   Definitions

Starter: choose good inventions.

Listen to definitions of inventions and fill in gaps with *that, which, who.*

Defining relative clause with *which, that, who*. Form of definition: *be* + generic (type) noun + defining relative clause, eg *An iPod is a device that downloads and plays music.*

Word list: *adjuster, alarm system, booster car seat, device, download, electronic, man overboard (MOB), mix (music), website*

Vocabulary: 'type' nouns used in definitions: *device, machine*, etc. (a) Complete pairs of sentences. (b) Join pairs of sentences into single definitions using *that, which, who*. Then rephrase definitions using *(used) for + -ing.*

Reading passage about man-overboard alarm system. Task: answer questions.

Group task: think of an idea for an invention, then write a definition and explanation. Finally, with group, explain idea to the class.

Word list: *controller, device, digital, display unit, instrument, GPS, hydrophone, machine, material, pins, pod, process, receiver, sonar, system, tool, transducer, transmitter, vehicle*

Briefing

This unit looks at ways of describing and defining things in terms of their function and appearance or shape.

Section 1 looks at advertisements about useful tools or machines. The X-beam wrench (or spanner) has a ninety-degree twist in the shaft so that the user's hand pushes against a flat surface. The Simple Start is a self-contained battery booster that plugs into the accessory outlet in the car and recharges a car battery. The device makes a beeping sound when the battery is charged. The Innespace Sea Breacher can move fast under and over the water like a dolphin. Joysticks control the mechanical fins, and foot pedals operate the tail. The extra-large windows allow passengers to see all around them. To use the Loc8tor (pronounced *locator*) you first attach a small radio-frequency-emitting tag to the object you want to locate, such as car keys. Later, if you lose the keys, you switch on the Loc8tor and it receives signals from the tag, showing you where the tag is. At the same time the tag emits a beeping sound.

The unusual devices shown in 7, on page 37 are: **1** A rotary cutter for cutting textiles and other materials. When you release the trigger, the circular blade moves back for safety. **2** A waterproof MP3 player for listening to music underwater. **3** A hand held anemometer for measuring wind speed. **4** A car inclinometer, to show the angle of a 4x4 when it drives on a hillside. **5** A bionic wrench. When you squeeze the two handles together, the six jaws in the head move inwards.

Section 2 deals with the shape and appearance of some famous buildings around the world. The remarkable shape of the Guggenheim Museum in Bilbao, Northern Spain, was designed by the architect Frank Gehry. The seat of government in Brazil is centred on the Plaza of the Three Powers (legislative, executive and judicial), in Brasilia. The building is 'H' shaped, with two dome-like accompaniments. The Central Chinese Television (CCTV) Tower in Beijing, China, is remarkable not for its height, but for its form, which projects outwards in an unsupported **cantilever** structure, and then descends again, all in one continuous **loop**. The structure is surprisingly strong and **earthquake-resistant**. The Vocabulary activities refer to structures shaped like letters. An **A-frame** is a basic building structure designed to bear a load in a lightweight economical manner. A **V-engine** refers to an internal combustion engine where the cylinders are at an angle to each other instead of in a straight line: the V configuration reduces the overall engine length and weight. **E-clips** are used to lock nuts in position. **G-clamps** are used to hold parts together while glue is setting. A **U-bend** is a pipe under a toilet or sink which traps water and prevents unpleasant gases from escaping.

Section 3 deals with inventions and ideas for new products by entrepreneurs. It begins by referring to a TV programme based on the BBC TV programme *Dragons' Den*. In the show, entrepreneurs explain their business ideas to a team of business experts (called the 'Dragons'), and try to obtain investment finance from them for their idea. The entrepreneurs explain their idea, and then the 'dragons' question them. The reading text describes the Man-Overboard (MOB) alarm system, based on the Mermaid system, by Matt Hazell. *Man overboard!* is what you shout if you see someone fall off a boat into the water. In this system, everyone on a boat wears a **pod**, a small egg-shaped device that is linked to the boat's **GPS (global positioning system)** and emits a **sonar** (sound) signal if it is covered with water. This signal is received on the boat by a **hydrophone**, which is a **transducer** (a device that converts an input signal of one form into an output signal of another form). The hydrophone detects the underwater signal and sends the data to a **display** at the **helm** (or steering unit) of the boat. This display sounds an alarm, displays the location of the MOB, and lights up lines of **LED**s (light emitting diodes) which show the captain the direction to the MOB.

Time magazine innovations: http://www.time.com/time/2006/techguide/bestinventions/

Great buildings: http://architecture.about.com/od/greatbuildings/Great_Buildings_and_Structures.htm

Dragons' Den BBC TV: http://www.bbc.co.uk/dragonsden/

Man Overboard alarm system: http://firstlightsolutions.co.uk/mermaid.html

---

Teacher's notes

1 Uses

Start here

1 Ask students to think of tools and devices that they use everyday. Ask them to think about what they use them for and why they are useful. Then put students in pairs to talk to their partner about them. Go round monitoring. Then ask students that have any interesting or unusual tools to tell the class about them.

> **Extra activity**
>
> You could start the lesson off by revising the names of tools that students are familiar with.
>
> Put the class into groups and ask them to write down as many tools that they know in two minutes. Then feedback with the class and find out which group has the most tools. Write the names of the tools on the board. Ask students what the tools are for.

Reading

2 Focus students' attention on the pictues of the unusual objects. Ask them what they think they are for and how they think they work. Then ask students to read the advertisements about them and match each advert to the objects in the pictures.

> A 2   B 4   C 1   D 3

> **Extra activity**
>
> Ask the class these follow-up questions on the text:
>
> *What does the wrench do?*
>
> *What do you normally do when your car battery goes flat?*
>
> Ask them to mime the words *jump*, *dive*, *roll*.
>
> Ask: *'What does rocket across water' mean?*
>
> Ask them to find another word in the text for *hold tightly*, *help* and *send out*.

Speaking

3 Ask students to look back at the advertisements and the pictures of the objects in 2 and discuss with a partner what they think of these items and give reasons why they think they might or might not be useful for them.

Then ask students if they know of any other unusual tools and what they are used for.

Listening

4 ▶ 🔘 13

Tell students that you're going to play a recording which will tell them about three of the inventions from 2. Ask students to listen to the recording and write down the number of the advertisement for that invention. They could then compare their answers with a partner before you check with the class.

> **a)** 4   **b)** 2   **c)** 3

▶ 🔘 13

a) A: So, tell me about your invention. What's it for?
 B: It's for finding lost items.
b) A: OK. And what about this device. What's it used for?
 B: It's used for charging a flat battery from inside the car.
c) A: Tell me about this invention. What can it be used for?
 B: You can use it to move quickly over and under water.

5 Students listen to the recording again and complete the dialogues.

> **1** for finding lost items
> **2** used for charging a flat battery from inside the car
> **3** can use it to move quickly over and under water.

Language

Describing uses and functions

Go through the Language box with the class, which shows different ways of talking about the use or function of a device. Ask students to look back at the text in 2 and underline examples of the present simple (e.g. *It shows you where your key is.*), for + verb *-ing* (*The X-beam wrench is great for turning nuts and bolts*), and *to* + verb (*This is designed to jump, dive, roll and rocket across water*).

Tell students that they'll find more information about describing the use or function of a device in the Grammar summary on page 106.

Speaking

6 Put students in pairs. Tell them that they're going to make questions and answers about the functions of the devices in 2, and that they should use all the structures in the Language box to explain the uses for the inventions. Go through the example with the class so that they know what to do. Then students take it in turns to ask and answer questions about the devices.

7 Students now discuss the uses of a new set of devices in the photos with a partner. They should use a mixture of structures like they did in 6. Alternatively, ask students to describe the devices and get their partner to guess the device that they're describing.

> The devices are: **1** a rotary cutter, **2** a waterproof MP3 player, **3** an anemometer, **4** an inclinometer, and **5** a bionic wrench. See page 49 for an explanation of what these devices are for.

Vocabulary

Go through the information in the box and spelling rules about *-er* and *-or* agent nouns with the class first before they do 8 and 9.

8 Ask students to change the verbs in the box into agent nouns. Allow them to use a dictionary to help them if necessary. Point out that the *-er/-or* ending has a weak sound /ə/. Tell them that there are no rules to say why one noun ends in *-er* or *-or* and they'll just have to learn them as they go along.

> calculate – calculator
> conduct – conductor
> contain – container
> generate – generator
> receive – receiver
> stabilise – stabiliser
> transmit – transmitter

9 Students complete the sentences with nouns from the list in 8.

10
> **1** calculator
> **2** conductor
> **3** generator
> **4** receiver, transmitter

Task

Put students in small groups. Ask the groups to choose one of the objects listed and brainstorm as many unusual uses for them as they can. Go through the example with the class first to help them with ideas. Give them a time limit of three to four minutes to do this. Then ask them to choose the best ideas and write these down. Ask groups in turn to tell the rest of the class about their best ideas.

2 Appearance

Start here

1 Ask students to look at the buildings and identify them. They can then discuss their ideas with a partner before turning to page 115 where they can find the answers. Find out from the class if anyone has seen these buildings and what they know about them. Do they like them?

> **A** Plaza of the Three Powers, Brasilia, Brazil
> **B** Guggenheim Museum, Bilbao, Spain
> **C** Central Chinese Television (CCTV) Tower in Beijing, China
> **D** Oriental Pearl Tower, Shanghai, China
> **E** The Shanghai World Financial Center, Shanghai, China
> **F** Burj Al Arab, Dubai

2 Put students into pairs. Ask them to choose one of the buildings in the photos, but not to tell their partner which one they've chosen. They then describe the building to their partner in as much detail as they can. Their partner tries to identify the building from the description they're given. They could then go on and describe another building from the photos.

Reading

3 Tell students that the newspaper cuttings are about the buildings in the photos. Ask them to read the newspaper cuttings quickly and match them with the buildings. Don't check their answers yet.

Go through some of the vocabulary that describes the features of the buildings, e.g. *hulls*, *decks* and *bridge* (of a ship); *ladder*, *skewer* and *tripod*; *chisel* and *blade*, *sail* and *surfboard*, *dome*, *plate* and *soup bowl*; *link in a chain*. Ask them to point to these features in the pictures and then check their answers. Tell them to correct any of their answers to the matching activity and then check their answers to it.

> **1** B **2** D **3** E **4** F **5** A **6** C

Language

Describing the shape and appearance of something

Go through the Language box with the class, which shows different ways of describing the shape or appearance of something.

4 Ask students to cover the text in 3 and try and remember what they read about the buildings in the newspaper cuttings. Tell them to use the phrases from the Language box and describe each of the buildings at the top of the page.
You could build up each description about the buildings on the board, eliciting information from students. They then compare the descriptions with the one in the text in 3.

Ask students to underline the sentences in the newspaper cuttings that use the ways to describe shape or appearance from the Language box in the text.

Extra activity

Ask students to think of a building that they are familiar with or one in their home town and describe it to the class.

Vocabulary

5 Students could work in pairs. Ask them to look at the illustrations of the shapes and match them with the nouns in the box. You could set this as a competition and ask students to raise their hands when they've finished matching the nouns to the shapes.

1 cylinder
2 rectangle
3 triangle
4 cube
5 cone
6 semi-circle
7 sphere
8 square
9 circle
10 hemisphere

6 Students now work on their own and write an adjective for each of the nouns in the box in 5.

1 cylinder – cylindrical
2 rectangle – rectangular
3 triangle – triangular
4 cube – cubic
5 cone – conical
6 semi-circle – semi-circular
7 sphere – spherical
8 square – square
9 circle – circular
10 hemisphere – hemispherical

7 Ask students to underline the stressed syllable in each word. Tell them to say each word out loud as they do so, as this will help them to identify what sounds right. Don't confirm answers at this stage as they'll be listening to the words and checking them in the next exercise.

8 ▶ 🔊 14

Play the recording for students to listen and check their answers to 7.

(See underlined answers in the audio script below.)

▶ 🔊 14

1 <u>tri</u>angle
2 rect<u>an</u>gular
3 <u>cir</u>cular
4 <u>cy</u>linder
5 tri<u>an</u>gular
6 <u>cir</u>cle
7 <u>rect</u>angle
8 cy<u>lin</u>drical

Extra activity

Ask students to group the words under the following columns according to their stress pattern:

▢▫   ▢▫▫   ▫▢▫   ▫▢▫▫

---

9 Students complete the sentences by underlining the correct word from the options given. When checking students' answers, make sure that they are putting the stress on the correct syllable.

1 triangular
2 cylinder
3 rectangular
4 circular
5 cubic
6 sphere
7 cone
8 semi-circular

10 Ask students to look at the names of the objects in the box and match them with the pictures. They can then compare their answers in pairs before you check with the class.

1 A-frame
2 U-bend
3 V-engine
4 T-junction
5 E-clip
6 G-clip
7 G-clamp
8 U-bolt

Task

11 Put students in pairs. Go through the instructions with the class. Point out that Student A must not tell their partner what the object is, and that Student B can't ask Student A directly what the object is. Read out the type of questions Student B can ask for each category. Remind them of the language from the lesson used to describe the shape and appearance of an object, i.e. *it looks like …*; *it's shaped like*, etc.

To make sure that students know what to do, you could start the activity off by thinking of an object yourself, and getting students to ask you about it. Then allow students to work in pairs and play the game.

3 Definitions

Start here

1 Ask students to look at the photo and explain that it shows five business experts who are taking part in a British TV programme called *Dragon's Den*. Explain that *an entrepreneur* is a person who starts up a commercial business to make a profit. Tell students that in this programme inventors and entrepreneurs try to persuade the business experts to help them to invest their money in their business idea. They present their idea to the experts who decide whether or not to invest their money in the invention and how much money they want to invest in it.

Put students in pairs. Ask them to read the advertisement and discuss with their partner which ideas were successful in the programme.

> These four ideas were all successful in the TV show, *Dragon's Den*.

Listening

2 ▶ 🎧 15

Tell students that they're going to listen to the four inventors from 1 making their opening statements about their invention in the programme. Either play the recording for students to complete the sentences, or ask students to read the statements first and complete them with *which*, *who* or *that*. Then play the recording for students to check their answers.

Go through the Language box with the class. Remind students of the work they did on non-defining relative clauses in Unit 4 Part 3. Here students are presented with defining relative clauses, which help to define the topic of the sentence. Tell them that *that* can replace *which* and *who* as the relative pronoun, and that it's a bit more informal. Point out that you do not put a comma after the relative pronoun in defining relative clauses.

Tell students that they'll find more information about defining relative clauses in the Grammar summary on pages 103 and 107.

> **1** which
> **2** that
> **3** who
> **4** which
> **5** that

🎧 15

1 A: So, tell me all about your invention. What does it do?
   B: My invention is an electronic device which can boil eggs without using water.

2 A: So, tell me about your invention. What is it? What's it for?
   B: LifeGuard is an alarm system that can find someone who has fallen off a boat.

3 A: So, let's hear about your invention. What is it and what's its purpose?
   B: This is a music website which allows you to download and mix dance music.

4 A: So, why don't you tell me about your invention. What exactly is it for?
   B: It's a seat belt adjuster that protects children in car booster seats.

Vocabulary

3 Explain to students that the words in the box are all 'type' nouns. For example, you can categorise a car as a type of vehicle.

Ask students to fill in the blanks with the appropriate type noun in the box. They could then check their answers with a partner before you check with the class.

> 1 device
> 2 vehicle
> 3 technician
> 4 tool
> 5 system
> 6 instrument

4 Students work on their own to make definitions by combining each of the sentences in 3 into a single sentence, using the relative pronouns *which*, *who* or *that*.

> 1 A solar panel is a device which/that converts sunlight into electricity.
> 2 The hovercraft is a vehicle which/that carries people over land and sea.
> 3 A lab assistant is a technician who/that maintains the equipment in a laboratory.
> 4 A torque wrench is a tool which/that tightens nuts and bolts.
> 5 GPS is a satellite which/that gives the location of objects on the ground.
> 6 An ammeter is an instrument which/that measures electric current.

Extra activity

Ask students to write two sentences using defining relative clauses, one to describe an object and the other to describe a person's job. Tell them to look back through Units 1–5 and choose objects and people from these units. Tell them not to name the object or the job title of the person in their description, but to leave this information blank. They then take it in turns to read out their sentences and the class guess the name of the object or the person.

For example:

… is a hard hat which protects your head. (*a safety helmet*)

… is a person who repairs oil rig platforms. (*a sub-sea engineer*)

Tell students that when they come across new vocabulary, writing a definition for it in English is a good way to record the word.

Reading

5 Explain to students that they're going to read an advert about one of the inventions from *Dragon's Den*. Draw their attention to the diagrams in the margin, which shows the Man Overboard system, and ask them to answer the questions about it by reading the advert. When they've finished, they can compare their answers with a partner before you check with the class.

> 1 a) the alarm pod
>   b) the hydrophone
>   c) the display
> 2 a) the hydrophone
>   b) the alarm pod
>   c) the display
> 3 No, because the two pins have to make contact with water for one second and the contact has to be constant across the two pins.
> 4 b) via the hydrophone
> 5 a) visible
>   b) audible

Task

6 Put students into small groups. Tell them to decide on a new invention between them. When they've done this, they should write a short definition of the device in a single sentence, like the ones in the opening statements in 2. Then tell them that they should write a few sentences explaining how the invention works.

Extra activity

In their groups, ask students to decide on one person who is going to present their invention to the rest of the class. These students then take it in turns to explain their invention to the rest of the class, who will be 'the dragons' and who will decide whether or not they should invest money in the invention.

Contents

1   Safety

Identify hazards in picture of a warehouse.

Reading: match warehouse safety rules with the identified hazards.

Language: passives following modals (*must/ should*) and semi-modals (*need to/ have to*).

Wordlist: *aisle, blockage, chain* (vb), *fork, forklift truck, gas cylinder, hand truck, overload, ramp, shelf, stack* (vb), *strap* (vb)

Discuss meaning of carton labels and what cartons might contain.

Complete the explanations of carton labels (*fragile, this way up*, etc.): *This item needs to be handled carefully.* Practising modal + passive.

Change passives in previous instructions to active form: *You need to handle this item carefully.*

Task: in pairs, unjumble three sets of safety procedures and put them under correct headings and in correct order.

Writing: safety rules for own workplace.

Word list: *artificial respiration, authorised, condition, CPR (cardio-pulmonary resuscitation), fragile, freeze, freezer, non-fragile, recovery position, pulse, this way up, upside down*

2   Emergency

Group starter: decide on a plan to rescue a trapped diver.

Listen to a brainstorming session. Task: identify the points on a spidergram, in order points are spoken.

Word list: *artificial respiration, available, buoyant, casualty, first aid, locate, oxygen, scuba diver, surface, trapped, tow*

Listen to a discussion following the brainstorm. Number the notes in the correct order.

Speaking: *What should we do if ...? We should ...*

Language: *must* (necessity) and *should* (recommendation). Modals + passives.

Reading: email. Task: identify the old info/ new info/ action sections.

Writing: write a reply to the email in same way, including recommendations.

Word list: *carbon emission, decision, global warming, improve, on board, reduce, renewable energy, rescue operation, safe, update*

3   Directions

Starter: landmarks on road, e.g. *roundabout, slip road.*

Match directions with sketch maps: *Take the second turning on the left* etc.

Language: make directions clearer: *describe the situation* then *give the instruction*. Eg: *There's a stop sign at the junction. Turn left here.*

Wordlist: *flyover, gantry, go straight ahead, motorway, police station, roundabout, slip road, stop sign, take the (second) turning on the left, take the first exit, (set of) traffic lights, turn (left, right), underpass, U-turn*

Reading: an e-mail giving directions. Task: find location on map.

Listen to directions around a university campus and identify destinations on a map.

Speaking: students give each other directions on a map.

Task: students give each other directions to places they know.

Wordlist: *campus, directions, entrance, junction, located, reception desk*

Briefing

This unit looks at safety rules, emergency and rescue procedures, and directions.

Section 1 deals with safety procedures, particularly in **warehouses** (large storage buildings). Safety is an important issue in warehouses because goods are constantly being moved around and lifted, and also because the goods themselves (such as chemicals or gas cylinders) may be dangerous. Safety procedures must therefore be followed carefully. Warehouses have **racks** (frameworks) of **shelves**, separated by **aisles** (long passages pronounced like 'isles'). Goods are packed in wooden **crates** or cardboard **boxes**, often attached to wooden **pallets**, which give them a flat and firm surface underneath and allows them to be lifted by **forklift trucks** without damaging the product inside. Goods can also be moved around on **hand trucks**, which the **warehousemen** pull or push around. Sloping **ramps** are used (instead of steps) between higher and lower levels of the warehouse, so that the trucks can go up or down them. Gas cylinders must be fastened to hand trucks in case they roll off. Hand trucks must not be pulled down ramps (or pushed up them) in case they move out of control and cause an accident. Boxes and crates have **labels** on them which give instructions for safety and to protect the product: for instance **frozen** goods must be kept inside a freezer, **perishable** goods (such as fruit or meat) must be delivered quickly (for example within three days). The Task deals with three emergency procedures: escaping from a building during a fire, giving someone first aid after electric shock, and what to do if chemicals spill out of their containers. **Cardio-pulmonary resuscitation** (or **CPR**) is done if someone's heart beat (or **pulse**) and breathing have stopped: the heart is massaged and **artificial respiration** is carried out to start them breathing. Unconscious people who do not need CPR are placed in the **recovery position**, as illustrated in the unit. (Note: special training is required before attempting these procedures).

Section 2 deals with a diving instructor training her team about emergency procedures to rescue a **scuba diver** who is trapped underwater. A scuba diver breathes from **cylinders** containing **breathing gas** (mainly oxygen). (There is a photograph of a scuba diver's equipment in Revision Unit C). The instructor conducts a **brainstorming** session, in which she encourages the trainees to mention everything they can think of, in any order. Then, in the next exercise, the instructor gets the trainees to put their ideas into the best order, so that they are sequenced as a procedure. The first thing the rescuers have to do is to **locate** the trapped diver, that is to find out exactly where the diver is. They then **mark** the diver's position on the surface of the sea, usually by placing a small **buoy** directly above the diver, attached by a **line** to the sea bed. When the diver has been brought up to the surface, he or she may not be **buoyant**, that is they may not float on the surface but begin to sink. To prevent this, the rescuers have to **inflate** the diver's **wet suit** by pumping air into it.

Section 3 deals with giving and following directions from one place to another. The section begins with some terms in **highway engineering**, which can be used as **landmarks** when giving directions to someone travelling by **motorway** or other major road: a **roundabout**, a **slip road** (where you exit or enter the motorway), a **gantry** (a metal structure supporting road signs above a road), a **flyover** (a bridge) and an **underpass** (a short tunnel). When giving directions using roundabouts it is often possible to say *turn left* at the roundabout, but where there are multiple exits it is clearer to say *take the first/second/third exit*.

Warehouse safety: http://www.blr.com/samples/15400200/product%20sample.pdf

Pallet identification labels: http://www.markartproductions.com/lapallet.html

Health and safety at work: http://www.hse.gov.uk/pubns/leaflets.htm

Diving equipment: http://en.wikipedia.org/wiki/Diving_equipment

Diver rescue: http://en.wikipedia.org/wiki/Diver_rescue

Teacher's notes

1 | Safety

Start here

1 Focus students' attention on the picture. Elicit from students that it's a warehouse. Tell them that the warehouse contains lots of hazards, i.e. things that are dangerous. Ask students to make a list of the hazards that they see in the picture in note form. Pre-teach some vocabulary which they'll need to help them describe the hazards: e.g. *overload*, *block*, *stick out*, *stack*, *strap* or *chain* to something.

Allow students a few minutes to complete their list. Then put them in pairs to compare the notes on their lists and to add items they missed to them. They can then join up with another pair and compare their lists again, again adding any new items to their list. Finally, elicit the items students identified on the board. Keep these on the board for 2.

A: There are some large boxes stacked dangerously on the top shelves.

B: There are some long boxes sticking out from shelves into aisle.

C: A man is lifting two boxes at same time from shelf.

D: A man is standing on bare forks of a fork-lift truck.

E: There are some empty pallets stacked up in the aisle blocking the passage.

F: There are some gas cylinders on hand truck, not strapped to it.

G: A worker has overloaded a hand truck with items above handles.

H: A man is pushing the hand truck with the cylinders up a ramp.

Reading

2 Ask students to look at the safety poster and explain that it gives a list of safety rules for the warehouse in 1 that should have been followed. Ask students to match the rules to the hazards in the picture. When checking their answers, tell students to explain their answers, e.g. rule number 1 matches G, because the hand trucks are overloaded.

1 G   2 E   3 B   4 F   5 D   6 A   7 H   8 C

Language

Modal verb + passive

Go through the Language box with the class, which presents the modal verbs *must*, *should*, *have to* and *need to* followed by passive verbs. Explain to students that these forms are often used in safety rules and procedures and that they express obligation, i.e. that something is necessary. There is no difference between *must* and *have to* in written English. There's a small difference in spoken English, but it's not necessary to draw their attention to this at this level. Students will have more practice on *must* and *should* in the next lesson.

Tell students that they'll find more information about modal verbs in the Grammar summary on page 102.

3 Ask students to look at the container labels. Tell them to try and explain what each label means.

> *Possible answers:*
> You can see these labels on containers of goods that are ready to be delivered or which have just been delivered.
> 1 fragile – be careful, the objects in the container can be broken easily
> 2 the container should be placed rightside up
> 3 keep dry – keep the container inside, away from rain
> 4 perishable – these things can go bad quickly. They must be delivered as soon as possible
> 5 keep frozen – these things are frozen, i.e. put them in a freezer

4 Ask students to say what they think is in the container for each of these labels, using the words in the box. Tell them that they can use more than one item from the box.

> 1 glass, bottles of liquid   4 food, fruit
> 2 bottles of liquid, plants   5 food
> 3 hats, electrical goods

5 Students complete the explanations for each of the labels in the illustrations. Tell them to use the correct form of the modal verbs and the passive form of the other verbs in brackets. Go through the example with the class first, to make sure that they understand what to do. They can work in pairs to do this exercise if they wish.

> 1 needs to be handled, must not/mustn't be dropped or thrown
> 2 needs to be carried, must not/mustn't be turned
> 3 should be kept, has to be protected
> 4 should be delivered, must not/mustn't be left
> 5 has to be frozen, must not/mustn't be left

6 Students rewrite the instructions in 5, changing the passive form into the active form. Go through the example with the class first.

> 1 You need to handle this item carefully. You mustn't drop ot throw it.
> 2 You need to carry this item this way up. You mustn't turn it upside down.
> 3 You should keep this item inside the warehouse. You have to protect it from the rain.
> 4 You should deliver this box as soon as possible. You mustn't leave it for more than three days.
> 5 You must freeze this box. You mustn't leave it outside the freezer.

Task

7 Ask students to look at the notes at the bottom of the page. Tell them that they are notes for three different safety procedures. Explain that they have become mixed up. Tell students that they must sort out the procedures and put them in a logical order. Student B's notes are on the page. Ask Student A to turn to page 112 at the back of the book where they will find their set of notes.

Ask students to write the following headings on a piece of paper: *First aid after electric shock, Fire evacuation procedure* and *Chemical spill procedure*. In their pairs, students work out between them which procedure goes under which heading from their notes. Point out that each procedure has eight notes. Finally, ask students to put the notes in the correct order.

> **First aid after electric shock**
> 1 Switch off the electricity.
> 2 Check the person's condition.
> 3 Call 112.
> 4 If the person is not breathing, start artificial respiration.
> 5 If there is no pulse, give the person CPR.
> 6 If the person is breathing, they should be placed in the recovery position.
> 7 Cover the person with a blanket and keep them warm.
> 8 Stay with person until emergency services arrive.
>
> **Chemical spill procedure**
> 1 Stop work.
> 2 Turn off any ignition sources.
> 3 Attend to any injured persons, if you can do so safely.
> 4 Call 999 to evacuate injured persons.
> 5 Evacuate the workroom and close the door behind you.
> 6 The workroom must be secured to keep others out.
> 7 Call Chemical Safety department.
> 8 Remain near workroom until Chemical Safety staff arrives.
>
> **Fire evacuation procedure**
> 1 If you hear an alarm, remain calm.
> 2 Leave the building by the safest route.
> 3 Do not stop to collect your belongings.
> 4 Lifts must not be used.
> 5 Close all the doors behind you.
> 6 Move at least 30 metres from building.
> 7 Report to the assembly point.
> 8 Do not return to the building unless you are authorised by the fire department.

> **Extra activity**
>
> Put students in pairs and ask them to discuss what safety issues there are in their own workplace or college, and what safety rules they think can solve these problems. Ask them to make notes of their ideas.
>
> They work individually and write a set of safety rules for their workplace or college, using their notes. Refer them back to the warehouse safety poster on page 42.
>
> Finally, ask them to swap their safety rules with a different partner. Tell students to check their partner's rules and make suggestions to improve them. Ask them to make sure that they are clear and simple and in correct English. They could then design up the posters and put them on the wall for the rest of the class to read.

2 Emergency

Start here

1 Put students in small groups. Ask them to read the situation concerning Mike and Ben. Then check that they understand what's happened. Ask: *Where's Ben?* (*On a motorboat, 2 km from land*), *What's happened to Mike?* (*He's had an accident and injured his leg. He's on the seabed.*) *What's Ben going to do?* (*He's going to rescue Mike.*) Then ask them to decide between them on a plan to rescue the diver.

Students should brainstorm tasks that Ben has to do in order to rescue Mike and make a list of them. Tell them not to worry if the list of ideas is not in a logical order to begin with. Then after they've thought of everything they could do to rescue the diver, ask them to decide on the best order in which to do the tasks. Feedback from the class by getting groups to read out their lists. Ask students if they agree with the order each group has put their tasks in.

Listening

2 ▶ 💿 16

Tell students that they're now going to listen to a diving instructor brainstorming ideas with her trainees on how to rescue someone trapped under water. Ask them to look at the diagram and number the points in the order in which they are mentioned. Make sure they understand this is the order that the trainees give in the brainstorming session and not the correct order in which they should carry out the procedure. They can then compare their answers with a partner. If necessary, play the recording a second time.

1	free diver's leg
2	bring to surface
3	remove from water
4	locate diver
5	mark position
6	provide extra air
7	do artificial respiration
8	make diver buoyant
9	tow diver to safety
10	attract help at surface
11	take to hospital
12	give first aid

💿 16

A: Right, let's brainstorm for a moment. Your diving partner is trapped under water. What do you need to do? Just come up with ideas, quickly, in any order.

B: Get his leg free from the wreckage, or rocks, or whatever.

C: We've gotta bring him up from the bottom of the sea to the surface.

D: You gotta get him OUT of the water.

A: Mm. Right, good. Any other ideas?

B: Well, you have to find him first. You need to locate him.

D: Yeah, you find him and then you've got to mark his position. Use a buoy on the surface.

C: You should give him extra oxygen, more gas, if his own oxygen is low.

A: Good, you're doing well. What else do you need to do?

D: Give him artificial respiration, if he's not breathing.

C: When he's on the surface of the sea, you have to make him float, make him buoyant.

B: When he's on the surface, you need to tow him to safety, you know, pull him to a boat or something.

A: Yeah, this is good stuff. Anything else?

B: You may have to attract help at the surface. Shout or shine a light to other boats.

C: Take him to hospital.

D: Yeah, but give him first aid, if he needs it.

A: Great. OK, let's look at these ideas again.

3 ▶ 💿 17

Tell students that they will now listen to the trainees putting their ideas into the best order. Ask them to listen to the recording and number the notes in the correct order. If necessary, play the recording again before you check their answers. They can then compare the order from the listening with the notes they made in 1.

1	Diver's location under water unknown? Locate diver and mark their position.
2	Diver trapped underwater? Free diver with knife.
3	Diver's air supply low? Give extra gas cylinder to diver.
4	Diver submerged in water? Bring to surface carefully.
5	Diver not buoyant at the surface? Inflate diver's wet suit.
6	Not breathing? Give artificial respiration.
7	Other boats in area? Send signal for help.
8	No help available at surface? Tow diver to boat or land.
9	Diver close to boat or land? Remove from water.
10	Diver needs immediate treatment? Give first aid.
11	Serious injury? Call helicopter to take to hospital.

▶ 💿 17

A: OK, now let's look at all the ideas in this spidergram, and put them in the best order, the best sequence of events. So, let's start at the beginning. What if we don't know exactly where the diver is? If his location underwater is unknown? What should we do first?

B: We have to locate the diver, and then mark his position with a buoy on the surface.

C: And then we can cut him free, with a knife, if he's trapped.

A: Right, and what about his oxygen supply?

D: If his breathing gas is low, we have to give him some more gas. We can use an extra oxygen tank.

B: And then we should bring him up to the surface, very carefully and not too quickly.

A: Right, good, so you're at the surface, and you're holding the diver there. What if he sinks again?

C: We need to make him float, make him buoyant at the surface. We can inflate his wet suit.

D: If he's not breathing, we may have to give him artificial respiration there on the surface.

B: And call for help, if there are any other boats around. Or send a signal for help.

A: What if there's no help available? You're on the surface, but there are no other boats around?

B: Tow him to the boat, or to the land if it's close.

C: Then remove him from the water and get him into the boat or onto land.

D: If he needs immediate treatment, give him first aid.

B: And if the injury is serious, call a helicopter to take him to hospital.

A: Good, well done.

Speaking

4 Go through the example question and answer with the class first. Point out that they should write the questions and answers in the correct order that the tasks should be done. They could then take it in turns to read out their questions and answers with a partner.

1 What should you do if the diver's location under water is unknown?
You should locate them and mark their position.

2 What should you do if the diver is trapped underwater?
You should free the diver with a knife.

3 What should you do if the diver's air supply is low?
You should give an extra gas cylinder to the diver.

4 What should you do if the diver is submerged in water?
You should bring the diver to the surface carefully.

5 What should you do if the diver isn't buoyant at the surface?
You should inflate the diver's wet suit.

6 What should you do if the diver isn't breathing?
You should give the diver artificial respiration.

7 What should you do if there are other boats in the area?
You should send a signal for help.

8 What should you do if there is no help available at surface?
You should tow the diver to a boat or to land.

9 What should you do if the diver is close to a boat or land?
You should remove the diver from the water.

10 What should you do if the diver needs immediate treatment?
You should give the diver first aid.

11 What should you do if there is serious injury?
You should call a helicopter to take the diver to hospital.

Language

must and *should*

Go through the Language box with the class, which shows the difference between *must* and *should*. Explain that these words are often used in safety rules and procedures.

Reading

5 Ask students to read the email and answer the questions.

> Old information: You'll remember that …
> New information: The rescue leader has just told me …
> I'm holding a meeting next week …
> Action: Could you please send me …

Writing

6 Students write Jon's reply to Don's email. Point out that the email must include old information, new information (which includes six recommendations) and the action they are going to take. Tell them that they can include six items from the notes in 3, or they can provide their own ideas for the recommendations.

Extra activity

Put students in small groups. Ask them to choose a problem or an issue that interests them and brainstorm some solutions. Then ask them to write the solutions as a set of recommendations.

Examples of issues: *global warming, transport safety, renewable energy, public transport, safety in buildings, computer viruses, mobile phone prices.*

Students then present the recommendations with their group to the rest of the class.

---

3 Directions

Start here

1 Ask students to look at the photo of the motorway and to use the words in the box to identify the landmarks in the photo. They can then compare their answers with a partner before you check with the class.

> **Extra activity**
>
> Ask them if they know any other words which can be used in a motorway and other road contexts, e.g. *fast lane/slow lane*, *hard shoulder*, *crash barrier*, *road signs*, *traffic lights*, *zebra crossings*, etc.

1 slip road
2 flyover
3 gantry
4 motorway
5 roundabout
6 underpass

Reading

2 Ask students to look at the small maps and match them with the directions that they show. Ask them how many exits there are on the roundabout in photo F.

1 D   2 F   3 A   4 C   5 B   6 H   7 G   8 E

Language

Directions

Go through the Language box with the class. Tell students that to make your directions clear, you should describe the situation first and then give the instruction.

> **Extra activity**
>
> Ask students to look back at the directions in 2. Ask them to try and make them clearer by describing the situation first and then giving the instruction. For example: *A When you come to the T-junction, turn left.* Tell them that you can also say: *At the T-junction, turn left.* (N.B. it's not possible to change number D.)
>
> (Possible answers:
>
> **B** *At the crossroads, go straight ahead.*
>
> **C** *When you come out of the building, turn right.*
>
> **E** *When you come out of the car park, you'll see a flyover. Turn left under it.*
>
> **F** *You'll see a roundabout. Take the third exit.*
>
> **G** *At the bridge, go over it and take the first road on the right.*
>
> **H** *When you come to the slip road, leave the motorway. You'll then see a roundabout. Turn left.)*

Reading

3 Ask students to read the email and follow the directions in it on the map. Tell them to raise their hands once they've marked TurboTech on the map.

> B

> **Extra activity**
>
> As a quick warmer to this exercise, ask students who they think are better at giving and following directions: men or women.

Listening

4 ▶ 💿 **18**

Tell students that they're now going to listen to a recording and tell them to follow the directions that are given on the map. They have to mark the Engineering Department and the Sports Centre on it. Point out that the university is in a country which drives on the left.

> Call 1: 6
> Call 2: 4

▶ 💿 **18**

[C1 = Caller 1; C2 = Caller 2; R = Receptionist]

1

C1: Oh, hello, erm, do you think you could tell me how to get to the Engineering Department in the university?

R: Of course. Where are you at the moment?

C1: I'm driving up the M95 motorway from the South.

R: OK. Well, you have to leave the motorway at Junction 3. You'll see the sign.

C1: Right. So I leave the M95 at Junction 3.

R: Yeah. Then when you come off the slip road of the motorway, you'll come to a large roundabout.

C1: OK?

R: Take the ... how many? ... er, ... the fifth exit. Yes, the fifth exit from the roundabout. One of the exits is no entry because it's a slip road from the motorway.

C1: OK. Fifth exit.

R: Then almost immediately, you'll come to the main entrance to the South Campus.

C1: Right.

R: So then, turn left into the campus and go straight ahead.

C1: OK.

R: You'll see four buildings on your left.

C1: Four buildings on my left.

R: Yes. And the Engineering Department is the last building on your left.

C1: Great. Thanks very much.

R: You're welcome.

2

C2: Hi, yeah, er, could you please tell me how to get to the Sports Centre in the university?

R: Sure. Where are you now?

C2: I'm coming out of the entrance to the South Campus.

R: Are you driving a car?

C2: Yes, I am.

R: OK ... well, erm, come out of the entrance and turn right at the T-junction.

C2: OK.

R: Soon you'll come to a large roundabout over the M95 motorway.

C2: Right ...?

R: Go round the roundabout, pass the no-entry slip road, and take the second main exit. You're in Comet Way. Keep going until you come to the next roundabout.

C2: OK.

R: So, turn left at this roundabout. It's the first exit. Soon you'll come to another small roundabout. There's a hotel on your left at the roundabout.

C2: OK.

R: At this roundabout, take the second exit.

C2: OK.

R: There's another roundabout ahead of you. Go straight ahead at this roundabout, second exit. Now you're going past the main entrance of the North Campus.

C2: Yeah.

R: At the next roundabout, turn left. Follow the road around to the left. You'll see the North Campus on your left.

C2: OK.

R: Just before you come to the next crossroads, you'll see a large building on your left.

C2: OK. A large building on my left. Just before the crossroads.

R: That's right. That building is the Sports Centre.

C2: Thanks. Got it!

Speaking

5 Put students in A and B pairs. Explain that they're going to give each other telephone directions to places on the map in 4. Tell students to turn to their pages at the back of the book.

Students read the instructions and roleplay their conversations. When they're doing their roleplay, encourage them to sit back to back so that they can't see each other speaking.

When they've finished, ask them to check that they've correctly found the places on their maps with their partner.

Task

6 Students can work with the same partner. Tell them to list three local places that they know how to give directions to. They then take turns to give their partner directions to that place. Their partner listens and draws a map showing the directions that they're being given. Finally, they swap their maps with their partner and check that they've followed the directions correctly.

Review Unit C

Answer key

1
1 starting
2 detect
3 convert
4 treating
5 carry

3
1 The demand valve is for controlling the flow of air to the diver.
2 The cylinder is used to store air under high pressure.
3 The pressure gauge indicates the amount of compressed air in the cylinder.
4 The cylinder is used for transporting compressed air with the diver.
5 The depth gauge is designed to indicate the depth of the water.
6 The harness is for fastening the equipment to the diver.
7 The diving mask is designed to allow the diver to see clearly underwater.
8 The pressure gauge acts as a warning for the diver.
9 The demand valve supplies compressed air to the diver.
10 The harness acts as a support for the scuba equipment.

4
1 it called
2 it for
3 does it work
4 is a hydrophone/does the hydrophone do
5 is it designed
6 is it
7 big is it
8 do you put it
9 is it made of
10 colour is it

7
1 An MP3 player is a device which downloads and plays music from a computer.
2 Fibreglass is a material which is used for making hulls of boats.
3 Artificial respiration is a procedure which helps a casualty to breathe.
4 GPS is a system which uses satellites to locate your position.
5 A sub-sea mechanic is a technician who repairs underwater pipes and machines.
6 A solar-powered car is a vehicle which is powered by electricity from a solar panel.
7 A wheel wrench is a tool which loosens and tightens nuts on wheels.
8 A depth gauge is an instrument which calculates a diver's depth in the water.

8 *Sample answer:*
Continue along 156th Ave NE until you come to NE 36th St. Turn right. Go straight ahead at the crossroads. Then take the first turning on the right. Go straight ahead along NE 36th Way. You'll pass a turning to the right. After the turning, the road becomes 163rd Ave NE and you'll see Building 31 on your right.

9
1 Two air cylinders must be carried at all times during a dive.
2 Lifejackets have to be worn on board this oil rig (by all staff).
3 Boxes or crates must not be stacked in the aisles.
4 All this food needs to be frozen before you send it to the warehouse.
5 Forklift trucks should never be used as people carriers (by workers).
6 Trucks have to be pushed down a ramp. They must never be pulled down.

Project

13 At the end of every review Unit is a project. Students should use a good dictionary or an internet search engine.

Tip: To find the meaning of a word in Google, type *definition* and then the word.

Quick test answer key

Part 1: Vocabulary & grammar

1
1 buoy
2 fragile
3 gantry
4 casualty
5 ramp

2
1 vehicle
2 instrument
3 tool
4 system
5 device

3
1 square
2 rectangular
3 circular
4 cubes

4
1 sign
2 roundabout
3 motorway
4 underpass
5 flyover

5
1 to open
2 as a conductor
3 measuring
4 to start
5 controlling

6
1 It looks like an ocean liner.
2 It's dome-shaped.
3 The pipe is S-shaped.
4 It's shaped like a square.
5 It's triangular shaped.

7
1 A sub-engineer is a person who repairs oil pipes under the sea.
2 A jack is a device which lifts heavy objects.
3 A tunnel drill is a powerful machine which cuts holes into rocks.
4 The wheel-gun team are mechanics who tighten nuts on wheels.
5 A feed horn is an antenna which transmits radio waves.

8
1 You needn't finish the job today.
2 These objects must be carried carefully. They're fragile.
3 The equipment has to be checked every day.
4 Jamal should wear gloves when he operates the machine.
5 Tools should not be left on the ground.

9
1 is, don't use
2 breaks, don't move
3 burns, cool
4 have, wash
5 are, don't stand

1 turn/go
2 will
3 exit
4 over/under
5 turning/road

10 Part 2: Reading and writing

Reading

1 They aren't used after the Olympic Games are over.
2 It's designed to convert into a smaller permanent stadium.
3 A 65-foot plastic structure goes around the stadium.
4 Two-thirds of the people are protected from the rain.
5 Some people think it looks like the Roman Colosseum, some people think it looks like a gasometer and some people think it looks like a fruit bowl.

Writing

Hi Pete
You'll remember that a safety officer inspected the warehouse last week. He has just told me that one of the fire extinguishers doesn't work. We should get it repaired or replaced as soon as possible. I'm holding a meeting next Thursday on checking and maintaining all safety equipment. Could you let me know if you can attend this meeting?
Kind regards
Jon

Review Unit C Quick test

Total _____/60

Part 1: Vocabulary and grammar

1 Write the correct word for these definitions.

1 An object that floats on the water to warn ships about objects or dangerous areas in the sea. b_____

2 Easy to break. f_____

3 A frame to display road signals on a motorway. g_____

4 Somebody who is seriously injured in an accident. c_____

5 A sloping surface that allows you to go from a lower level to a higher level. r_____

(5 marks)

2 Complete the sentences with a 'type' noun in the box.

device   instrument   system   tool   vehicle

1 A forklift truck is a _____.

2 A thermometer is an _____.

3 A G-clamp is a _____.

4 A solar panel is a heating _____.

5 An MP3 player is a _____.

(5 marks)

3 The words in italics are incorrect. Correct them.

1 A *triangle* has four sides. _____

2 Windscreens of a car are *square* in shape. _____

3 CDs are *spherical* in shape. _____

4 You put *spheres* of ice in drinks. _____

(4 marks)

4 Complete the text with the words in the box.

flyover   motorway   roundabout   sign   underpass

1 At the end of the road there's a stop (3) _____.

2 When you come to a (4) _____. Take the third exit.

3 Come off the _____ at junction 10.

4 Drive through the _____. The M32 is above you.

5 Take the A30 – it goes under a _____ – and continue for a mile.

(6 marks)

5 Underline the correct option.

1 A tin opener is designed **to open/opening** tins.

2 Trees act **to conduct/as a conductor** of electricity.

3 It can be used for **measure/measuring** very large and difficult walls.

4 You use this lever **to start/starting** the machine.

5 This device is for **control/controlling** the temperature of the liquid.

(5 marks)

6 Complete the second sentence to mean the same as the first.

1 It's similar in appearance to an ocean liner.
It _____.

2 It's shaped like a dome.
It's _____.

3 It's an S-shaped pipe.
The pipe is _____.

4 It's square shaped.
It's _____.

5 The building is in the shape of a triangle.
It's _____.

(5 marks)

7 Join the first half of the sentence with the second and rewrite them using relative pronouns: *who*, *which* or *that*.

1 A sub-sea engineer is a person | He repairs oil pipes under the sea.

2 A jack is a device. | It lifts heavy objects.

3 A tunnel drill is a powerful machine. | It cuts holes into rocks.

4 The wheel-gun team are mechanics. | They tighten nuts on wheels.

5 A feed horn is an antenna. | It transmits radio waves.

(5 marks)

8 Complete each sentence with the modal verb in brackets in the active or passive form.

1 It's not necessary to finish the job today.
You _____. (needn't)

2 It's essential to carry these object carefully. They're fragile.
These objects _____. (must)

3 It's essential to check the equipment every day.
The equipment _____. (have to)

4 It's a good idea that Jamal wears gloves when he operates the machine.

Jamal _____. (should)

5 We recommend that you do not leave tools on the ground.

Tools _____. (should not)

(5 marks)

9 Complete the sentences with the words in brackets. Use the affirmative or negative.

1 If there _____ a fire in the building, _____ the lifts. (be/use)

2 If someone _____ their leg, _____ them. (break/move)

3 If someone _____ their hand, _____ it with cold water immediately. (burn/cool)

4 If you _____ chemicals in your eye, _____ the eye out with sterile fluid for 10 minutes. (have/wash)

5 If you _____ in a lightning storm, _____ under a tree. (be/stand)

(5 marks)

10 Complete the sentences with an appropriate word.

When you come out of the car park, (1) _____ left. Go to the end of the road and you (2) _____ see a roundabout. Take the third (3) _____ from the roundabout. Continue along this road for one kilometre. Go (4) _____ the bridge. Then take the second (5) _____ on the right. Our house is on your left.

(5 marks)

Part 2: Reading and writing

Reading

Read the text and answer the questions below.

> The problem with most Olympic stadiums is that they aren't used when the Games are over. The new London Olympic stadium for the 2012 Games is designed to convert from a temporary stadium used for the Olympic Games to a smaller permanent stadium used for holding sporting and other local community events after the games are finished.
>
> The stadium has two oval-shaped layers. The bottom layer is shaped like a bowl, which has been dug into the ground. This part is for the running tracks and field area, and has seats for 25,000 people. The top section has a structure made of steel, which has a further 55,000 seats. The organisers plan to remove these seats and sell them as soon as the Games finish. There is a cable-supported roof, which covers two-thirds of the seats. A 65-foot structure made of plastic is attached to the outside of the stadium and wraps around it like a curtain. The organisers plan to decorate the material with pictures of former Olympic winners. After the Games they plan to cut up the fabric and make them into souvenir bags.

> People have different opinions about the design of the stadium. Some people think it looks like the Roman Colosseum, others think it looks like a gasometer, and for some it looks like a fruit bowl.

1 What is the main problem Olympic stadiums have?

_____

_____

2 What is the London Olympic stadium designed to do?

_____

_____

3 What is designed to go around the stadium?

_____

_____

4 How many people does the roof protect from the rain?

_____

_____

5 What do people think the stadium looks like?

_____

_____

(5 marks)

Writing

Put the sentences in the correct order and rewrite the email below.

1 We should get it repaired or replaced as soon as possible.

2 I'm holding a meeting next Thursday on checking and maintaining all safety equipment.

3 He has just told me that one of the fire extinguishers doesn't work.

4 You'll remember that a safety officer inspected the warehouse last week.

5 Could you let me know if you can attend this meeting?

Hi Pete

_____

_____

_____

_____

_____

_____

_____

_____

Kind regards

Jon

(5 marks)

7 | Services

Contents

1 | Technical support

Task: decide best solutions to common computer problems.

Listen to phone calls about computer problems and complete IT technician's report about *problem, diagnosis* and *solution*.

Word list: *access (vb), attachment, click, firewall, icons, incoming, interfere with, IP address, link, log in(to), monitor, network, password, reboot, reject, router, screen resolution, security level, setting, uncheck (a box), website, wireless, wirelessly*

Listen and fill gaps: *must, may, might, could + be,* present continuous or present perfect

Identify which modals indicate *certainty* or *possibility*.

Listen and fill gaps: verbs with *–ing* ending after *try*

Language: possibility in present: *may/might be*; certainty in present: *must be*; use of *may/might/must* + present perfect: *You must have broken it.* Making suggestions: *(I suggest you)/(You could)/(Why don't you) try –ing.*

Make diagnosis + suggestion: *Your switch might be broken. Try changing it.*

Word list: *compress, disconnect, reconnect*

2 | Reporting to clients

Brainstorm ideas for making tall buildings safe.

Group task: discuss a diagram which has ideas for safer skyscrapers. Decide what the purpose of each idea is. Decide which ideas will/will not work.

Present group's decisions orally.

Word list: *backup power, beam, CCTV camera, column, fire drill, fireproof, loudspeakers, parachute, reinforced, sensors, skybridge, sprinklers, strain*

Read a covering letter and answer questions.

Read the attachment to the letter reporting on work done, and match points to the diagram of building.

Language: form of past passive.

Speaking: phone call going through all the points in the report, changing passives to actives. *CCTV cameras were installed. How many did you install? We installed twenty.*

Word list: *attach, compulsory, cross over, expand, fire-resistant, install, monitor, practical, regular, shorten, smoke detector, structural, widen*

3 | Dealing with complaints

Starter: common customer complaints and how to deal with them.

Listen to phone call with complaint. Task: complete complaints form with details.

Read behavioural guide on how to deal with complaints, listen again and decide if guide is followed.

Role play phone calls between service staff and complaining customer.

Word list: *complain/complaint, offer, record (details), reduce, refund, repair, replace, summarise, sympathy*

Describe damage to suitcase (pictured). Revision of *dented surface, corner, edge*, etc.

Read reply to customer's letter of complaint. Answer questions. Focus on phrases showing sympathy, apologising, introducing good/bad news, offering.

Write a reply to letter of complaint.

Word list: *apologise, broken, cracked, cracked, crushed, dented, gesture of good will, I am pleased to inform you that, I look forward to, in stock, inconvenience, please do not hesitate to, purchase, split, torn, twisted, unfortunately*

Briefing

This unit looks at aspects of dealing effectively with customers and clients.

Section 1 deals with **technical support** using a telephone hotline. The six staff who talk to Lisa, an IT support technician in their company, have problems using the company computer **network**. The first caller's **password** is rejected by the network. This is because the caller must have keyed in the wrong password at an earlier time. The system remembers it because the caller **checked** (put a tick in) the REMEMBER PASSWORD box. The second caller has the wrong **screen resolution settings**: everything appears too large on the screen. To solve this using a PC, go to CONTROL PANEL – DISPLAY – SETTINGS. The third caller's email **security setting** is too high: it blocks all email **attachments** to protect the computer from **viruses**. The security settings need to be lowered in the internet browser. The fourth caller's **firewall** program has been configured to **block** all **pop-up adverts** and pop-up links. Simply **unchecking** BLOCK POP-UPS in the browser is not enough: you then have to clear the **cache** (stored web pages), then **refresh** the page. Computers transmit radio waves to wireless **routers**, but the signals can be blocked by steel filing cabinets or cordless phones. Moving the router to another location can solve the problem. The **IP address** must be the same between computer and router. If they are different they will not be able to communicate with each other. If the computer is set to find the IP address automatically, **re-boot** (re-start) the computer and/or the router.

Section 2 deals with **reporting to clients** about ways of making **skyscrapers** safer in emergencies. A **control centre** away from the building would allow emergency services to coordinate the rescue, watching images from **CCTV** (**closed-circuit TV**) cameras throughout the building. **Skybridges** (covered **walkways**) between towers would allow people to escape from one building to another. Wireless loudspeakers could give escape instructions to people. Structural improvements to the buildings would include: wider stairs, **reinforced** with steel, so that more people could use them; gaps between (horizontal) **beams** and (vertical) **columns** to allow safe **expansion** when heated in a fire; wider doors at **exits** would prevent accidents from overcrowding; the mechanical and electrical systems in lifts would be made **fireproof** so that they could be used in a fire; steel beams and columns would be given fireproof **coatings** to protect the building structure; **sprinklers** would be made stronger and provided with backup power and water supplies so that they continued to work in a fire; **strain gauges** (detecting pressures on the structure), smoke and heat **detectors** and microphones would send information to the control centre; **parachutes** would allow people to jump from high floors; people could put on magnetic **lifejackets** and jump into vertical escape shafts lined with **electromagnets** to control their descent to the ground.

Section 3 features a company handbook which tells customer service staff how to deal with **customer complaints**. It explains the importance of treating customers politely and helpfully. Staff should offer solutions for genuine complaints: either to **repair** the faulty or damaged item, to **replace** it with a new one, to **refund** (give back) the money paid by the customer, or to offer a **reduction** in the price of the next purchase by the customer. Service staff are trained to distinguish between showing **sympathy** (or empathy) with the customer for the inconvenience they have suffered, and **apologising** (which should only be done if the company, rather than the customer, is to blame for the damage). This is why it is important to collect and record all the details of the customer's complaint and try to find out who is to blame before apologising and admitting fault.

Computer network protection: http://dailycupoftech. com/10-ways-to-protect-your-home-network/

Computing terms, problems and solutions: http:// www.pchell.com/

Safer skyscrapers: http://technology.newscientist. com/article.ns?id=mg18925381.400&print=true

Teacher's notes

1 | Technical support

Start here

1 Ask students to brainstorm all the problems they've had with computers, e.g. setting up their computer, connecting to the internet, etc., and tell the class what the solutions were to the problems.

2 Put students into pairs. Ask them to read the list of problems and decide what the best solution for each one is.

Listening

3 ▶ 🎧 19

Tell students that they're going to listen to Lisa, an IT support technician, who's helping people in her company with their computer problems. Focus students' attention on the report form and tell them they have to complete it with the number of the diagnosis and the number of the solution from the list below. Explain *diagnosis* if necessary (the identification of the cause of a problem). Then play the recording for students to complete the form.

1 D3, S2	**4** D5, S4
2 D4, S3	**5** D2, S5
3 D6, S6	**6** D1, S1

▶ 🎧 19

[L = Lisa; C1 = caller 1; C2 = caller 2; C3 = caller 3;
1
C4 = caller 4; C5 = caller 5; C6 = caller 6]
L: Technical support. Lisa here. What's up?
C1: Hi, Lisa. I can't log into the network. It says WRONG PASSWORD.
L: Right. Are you sure that you're typing the correct password.
C1: The password appears automatically.
L: Oh right. You must have checked the REMEMBER PASSWORD box.
C1: Ah, yes, I have. So what do I do?
L: Uncheck the box, OK?
C1: Yes.
L: Now try typing in the correct password.
C1: Right. Yes, I've done it. I've logged in. Thanks, Lisa.
2
L: Technical support. Lisa here.
C2: Oh hi, Lisa. It's Rod.
L: You again! So what's wrong now?
C2: Hi, Lisa. Yeah, sorry, it's me. Well, this time my monitor isn't working. I can't see the whole page. I can only see part of the page.
L: Aha. And are the icons and words too big?
C2: Yep. That's right.
L: OK. Well, your computer must be using the wrong screen resolution settings.
C2: Oh, right. So what should I do?

L: You should go to *Control panel*. Click on *Display*, then *Settings*.
C2: Right, I've done that …
L: Then you should move the slider up. Increase the screen resolution.
C2: OK, done it.
3
L: Technical support. Lisa here. What's the problem?
C3: Hi, Lisa. Well, I can't open any email attachments.
L: OK. How about the emails themselves? Can you open them all right?
C3: Yes, the emails are fine. But when I double-click on the attachments, nothing happens.
L: Well, your email program may be blocking the attachments.
C3: Oh, right. So, what can I do?
L: Open *Tools – Options – Security*. Try lowering your security level.
C3: OK. I'll try that. Thanks.
4
L: Technical support. Lisa here. How can I help?
C4: Hi, Lisa. I'm using the internet. When I click on a link, nothing happens.
L: OK. Is it a pop-up?
C4: I don't know. It says CLICK HERE TO SEE PHOTO. But when I click I don't see the photo.
L: It may be a pop-up. Do you have a firewall?
C4: Yes.
L: OK, your firewall might be blocking the pop-ups.
C4: Right. So, what should I do now?
L: I suggest you try unblocking the pop-ups. Open your firewall program.
C4: OK, I've done that.
L: Does it say BLOCK POP-UP ADVERTS?
C4: Yes.
L: Try unchecking the box. Then clear your cache, refresh your web page and try again.
C4: OK, I'll try that. Thanks, Lisa.
5
L: Technical support. Lisa here. What's the problem?
C5: Hi, Lisa. Yeah. Bill here. I've set up a wireless router in the next room to my computer. But I can't get a connection between the router and the computer.
L: Aha. How far is the router from the computer?
C5: It's only about eight metres away.
L: Well, another electronic device could be interfering with the connection.
C5: Oh, right. What kind of device?
L: It could be a cordless phone, a microwave oven, anything really. Do you have a cordless phone?
C5: Yes, I do.
L: It must be that.
C5: So, what should I do?
L: Well, you could move the phone away. Or why don't you move the router around? I suggest you try moving the router to a different location. Then try the connection again.
C5: OK, I'll try moving the router. Thanks, Lisa.
6
C6: Technical support. Lisa here. What's up?

Bill: Hi, Lisa. It's Bill again.
C6: Aha, hello Bill. Is it your wireless connection?
Bill: Yes. I've connected my computer to the router. Thanks.
C6: Good.
Bill: But I can't access the internet.
C6: Is there a message on the screen?
Bill: Yes. It says LITTLE OR NO CONNECTIVITY.
C6: Aha. Well, it must be an IP problem. You must have given the computer a different IP address from the router.
Bill: Right. So, how can I fix that?
C6: Why don't you try rebooting the router first. If that doesn't work, try rebooting the computer and then the router again.
Bill: OK, I'll do that. Thanks.

Listening

4 ▶ 🔊 20

Tell students that they're going to listen to Lisa giving an explanation of why the callers are experiencing their problems. Ask them to read through the statements first. Then play the recording for students to complete the statements with the words in the box.

1 must	**4** might
2 must	**5** could
3 may	**6** must

▶ 🔊 20

1 You must have checked the REMEMBER PASSWORD box.
2 Your computer must be using the wrong screen resolution settings.
3 Your email program may be blocking the attachments.
4 Your firewall might be blocking the pop-ups.
5 Another electronic device could be interfering with the connection.
6 You must have given the computer a different IP address from the router.

5 Ask students to look back at the statements in 4 and decide which of her diagnoses are certainly correct and which are possibly correct. Tell them to write *C* for *Certainly* and *P* for *Possibly* after the statements.

Sentences 1, 2 and 6 – C
Sentences 3, 4 and 5 – P

6 ▶ 🔊 21

Tell students that they're now going to listen to four different ways in which Lisa suggests a solution. Play the recording for students to complete the sentences with the correct form of the words in the box.

1 typing	**3** could, don't
2 lowering	**4** suggest, try

▶ 🔊 21

1 Now try typing in the correct password.
2 Try lowering your security level.

3 Well, you could move the phone away. Or why don't you move the router around?
4 I suggest you try moving the router to a different location.

> **Extra activity**
> You could then ask students to rewrite each of the sentences using a different way of making the suggestion.

Language

Diagnosing problems

Go through the Language box with the class. First go through the different ways of diagnosing a problem, using the modal verbs *must* to express that you know something is certain because of the facts, and *may*, *might* and *could* to express possibility. N.B. you may have to tell students that the negative of *must* is *can't* to express uncertainty not ~~mustn't~~. Point out that modal verbs to express certainty and possibility need to be followed by *be* in the present and by the present perfect in the past.

Go through the three different ways of suggesting a solution, using *try* + verb + *-ing*, *Why don't you* and *could* followed by verb (without *to*).

Tell students that they'll find more information on diagnosing a problem and suggesting a solution on page 107.

7 Go through the example with the class. Tell students to refer to the Language box and rewrite 2–6, giving a diagnosis and a suggestion.

1 Your switch might be broken. Try changing it.
2 Your cable may be loose. Try pushing it firmly into the socket. (or You could/Why don't you push it …)
3 You must be using the wrong IP address. Try rebooting the router. (or You could/Why don't you reboot …)
4 The program may be frozen. Try pressing CTRL-ALT-DEL. (or You could/Why don't you press …)
5 The mouse must have stopped working. Try disconnecting and reconnecting it. (or You could/Why don't you disconnect …)
6 Your file must be too large for the disk. Try compressing it. (or You could compress it/Why don't you compress it?)

> **Extra activity**
> Put students into pairs or small groups. Ask them to make a list of typical problems in their own technical field. Then ask them to brainstorm a diagnosis for each problem, and finally ask them to find a solution for each diagnosis.
>
> They could then choose one of the problems from their list. They then take it in turns to be the customer with the problem and the technical support officer and roleplay a telephone conversation between them.

2 Reporting to clients

Start here

1 Explain to students that they will be looking at ways to make tall buildings safer in this lesson. First ask them for another name for tall buildings (*skyscrapers*). Then ask students to work in groups of four to six and brainstorm some ideas about making tall buildings safer in the event of a fire or other emergencies. Then ask students to tell the class their ideas.

Task

2 Ask students to look at the diagram and read through the information on it. Then refer students to the table, showing two of the ideas in the diagram and the purpose of those ideas. Ask students to copy the table. Then ask them to discuss the other purposes of the ideas in the diagram in their groups and complete the table with the idea and its purpose.

3 Ask students to discuss the three questions with their group. Tell them to tick the safety features they think will work, and put a cross against the ones they don't think will work or be too difficult to install, and give reasons why. Tell them that they can make brief notes for their reasons against the ideas in the table.

4 Students then take it in turns to present their group's decisions to the class.

Model answer:

Idea	Purpose
(a) CCTV cameras	to check everyone's location; to allow controllers to monitor the situation
(b) parachutes	to allow people to escape quickly from the top floors
(c) fireproof ceilings	to prevent the fire from spreading to other areas and floors
(d) control centre (away from building)	so that the controllers can operate safely away from the affected building
(e) fire drills	so that everyone is aware about what to do and where to go in the event of a fire
(f) wider doors	to allow the maximum number of people to escape quickly
(g) sensors (of smoke, heat, strain)	to detect changes in temperature and warn people about a fire
(h) magnetic shafts (with magnetic lifejackets)	to allow people to jump down magnetic shafts. They wear magnetic lifejackets so that the electro-magnets can control their fall.
(i) stronger sprinklers (with backup power and water)	to make sure that there is a continual sprinkling of water on the fire
(j) fireproof lifts	so that the lifts can operate in the event of a fire
(k) skybridges	to help people to escape to another building
(l) gaps between beams and columns	to prevent fire from spreading
(m) wider stairs (reinforced with steel)	to allow more people to escape quickly and prevent overcrowding; to make sure that the stairs don't collapse in the fire
(n) loudspeakers	to warn everyone in the building about the fire and to tell them what to do and where to go

Reading

5 Ask students to read the covering letter and answer the questions. You may have to explain what a covering letter is. (It's a letter explaining what is in another document, like a report or a CV, which has been attached to it.) When they've finished the activity, ask them what *enc.* at the end of the letter means. (It's is an abbreviation for *enclosed.*)

> 1 (a) John Hu, (b) Pierre Van Ek
> 2 He asked him to upgrade the safety of the Hu building. He asked him on 24th January.
> 3 He has completed the work and he has written a report on it.
> 4 It's enclosed with the letter.
> 5 He has asked him to let him know if he needs any clarification of any of the points in the report.
> 6 I am pleased to inform you …

6 Ask students to read the contractor's report about the safety upgrading of the Hu Building. Ask them to look back at the diagram in 3 and write a letter from it next to each of the jobs in the report.

> 1 k 2 m 3 c 4 f 5 j 6 l 7 g 8 b and h

7 Look at the Language box with the class first. Then ask students to look back at the report and tell them to underline all the passive structures as in the example.

> 1 Three walkways <u>were built</u> between the towers …
> 2 The width of stairs <u>was increased</u> by 25 cm …
> 3 Fire-resistant material <u>was placed</u> between floors …
> 4 Exits on the ground floor <u>were widened</u> by 1 m …
> 5 Elevators <u>were covered</u> with fire-resistant material …
> 6 Structural beams <u>were shortened</u> by 8 cm …
> 7 Smoke detectors <u>were installed</u> …
> 8 No equipment for jumping <u>was provided</u> …

Language

Past simple passive

Go through the Language box on the past simple passive with the class and point out that passives in the past use *was/were* + the past participle.

Tell students that they'll find more information on the past simple passive on page 102.

8 Ask students to look back at the passive structures they underlined in the report in 6 and tell them to change them into the active. Refer students the first item in the report and go through the example with the class first.

> 1 We built three walkways between the towers to allow people to cross over.
> 2 We increased the width of stairs by 25 cm to allow more people to use them.
> 3 We placed fire-resistant material between floors to stop fires from spreading.
> 4 We widened the exits on the ground floor by 1 m to allow people to escape more easily.
> 5 We covered the elevators with fire-resistant material to protect them.
> 6 We shortened the structural beams by 8 cm to allow them to expand in a fire
> 7 We installed smoke detectors to give early warning of fire.
> 8 We provided no equipment for jumping since we decided it was impractical.

Speaking

9 Ask students to work in the same groups as they did in 1–4 and ask them to look back at the table they completed in 3. Tell them that they're going to prepare for a meeting between the client John Hu and a member of the team of contractors working for Safety Designs Ltd. Then ask them to read the information.

Tell students to divide their group up into two so that half of the group prepares what John Hu is going to say in the meeting and the other half of the group prepares what the contractors are going to say. Allow them five minutes to do this.

Ask students to choose one student to be John Hu and one student to be the contractor. They then roleplay the meeting.

3 Dealing with complaints

Start here

1 Ask students to tell the class what the most common customer complaint is in their technical field.

2 Ask students how they think staff should deal with customer complaints and tell them to write some guidelines for staff in their company in note form.

If students are from the same technical field, you could ask them to make their lists in pairs or groups of three.

Listening

3 ▶ 🎧 22

Tell students that they're going to listen to a phone call from a customer who's complaining about a product they've just bought. Ask students to read through the form first, so that they know what information they need to listen out for. Play the recording for students to complete the form. They can then check their answers with their partner. Play the recording once more for students to check their answers.

Date and time of call	10.45 16/03
Name of customer	Maria Beck
Order number	89054
Description of goods	Printer
Model number	3845
Details of complaint	The AC adapter with the printer doesn't work
Solution offered	✓ replace ✓ reduce
Customer response	✓ accept

▶ 🎧 22

[S = Steve; C = Customer]

S: Good morning, customer service. My name is Steve. How can I help you?

C: Yes, good morning. I wish to complain about a printer I bought from you.

S: Oh, I'm sorry to hear that. What exactly is the problem?

C: The AC adapter with the printer doesn't work.

S: I see. Did it work the first time you switched it on?

C: No, it didn't.

S: Well, I do apologise for that. It must be our fault. What model of printer is it?

C: It's a 3845.

S: And could I have you name, please?

C: Yes, my name is Maria Beck.

S: ... And do you have your receipt there?

C: Yes.

S: That's great. Could you read out the order number, please? It's at the top on the right.

C: Errm. Yes, order number ... it's 89054.

S: Great. ... Right, Ms Beck. Let me just summarise the situation. You've told me that the adapter with your 3845 printer doesn't work, and has never worked. Is that correct?

C: Correct.

S: Well, I'm pleased to tell you that we will replace your adapter and the printer. You will receive the goods by the end of the week. We have your address. We'll collect the old printer at the same time.

C: Great.

S: And I'm happy to say that we're going to give you five euros discount off your next purchase.

C: That's very reasonable. Thank you.

S: You're welcome, Ms Beck. Have a nice day.

4 Ask students to read the company guidelines on dealing with complaints from the handbook. Then play the recording again for students to tick procedures which the customer service officer follows, and to put a cross next to the ones that he doesn't follow.

Ask students if they think these guidelines are a good way for dealing with customer complaints and if they could add any other rules to them.

> **(a)** rules followed:
> 1 be friendly, polite and helpful
> 2 listen carefully
> 3 show sympathy with the customer's problems
> 4 summarise what the customer has told you, and check that you have understood correctly
> 5 record the details and collect the evidence (e.g. receipts or damaged goods)
> 6 offer a solution (although he offers two solutions not one: to *replace* the printer and *reduce* the price of the next purchase)
>
> **(b)** rules broken:
> 3 don't admit the company's fault (he says 'It must be our fault')

Task

5 Put students in pairs. Tell them that they're going to roleplay a phone conversation between a customer service officer and a customer about a complaint. Ask them to decide who's going to be the customer service officer and who's going to be the customer, then tell them to read the information for their role. Refer them to the audio script of the phone call from 3 first on page 124, and tell them to underline any useful language they could use for their role.

Students then roleplay their conversation. When they've finished, ask the customers if they were satisfied with the answers they were given by the customer service officers, and what could be improved, referring to the guidelines in 4.

6 Ask students to look at the diagram of the damaged suitcase and to describe the damage on the suitcase.

> *Sample answer:*
> The handle on the top surface is twisted. The handle on right side of the suitcase is broken. One wheel is broken. The top left corner dented. All of the right-hand side of the suitcase is crushed. The front surface of the case is cracked. The front right edge is split open.

Reading

7 Ask students to read the reply to the customer's letter of complaint and answer the questions.

> **1** The top surface of the customer's new DVD player was scratched and the edge was cracked.
> **2** He offers a refund and a 10% discount off the customer's next purchase.
> **3** (a) I was sorry to hear … (b) I would like to apologise for …
> **4** (a) I'm pleased to inform you … (b) Unfortunately, …

Writing

8 Tell students that they're the manager of the computer company IT Online Ltd. Ask them to read the complaint letter and to write a reply to it.

> *Sample answer:*
> Dear Mr Bradwell
> Thank you for your letter complaining about your Mace notebook computer from our online store. I was sorry to hear that the adapter was missing from the box.
> Unfortunately, we do not have any more adapters in stock at the moment. However, I'm pleased to inform you that we will get a new stock next week, and we will send you the adapter immediately. In addition, as a gesture of good will, we will give you a 5% discount from your next purchase at our store.
> I would like to apologise for the inconvenience you have experienced. Please contact me if you have any further queries.
> Yours sincerely

Extra activity

Ask students to think about a typical complaint their company receives, and write a reply to it.

---

8 | Energy

Contents

1 Water power

Starter: brainstorm how to convert sea wave energy into electrical power.

Task: study diagram and work out how wave energy converter works. Present ideas to class.

Vocabulary: names of motions in task: *linear*, etc. Fill gaps with *oscillating* etc. Fill gaps with corresponding verbs: *oscillate* etc.

Word list: *anti-clockwise, clockwise, convert, energy, fluid, fossil fuel, gas, linear, liquid, motion, movement, oscillating, reciprocating, (non-) renewable, rotary, solar ray, source*

Scanning task: look for information about the wave energy converter.

Listen to an oral presentation on wave energy and complete notes.

Task: choose a wave energy system (diagram and notes supplied) and prepare and give a group presentation to class.

Write a description of the chosen system.

Word list: *buoy, coil, fall, induce (current), kPa, kW, lever, magnetic, oscillate, pendulum, psi, reciprocate, rise, rotate, shaft, turbine*

2 Engines

Starter: describe the motion in internal-combustion (IC) cylinder.

Put jumbled diagrams of stages of IC cycle into correct order.

Read description of four strokes in IC engine and check ordering of diagrams.

Word list: *cam, camshaft, crankshaft, cylinder, exhaust, explode, ignite, inlet valve, intake, internal combustion, piston*

Identify words/ clauses in text referred to by pro-forms: *this, which* etc. referring to whole clause, as well as words; *through which*.

Find synonyms in text for given phrases.

Language: *when* and *as* clauses of sequential and simultaneous action.

Join groups of three sentences into one, using *when/as* and *which* (referring to previous clause): *As the piston moves up, the exhaust valve opens, which lets the burnt gases escape.*

Write a description of a diagram of a hydrogen-fuelled IC engine.

Word list: *afterwards, at the same time, chamber, engine block, hydrogen, immediately, in sequence, injection, simultaneously, vacuum*

3 Cooling and heating

Starter: scientific principles underlying refrigerators. Make notes then present to class.

Reading: description of the heating operation of a heat pump. Tasks: (a) draw arrows on diagram to show flow direction (b) delete wrong words on diagram

Word list: *absorb, coil, compressor, condense, condenser, evaporate, evaporator, expansion valve, extract, give out, heat-exchanging pipe, maintain (pressure), reduce, refrigerant, refrigeration, refrigerator, reverse*

Match parts of heat pump with their definitions.

Vocabulary: verb/concept noun/agent noun families: *compress/compression/compressor* etc.

Write a follow-up paragraph on the cooling operation of the heat pump.

Group task: discuss a diagram of a geothermal heat pump, make notes and write a description of how it works.

Word list: *compress/compression/compressor, condense/condensation/condenser, decompress/decompression/decompressor, evaporate/evaporation/evaporator, extract/extraction/extractor*

Briefing

This unit deals with conversion of one form of **energy** to another.

Section 1 looks at ways of converting the energy in the movement of sea waves into electricity. Four types of **motion** are dealt with: **linear** (in a straight line); **reciprocating** (like a piston), **rotary** (circular) and **oscillating** (like a pendulum). In the **wave energy converter**, the oscillating waves make a flexible disc move up and down. The disc is attached to a large lever: this makes two pistons move up and down. This sucks sea water into a **chamber** and then through pipes at high pressure to drive a **turbine**, which generates electricity. The second device, the **wave energy buoy**, has an **electric coil** attached to its interior. Freely moving inside the coil is a **magnetic shaft**, connected to the sea bed. When the buoy moves on the sea, the coil moves over the shaft, generating electricity in the coil. The electricity is transferred from the buoy to an electricity **grid** on the sea bed, and fed to the shore. The third device, the **wave power station**, contains a turbine and generator. The waves push water into a lower chamber, which forces air through a valve into an upper chamber, which contains the turbine. The motion of the air turns the turbine and generates electricity. In the fourth device, the **wave roller**, the waves push metal plates forwards and backwards. This movement operates a **hydraulic piston pump**, which forces oil along a pipe and powers a turbine on land.

Section 2 deals with the **four-stroke internal combustion engine**. The **spark plug** ignites compressed fuel in the combustion chamber. The force of the explosion pushes the piston down the cylinder. This is the **power** stroke, which initiates all the motion of the engine. As the piston moves down, it turns the crankshaft, which is connected to it. As it rotates, the U-shape of the crankshaft moves the piston up, down and up again for the following three strokes (**exhaust**, **intake** and **compression**). The crankshaft is connected by a belt to the **camshaft**, which turns the **cams**. These are shaped in such a way that they make the intake and exhaust valves open and close at the right moments. Both valves are closed when the piston moves up for the compression stroke, which creates the conditions for ignition and the next power stroke. In the text and diagrams on page 60, the description of the cycle begins with the intake stroke, followed by the compression stroke, ignition, power stroke and exhaust stroke. The **hydrogen engine** in the writing task has a triangular rotor instead of a piston. Hydrogen and air are used as fuel; this mixture is ignited and the explosion pushes the rotor around inside the sealed chamber. As it rotates it pushes out exhaust, sucks in more air and turns the crankshaft.

Section 3 deals with **refrigeration**. The basic principle is that when gas is **compressed**, it **condenses** (turns into liquid), and gives out heat into the surrounding atmosphere. Conversely, when liquid is **expanded**, it **evaporates** (turns into gas), and **absorbs** (takes in) heat from the surrounding atmosphere, making it colder. In a refrigerator, a **compressor** (pump) forces the **refrigerant** (a fluid with a low boiling point) through a closed pipe system around the refrigerator and then back to the pump. In the pipe there is an **expansion valve** which makes the fluid slow down and puts it under pressure. As the pressure increases, the fluid condenses, giving heat out (at the back of the refrigerator). After the fluid passes through the expansion valve, the pressure suddenly decreases, and the fluid expands and evaporates, absorbing heat and making the interior of the refrigerator cold. A **heat pump** uses the refrigeration principle. It has a **reversing valve** which changes the direction of flow of the refrigerant so that the **evaporator** becomes the **condenser** and vice versa. The **geothermal heat pump** in the Task is essentially the same as the heat pump, but it has an extra pipe which draws heat from the ground. This heat is then absorbed into the refrigerant.

Wave energy: http://www.rise.org.au/info/Tech/wave/index.html#fix

Internal combustion: http://en.wikipedia.org/wiki/Internal_combustion_engine

Hydrogen combustion: http://www.hybrid-vehicles.net/mazda-rx8-renesis-hybrid.htm

Refrigeration: http://www.howstuffworks.com/refrigerator.htm/printable

Heat pump: http://en.wikipedia.org/wiki/Heat_pump

Teacher's notes

1 | Wave power

Start here

1 Put students into small groups. Ask them to read the question and then to brainstorm their answers in their groups. They should make notes on their ideas and illustrate them by drawing simple diagrams.

Task

2 Ask students to look at the diagram and tell them that it shows one method of converting wave energy into electric power. Tell students to discuss how the method works in their groups, and then explain their ideas to the rest of the class.

Vocabulary

3 Ask students to read the text through first then to fill in the gaps with the motion words in the box.

> **1** linear
> **2** reciprocating
> **3** oscillating
> **4** rotary

4 Ask students to look back at the diagram in 2 and match the numbered arrows in the diagram with the motion words in 3. They can compare their answers with a partner before you check with the class.

> **1** rotary
> **2** linear
> **3** reciprocating
> **4** oscillating
> **5** reciprocating
> **6** oscillating

5 Ask students to complete the sentences with the present simple of the verbs in the box.

> **1** rotate
> **2** reciprocates
> **3** oscillate
> **4** rotates

Extra activity

Write the four basic motion words: *linear*, *oscillating*, *rotary* and *reciprocating* on the board. Ask students to brainstorm things that have these motions. They then write them under the heading. Give them a three-minute time limit to do this.

Ask students to count up the number of items and find out which pair has the most. Then ask them to read out their list to the class.

Scanning

6 Go through the instructions for the task with students. Then ask them to turn to pages 118–119 and find the text on the Wave Energy Converter and the five advantages. Remind them to read the text as quickly as they can and just look for the advantages, and not to look at every word in the text. Ask students to put up their hand when they've finished, so that you know who is the winner of the Speed search competition. Then check their answers with the class.

> **1** It uses waves and wave power, which can be found all over the world.
> **2** It can produce electricity and fresh water.
> **3** The energy is clean and does not use fossil fuel.
> **4** The converter sits on the seabed, where it is invisible and safe from storms.
> **5** The system does not need a large pipe system. It requires only a small diameter pipe to carry high-pressure seawater ashore.

Listening

7 ▶ 💿 23

Tell students that they're going to listen to someone giving a presentation on the CETO Wave Energy Converter. Ask them to look at the listeners' notes which they have to complete. Ask them to read through the notes first, so that they know what information they have to listen out for. Then play the recording for students to complete the notes. They can then check their answers with a partner. Play the recording one more time for students to check.

> **1** the energy
> **2** seabed
> **3** chamber
> **4** pistons
> **5** turbine
> **6** 20.4
> **7** 125
> **8** 7000
> **9** 100
> **10** down (in a linear motion)
> **11** high
> **12** rotates
> **13** renewable

▶ 💿 23

Good morning, everyone. Today I'm going to talk about the Wave Energy Converter.

You're probably wondering what a Wave Energy Converter is. So, let's have a simple definition to start with. Very simply, a Wave Energy Converter is a system which converts the energy from sea waves into electrical power.

Before I talk about the system itself, let me tell you where it is located, because some systems are located on the surface of the sea, and some on the sea shore. But not this system. The Wave Energy Converter is fixed to the seabed.

OK, now let's look at the main components. The Wave Energy Converter has five main components or parts. These are: a very large flexible disc, a lever, a chamber which takes in sea water, a set of pistons, many sea water pipes, and of course a turbine on the land.

The main specifications of the system are as follows. The whole system on the seabed is 4.6 metres high and 20.4 metres long; the main pipe is 125 millimetres wide; the pressure of the water in the pipes is 7000 kilopascals, or 1000 psi, that's pounds per square inch. The complete system can generate 100 kilowatts of electricity.

OK, that's enough number-crunching. Let's look at how the system works. Here's a very simple account of the operation of the system. Let's start with the sea. The sea wave oscillates. This oscillating motion pushes the disc down in a linear motion. The disc makes the lever oscillate. The oscillating lever makes the pistons move in a reciprocating motion. Then the pistons push sea water from the chamber through the pipe at high pressure. The high-pressure water then makes the turbine rotate. And of course this generates electricity.

So, that's how it works. And of course this system has great benefits. The most important benefit is that wave energy is a renewable energy resource; and of course it uses no fossil fuels.

Task

8 Divide the class into three or six small groups. Tell them which group is Group 1, 2 and 3. Explain that they're going to find out about different wave energy systems and that they're going to prepare a presentation about the system. Ask them to turn to the relevant pages at the back of the book where they'll find notes about their wave energy system.

9 Students give their group's presentation to the class. During the presentation, the students who are listening should make notes on any points they would like to ask the group questions about. When the presentation is finished, they can ask their questions.

Writing

10 Students write a description of their group's wave energy system and explain how it works. They could do this for homework if you are short of time.

2 Engines

Start here

1 Ask students to work in pairs or in small groups. Ask them to look at the diagram of the internal-combustion cylinder and tell them to draw arrows on it to show all the movements.

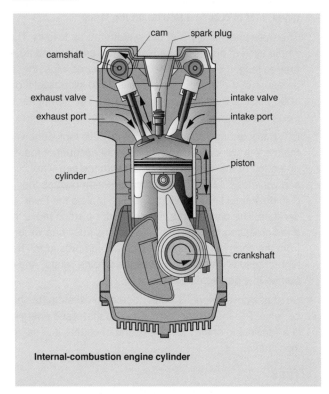

Internal-combustion engine cylinder

2 Revise motion words with students. Quickly ask them to describe each of the motions. Then ask them to look back at the diagram in exercise 1 and try and match the words to the parts of the internal-combustion engine which move. They can then check their answers with a partner before you check with the class.

> cams – rotary
> air out via exhaust valve – linear
> air in via intake valve – linear
> piston – reciprocating
> crankshaft – rotary
> valves – reciprocating

3 As a whole class, get students to explain what causes the movements of the valves, the pistons and the crankshaft.

> the valves: the cams rotate, which causes the valves to open and close.
> the piston: the crankshaft rotates, which causes the piston to move up and down.
> the crankshaft: the downward movement of the piston causes the crankshaft to rotate.

Task

4 Ask students to look at the diagrams. Explain that they show the four-stroke cycle of an internal combustion engine. Tell them that the first figure is in the correct order, but figures 2–5 are in the wrong order. Ask students to work in their groups and put them in the correct order. Don't confirm their answers yet, as they will find them in the reading text which follows.

Reading

5 Ask students to read the description of the four-stroke cycle and check their answers to 4.

> The correct order is: 1, 4, 6, 3, 5, 2.

8 Energy

6 Ask students to look at the words in the text in 5. Tell them that they'll find out what these words refer to by reading the sentence that goes before.

> **1** c **2** b **3** a **4** b **5** c

7 Ask students to look back at the text in 5 again and find words that mean the same as phrases 1–4.

> **1** simultaneously
> **2** torsion
> **3** intake port
> **4** exhaust valve

Language

Time clause

Go through the Language box with students, using *when* and *as* to indicate when two actions happen. Point out that these sentences begin with *When/As* and are used in the present simple.

8 Go through the example with the class first. Then ask them to join the other groups of sentences into a single sentence, using *when/as* and *which*. Point out that they must not include the words in italics in their sentences.

They can then compare their answers with a partner before you check with the class.

> **1** As the piston moves up, the exhaust valve opens, which lets the burnt gases escape.
> **2** When the spark plug ignites the fuel, there is an explosion, which makes the piston move down with great force.
> **3** As the camshaft rotates, the cam pushes the intake valve downwards, which allows the fuel to enter the cylinder.
> **4** When the piston moves away from the valves, it creates a vacuum in the cylinder, which sucks the fuel in.
> **5** When the piston moves up towards the valves, it puts the fuel under high pressure, which helps the gases to expand rapidly after ignition.
> **6** As the cam pushes the exhaust valve down, the piston moves up towards it, which forces the burnt gases out of the engine.

Writing

9 Ask students to look at the diagram on the right. Explain that it's a diagram of an internal combustion engine which uses hydrogen. You could ask students to work in small groups first to describe the engine and discuss how it works and what its benefits are. They could make brief notes while they're doing this.

Students then write up their notes describing the engine and how it works.

Students could write the description of the engine for homework if you are short of time.

Model answer:

The hydrogen internal-combustion engine uses hydrogen as a fuel.

It has a sealed chamber, a triangular rotor, an injector, two spark plugs, an exhaust port and an air intake port. The rotor has a seal at each corner. The rotor rotates inside the chamber.

The rotor rotates and pulls air into the chamber through the intake port. Hydrogen enters through the injector. The air and hydrogen mix. As the rotor rotates inside the chamber, it pulls the air and hydrogen to the spark plugs. The spark plugs ignite the gases. The gases expand, and push the rotor around the chamber. The rotor then pushes the burnt gas out through the exhaust port.

The main benefits of this engine are (1) it does not use a fossil fuel, and (2) its exhaust is cleaner than petrol exhaust.

3 | Cooling and heating

Start here

1 Put students in small groups. Ask them to look at the diagram of the refrigerating cycle and read the four scientific principles. Tell them to discuss in their groups which of the scientific principles the refrigerating cycle is based on.

> **2** When you compress a gas, it condenses. When you decompress a liquid, it evaporates.
>
> **4** As a gas condenses, it gives out heat. As a liquid evaporates, it absorbs (takes in) heat.

Ask students if they know what the other two principles could refer to.

2 Tell them that they're going to make notes about what happens to the fluid during a refrigeration cycle, using the two principles they found in 1. They can then explain their ideas to the class. Don't confirm their ideas yet as they will read the answer in the text that follows.

Reading

3 Ask students to work on their own and read the text about heat pumps right through. Then ask them: *What is the purpose of the heat pump?* and *What are the main parts of the pump?*

Ask students to look at the diagram of the heating operation of a heat pump. Tell them to draw an arrow on the pipes to show the direction of the flow of fluid as explained in the text. They then delete the words *high* or *low* in the brackets in the diagram. Students can then compare their answers with a partner before you check with the class.

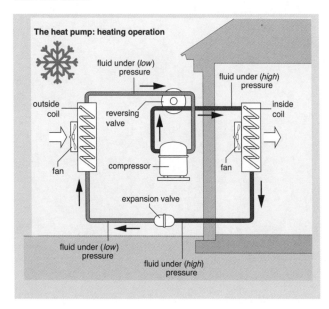

4 Ask students to work on their own and match the parts with their definitions. They can then work in pairs to check their answers. One student covers the right column and the other student covers the left column. They then take it in turns to read out their words or definitions for the other student to match up.

> **1** c **2** e **3** a **4** d **5** f **6** b

Vocabulary

5 Focus students' attention on the table and read out the example. Ask students to copy the table and add the other words from the box to it. Tell students that they can use a dictionary to help them if they wish.

verb	concept noun	agent noun
compress	compression	compressor
condense	condensation	condenser
decompress	decompression	decompressor
evaporate	evaporation	evaporator
extract	extraction	extractor
operate	operation	operator
refrigerate	refrigeration	refrigerator

> **Extra activity**
>
> Ask students to underline the stressed syllables in each of the words in the table.
>
> After you've checked their answers, ask students to look at the nouns ending in *-ion* and ask them where the stress is on these words. Explain that for words ending in *-ion*, the stress is on the syllable that comes immediately before *-ion*.

Writing

6 Ask students to read through the first part of the description of the cooling operation of the heat pump. Then ask students to work on their own and complete the description, using the diagram to help them.

> *Model answer:*
> **Cooling operation**
> During hot weather, the operation of the heat pump is reversed. The reversing valve changes the machine from a heater to an air conditioner. The outside coil acts as the condenser and the inside coil acts as the evaporator. The fluid in the evaporator is under low pressure, and so it evaporates and absorbs heat. The fan blows air over the evaporator. The evaporator cools the air. The cooled air is blown into the building. The compressor then pumps the heated fluid out of the building to the condenser. The condenser gives out the heat to the outside air.

Task

7 Put students into small groups. Ask them to look at the diagram of the geothermal pump and talk about it in their groups. Tell them to make notes on the pump, dividing their notes into three separate sections: (1) its function; (2) how it works and (3) how it is different from the heat pump.

8 Students write up their notes. Tell them to write three headings for the different sections of their notes.

Students could write the description of the pump for homework if you are short of time.

> *Model answer:*
> **The geothermal pump**
> The function of a geothermal pump is to transfer heat from the ground into a building. It has an evaporator, a condenser, a compressor, an expansion valve, and pipes which contain refrigerant. It operates like a heat pump, but in addition, it has a ground collector. This is a coiled pipe which is located under the ground. This pipe collects heat from the ground and transfers it into the evaporator.
> This is how it works. The refrigerant flows from the expansion valve under low pressure through the evaporator. Here it evaporates, and absorbs the heat from the ground collector. The compressor then pumps the heated refrigerant under high pressure through the condenser. Here the refrigerant gives out heat. This heats the water in the building. A pump makes the hot water flow to the heaters in the building.

Answer key

1

1 remembering	10 emptying
2 checked	11 interfering
3 unchecking	12 taking
4 typing	13 move
5 blocking	14 using
6 lowering	15 reboot
7 opening	16 rebooting
8 blocked	17 reboot
9 switching off	

4 (See exercise 5 for answers.)

5 *The correct order is:*

Two-stroke engine: the upstroke

As the crankshaft rotates, it drives the piston up.
This compresses the fuel in the cylinder.
At the same time, it creates a vacuum in the crankcase.
The vacuum opens the fuel valve.
As a result, fresh fuel is sucked into the crankcase.
Meanwhile, the piston moves up towards the top of the cylinder.
When it reaches the top, the spark plug fires.
Then the downstroke begins.

6 *Possible answer:*

When the spark plug fires, the fuel ignites. This drives the piston down. As it moves down, the piston compresses the fuel in the crankcase. As it moves down more, the piston uncovers the exhaust port. When the piston reaches the bottom of the cylinder, it uncovers the transfer port. Then fuel flows from the crankcase into the cylinder. At the same time, the fresh fuel pushes out the exhaust gas.

7
1 broken down
2 delivered, cracked
3 sent
4 received, scratched
5 ordered, delivered
6 bought, worn

8 **Inspector's report**

ACTIONS TAKEN
1 The site of the fire was examined.
2 Joints and connections were inspected.
3 The main lift was tested.
4 The gaps between beams were measured.
5 Parts of the wall were taken away and tested.
6 All fire exits were inspected.

FINDINGS
1 Four storeys were destroyed by the fire.
2 Three metal beams were sheared.
3 The main column was twisted.
4 Two lifts were jammed.
5 Two fire exits were blocked.
6 A large water tank (for sprinklers) was cracked by the heat.

RECOMMENDATIONS
1 Structural columns should be reinforced.
2 Water tanks should be strengthened.
3 A backup power system should be provided.
4 CCTV and monitors should be installed.
5 Stairs should be widened.
6 Ceilings should be covered with fireproof material.

9 *Sample answer:*

Dear Ms Williams

Thank you for your letter complaining about the Hotspot washing machine that you ordered from our city centre shop. I was sorry to hear that the machine doesn't work and that you are not happy with our service. Unfortunately, a lot of our staff are ill at the moment. However, we will send you a replacement washing machine. In addition, as a gesture of good will, we will offer you a free annual service next year.

I would like to apologise for the inconvenience you have experienced. Please contact me if you have any further queries.

Yours sincerely

11 *Model answer:*

How the Stirling Engine (Displacer Type) works (top diagram)

The engine has a sealed cylinder, a displacer piston, a power piston and a 90-degree phased crankshaft. One part of the cylinder is heated by a heat source, and the other part is cooled with water. The displacer piston moves air from the hot side to the cold side. When the air is on the hot side, it expands and pushes the power piston up. When it moves back to the cold side, it contracts and pulls the power piston down. The power piston makes the crankshaft rotate, and the crankshaft drives the displacer piston. It also drives the flywheel.

How the Stirling Engine (Two Piston Type) works (lower diagram)

This engine has two sealed cylinders, two pistons and a 90-degree phased crankshaft. The space above one cylinder is continuously heated by a heat source, and the space above the other cylinder is continuously cooled with water. The air in the hot cylinder expands and pushes the 'hot piston' down. The crankshaft also pulls the 'cold piston' down. Then the air in the cold cylinder contracts and pulls the 'cold piston' up. The crankshaft also pushes the 'hot piston' up. The crankshaft rotates and turns the flywheel.

Project

12 & 13 At the end of every Review Unit is a project. Students can do their research on the internet or in a library, and in their own language if they wish. They must then write their results in English.

Quick test answer key

Part 1: Vocabulary and grammar

1
1 log into		4 connect	
2 access		5 network	
3 Click on		6 screen	

2   1 d   2 c   3 e   4 f   5 b   6 a

3
1 crush	4 complaint
2 sprinkler	5 wheel
3 twisted	

4
1 evaporation	4 extraction
2 condenser	5 operation
3 decompressor	6 refrigerator

5
1 was spilt	4 was dented
2 were burnt	5 was torn
3 were crushed	

6
1 must	4 could
2 may	5 could be
3 must	6 upgrading

7
1 increasing	4 replacing
2 return	5 using
3 check	

8
1 Over half the cables were installed in the train tunnel last month.
2 A new shopping centre was built on the site last year.
3 The computer was taken back to the store to get repaired.
4 The car was driven around the track (by the mechanic).
4 The handle of my suitcase was broken at the airport.
5 The A30 superjumbo was flown from Singapore to Sydney on its first commercial flight.

9
1 When/As	4 At the same time
2 When/As	5 Meanwhile
3 After this	

Part 2: Reading and writing

Reading

Problem	Need to solve world energy crises, and reduce carbon emissions.
Solution	Building barrages to convert tidal energy into electricity.
Location	Narrow river estuaries
Operation	Seawater enters through sluices. It is held behind a barrage. When the tide falls the water flows out and drives the turbines. These rotate and create electricity.
Advantages	Clean, renewable power that doesn't produce any carbon dioxide.
Disadvantages	Expensive. Only 20 places in the world where you can have these. Damages wildlife and plants in the area.

Writing

Sample answer:

Dear Ms Benson

Thank you for your letter complaining about your suitcase. I'm sorry to hear about the damage to it and that you haven't had a reply to your letter.

However, I am please to inform you that we will replace your suitcase with another one. As an alternative, we will pay for the cost of your suitcase.

I would like to apologise again for the inconvenience you have experienced.

Yours sincerely

Review Unit D Quick test

Total _____/60

Part 1: Vocabulary and grammar

1 Replace the words in the sentences with a word in the box.

access   click on   connect   log into   network   screen

1 First, _____ the computer.

2 I can't _____ my account on the computer.

3 _____ the attachment.

4 I can't _____ to the internet.

5 The bank's _____ isn't working again.

6 The computer _____ goes black to save energy.

(6 marks)

2 Match the description of the movement with their words.

1 moving backwards and forwards
2 moving between two points in a rhythmic motion
3 the direction you loosen a screw is
4 move round a fixed point
5 go in a straight line
6 go round in the same way as a clock

a) clockwise
b) linear
c) oscillating
d) reciprocating
e) anticlockwise
f) rotary

(6 marks)

3 <u>Underline</u> the odd word out in each group.

1 condense   crush   evaporate   solidify
2 beam   brace   column   sprinkler
3 cracked   twisted   split   torn
4 complaint   refund   repair   replacement
5 cam   crankshaft   piston   wheel

(5 marks)

4 Write the missing noun for each verb.

	verb	noun	agent noun
1	evaporate	_____	evaporator
2	condense	condensation	_____
3	decompress	decompression	_____
4	extract	_____	extractor
5	operate	_____	operator
6	refrigerate	refrigeration	_____

(6 marks)

5 Complete these sentences with the correct form of the words in the box.

burn   crush   dent   spill   tear

1 Some coffee _____ on the table.

2 The documents _____ in the fire.

3 The boxes _____ because there was a heavy weight on them.

4 A van drove into the back of my car and the bumper _____ .

5 His report _____ . So, he printed out a new copy.

(5 marks)

Grammar

6 <u>Underline</u> the correct word in these sentences.

1 It's dark. It **must/may** be six o'clock by now.

2 I can't find my mobile phone. I **must/may** have left it at home or at work. I'm not sure.

3 I've got paint on my jacket. They **must/could** have just painted the door.

4 You **could/must** have disconnected the cable, but I'm not certain.

5 We have no electricity. It **could be/could have been** a problem with the electrical circuit. Will you check it?

6 I can't access my bank account details. They might be **upgrade/upgrading** the computer system.

(6 marks)

7 Complete these suggestions for the problems. Use the words in the box in the correct form.

check   increase   replace   return   use

1 A: I keep getting spam email in my inbox.
   B: Try _____ your security setting.

2 A: I bought this printer in a shop yesterday, but the tray is damaged.
   B: Why don't you _____ it to the shop and ask for a replacement.

3 A: Help! I can't connect to the internet.
   B: You could _____ the cables first.

4 A: My digital camera isn't working.
   B: I suggest you try _____ the batteries.

5 A: I can't download digital photos on my computer.
   B: Try _____ a different memory card.

(5 marks)

8 **Change these sentences from the active to the passive.**

1 They installed over half the cables in the train tunnel last month.

2 They built a new shopping centre on the site last year.

3 They took the computer back to the store to get it repaired.

4 The mechanic drove the car round the track.

5 They broke the handle of my suitcase at the airport.

6 Pilots flew the A30 superjumbo from Singapore to Sydney on its first commercial flight.

(6 marks)

9 **Complete the sentences with the words in the box.**

> after this   as   at the same time   meanwhile   when

1 _____ the intruder steps on the mat, the alarm sounds.

2 _____ you push the left-hand joystick up, the plane accelerates.

3 The cars are painted by the robots. _____ the body is checked by factory workers.

4 Lay the bricks. _____ check and adjust them so that they're level.

5 The program takes ten minutes to download. _____, can you check the price list in our new catalogue.

(5 marks)

Part 2: Reading and writing

Reading

Read the text and complete the form below

One solution to the problem of the world energy crisis and the need to reduce carbon emissions is tidal wave power. This is a system for converting the energy from seawater which is moved inland with the tides into electrical power. Narrow river estuaries, where the tide flows in from the sea, have the fastest and most powerful movements of water, and have big tidal ranges which are needed to convert the energy into electricty.

One way to convert tidal energy into electricity is by building barrages. These are long, concrete walls which stretch across the width of a river, like a dam. As the tide rises, the seawater flows into the river estuary. At the same time, sluices or valves, which control the flow of water, open. These allow the seawater to flow through the barrage. The water is then held behind the barrage until the tide falls. When the tide falls, the seawater flows out again. As it flows out, the water drives the turbines. These rotate and create electricity.

Tidal energy is a clean, renewable power that doesn't produce any carbon dioxide. However, only about 20 places in the world have the big tidal ranges which

can convert the energy into electricity. Barrages are also expensive to build and environmental groups believe they will damage the wildlife and plants of the area.

Problem	Need to solve world energy crisis, and reduce carbon emissions
Solution	
Location	
Operation	
Advantages	
Disadvantages	

(5 marks)

Writing

Read the letter of complaint below. Then write a reply to the letter using the notes below.

24th February 2008

Dear Sir/Madam

I'm writing again to complain about my suitcase. It was badly damaged during my 20.30 flight from Bangkok to London on 4th May. When I collected the suitcase, I found that the front surface was torn and the handle was broken. The suitcase was also crushed and dented in several places. I wrote to you on 10th May about the damage, but nobody has replied to my complaint. I'm unhappy about the damage to my suitcase and I'm not satisfied with the service from your company. I would like a reply from you soon.

I look forward to hearing from you.

Regards

Carla Benson

• acknowledge the letter

• apologise for the problem

• offer to replace the suitcase

• as an alternative, offer to pay for the cost of the suitcase

• apologise again and finish letter

Dear Ms Benson

_____

_____

_____

_____

Daniel Jameson

(5 marks)

Contents

1 Sports data

Read racing cyclist's blog with (a) description of measuring device (b) maintenance schedule, (c) table of distance covered. Task: check answers to starter questions about cycle race.

Word list: *adjust, altimeter, barometer, chain, data, display* (n), *frequency, gear, gizmo, lubricant, measurement, odometer, percentage, pressure, quick-release, tachometer, sensor, saddle, wheel rim*

Answer questions about the Web log.

Vocabulary: units of measurement, abbreviation and measuring instrument. Asking questions: *What do you use for measuring …? What does … stand for? What's the abbreviation for …? What's … for? What does… measure?*

Change percentages into approximate fractions: *almost one sixth of the distance*

Read a maintenance guide and answer questions on frequency: *every 3,000 km, at 3,000-km intervals, after … months, whichever is the sooner.*

Word list: *almost, approximately, exactly, just over/under, kilopascals (kPa), monitor, nearly, watts (W)*

2 Sensors

Starters: function of a sensor; write a definition. Discuss crash test sensors.

Read description of sensing equipment in crash test dummies. Task: complete statements about the function of the sensors.

Word list: *acceleration sensor, accelerometer, bending (force), compression, crash test dummy, deflection, impact, load sensor, motion sensor, rib, shear, tension*

Vocabulary: forces: *shear/bending/tension/compression/ torsion*

Language: noun + noun combinations: *side impact crash dummy*

Find noun + noun compounds in reading text.

Expand noun compounds into fuller phrases. Write these as full sentence definitions.

Task: talk about sensors in own industry.

Word list: *dial, fuel inlet port, gauge, indicator, meter, valve, inlet, outlet*

3 Positioning

Starter: what do systems (GSP, radar, etc) calculate: *distance, location* etc.

Read text about how GPS works. Text contains both noun phrases and indirect questions (e.g. *its location/ where it is*). Tasks: (1) match footnotes (indirect questions) with noun phrases in text; (2) choose mathematical formula matching words in text; (3) identify markers with meanings *and (in addition), but (however), for example (for instance, such as), in other words (that is, or)*

Word list: *altimeter, depth, distance, echo sounder, GPS, hand-held, height, lidar, location/position, multiply, orbit, pinger, precise, to within (= with a tolerance of), radar, speed, subtract*

Language: indirect question with same function/ position in sentence as object noun phrase: *your location/ where you are*).

Practice transformations between indirect questions and noun phrases.

Task: group work brainstorming and present applications of GPS.

Word list: *approach, ping/burst (of sound), reflect*

Briefing

This unit deals with ways of communicating about measurement systems.

Section 1 looks at measuring data in sports, with the Tour de France as an example. This is a cycle race of about 3,550 km around France every July, which lasts about three weeks, including two rest days. Much of the race takes place on mountain roads. The reading text mentions some measuring devices used by cyclists. An **odometer** measures the number of **rotations** of a cycle wheel, from which it calculates the total **distance** travelled in a given time. A **tachometer** measures the speed at which a mechanical device (such as a cycle wheel) rotates. Tachometers are used in a wide range of engineering fields to measure speed of rotation. A **laser tachometer** works by pulsing a tight beam of light against the rotating element. The rotating element has a reflective spot, and the tachometer measures the **rate** or speed at which the light beam is reflected back. A **barometer** measures the **pressure** of air in the atmosphere, useful when performing sports in changing altitudes. An **altimeter** measures altitude, or height above sea level; it can do this using a built-in barometer, or (in aeroplanes) by a **radar** device. The vocabulary exercise mentions a **power monitor**, which some sports people use to tell them how much **power** (measured in Watts) they are putting into a task. A **heart rate monitor** tells them how fast their heart is beating. A **quick-release lever** on a bicycle allows you to take a wheel off quickly.

Section 2 looks at sensors. A **sensor** is a type of **transducer**, a device that converts one type of energy to another for measurement or information transfer. Sensors **detect** changes in the environment, such as movement, smoke, heat or temperature and send data about them to a computer or display. The reading text is about **crash-test dummies**. Dummies are used in **destructive tests** to discover the strength and safety of vehicles. Three types of sensors are used in crash-test dummies to measure what happens to body parts during a crash: **motion sensors** measure the **distance** a dummy's 'body part' moves inwards or outwards; **acceleration sensors** measure its **speed** of movement; and **load sensors** measure the **force** exerted on the body part. The Vocabulary activity deals with four physical or mechanical forces: **shear force**, **torsion**, **compression** and **tension**. A shear force acts on a structure from two opposite directions, which may cause it to split. Scissors exert shear force when they cut something. Torsion is twisting. Tension is pulling apart or stretching. Compression is squeezing something into a smaller volume. Bending is a combination of compression and tension. When you bend a metal bar into a U shape, the inside of the U is under compression, and the outside is under tension. **Deformation** in a technical context means *changing shape*; the associated verb is to **deform**.

Section 3 looks at the **Global Positioning System** (**GPS**). This is a network of satellites which operate together to give accurate information about the position of any object on land or sea, or in the air. At least three satellites are needed to give an accurate positioning because of the mathematical principle of **triangulation**, which is used in surveying. If we know our exact distance from *one* satellite in space, we know we are somewhere on the *surface* of an imaginary sphere with a radius equal to the distance to the satellite. If we know our exact distance from *two* satellites, we know that we are located somewhere on an imaginary *line* where the two spheres intersect. And, if we take a third measurement from a *third* satellite, we can find the exact *point* where we are on the line. The web page reference below gives further information about GPS and triangulation.

Tour de France: http://www.letour.fr/2007/TDF/presentation/us/parcours.html

Measurement in sport: From: http://www.science.org.au/nova/033/033key.htm

Bike maintenance: http://news.bbc.co.uk/sport1/hi/other_sports/cycling/get_involved/4250522.stm

Sensors: http://en.wikipedia.org/wiki/Sensor

Crash-test dummies: http://auto.howstuffworks.com/crash-test.htm/printable

Forces acting on materials and structures: http://www.diydoctor.org.uk/projects/forces.htm

GPS: http://www.aero.org/education/primers/gps/index.html

Teacher's notes

1 Sports data

Start here

1 Put students in pairs. They discuss the questions about what they know about the Tour de France cycle race. Feedback with the class but do not confirm answers at this stage, as they will find them in the reading text which follows.

You could ask further questions about the race, e.g. *Who won the last Tour de France cycle race? What route did it take? Were there any problems in the race? Do you or any one you know take part in cycle races? Can you tell the class about the experience?*

Reading

2 Tell students that they're going to read a blog from a member of a cycling team about the Tour de France race. Ask students to read the blog and check their answers to the questions in 1.

> The route is 3,553 km long.
> It takes twenty days to complete.
> When they train for a cycle race they need to measure the distance they travel, their speed, their altitude and the atmospheric pressure.

> **Extra activity**
>
> Tell students to look back at the blog and ask these True and False questions:
> 1 The blog shows Team4Tour taking part in the Tour de France race.
> 2 You can click on a link to see the distances they have travelled.
> 3 You can click on a link to see the measuring devices they have.
> 4 They have completed three days of the tour.
> 5 Tomorrow they're going to Northern France.

3 Students work on their own and answer the questions on the text. They can then compare their answers with a partner before you check with the class.

> **1** (1) tachometer
>   (2) odometer
>   (3) altimeter
> **2** (1) accidents
>   (2) the wheels falling off
>   (3) the rider slipping down off the saddle
>   (4) the brakes from slipping
> **3** Yes, he/she should.

Vocabulary

4 Ask students to look at the table. Tell them the rows in the table are all mixed up. Tell them to match the sports measuring instruments with the correct items in each of the other columns in the table. You could do the first one with the class as an example.

Ask for full sentences when getting answers from the class, e.g. *A barometer measures pressure in kilopascals or kPa. A tachometer measures speed in kilometres per hour or km/h*, etc.

> **1** barometer – pressure – kilopascals – kPa
> **2** tachometer – speed – kilometres per hour – km/h
> **3** odometer – distance (cycling) – kilometres – km
> **4** altimeter – height (above sea level) – metres – m
> **5** stop watch – time – seconds – s
> **6** heart rate monitor – rate of heart beat – beats per second – bps
> **7** power monitor – power output – watts – W
> **8** scales – weight – kilograms – kg

5 Tell students to ask and answer questions about the table. Ask individual students to ask one of the questions listed and elicit the answer from other students, e.g. *What do you use for measuring your power output? You use a power monitor. What does kPa stand for? It stands for kilopascals*, etc.

Ask students to work in pairs and ask and answer further questions from the table.

6 Ask students to make a table about the units of measurement and measuring instruments in their own technical field, using the same headings as in 4. They can then ask and answer questions about their table with a partner, as they did in 5.

7 Ask students to look back at the distance table in the blog in 2. Tell them to complete it with the words in the box. Point out that they should use approximate fractions.

> *Possible answers:*
> 17% – almost one fifth
> 29% – more than a quarter
> 39% – more than a third
> 55% – just over half
> 65% – approximately two-thirds
> 76% – approximately three-quarters
> 89% – just under nine-tenths
> 96% – nearly all

8 Ask students to make some statements about themselves or a topic that interests them, using approximate fractions as in the example.

Reading

9 Ask students to read the text and answer the questions.

> **1** Yes, it should.
> **2** Yes, they should.

2 Sensors

Start here

1 Ask students to look at the photos and to identify the objects (*a microphone; a thermostat; a flashlight* and *a security beam*. Ask them which of the objects is not a sensor and to explain why they think so.

> **4** A flashlight.
> The others are devices that detect change in real-world conditions and convert it to analogue or digital signals, e.g. a microphone detects sound, a thermostat detects changes in heat and a security beam detects changes in light. A flashlight produces beams of light – it doesn't detect them.

2 Ask students to name other sensors they know about.

You could put students in pairs or groups of three and turn this exercise into a competition. Allow them three minutes to think of and write down as many different sensors as they can. Then find out who has the most sensors. That pair or group can then read out their list to the class. If any of the other students disagree about any of the objects they mention being a sensor, they can challenge the student.

Here are a few examples of sensors: a compass (detects magnetism); a thermometer (detects heat); a light sensor on a camera; a metal detector; a smoke detector; a solar cell (detects sunlight); a pressure mat (detects pressure when an intruder walks on it); an ammeter (detects electrical current); RADAR (detects aeroplanes and other objects); flow meters (detect water, oil, gas flowing through a pipe); speedometers (detect a car's speed).

3 Ask students to use the words and other words to complete the definition of a sensor.

> A sensor is a device that can detect change in the environment and convert it to data.

Reading

4 Put students in pairs. Ask them to look at the photo and discuss the questions. Then get feedback from the class.

> Engineers are conducting a car crash test.
> The effect of a front impact car crash and a side impact car crash on dummies.
> (See answers to 5 for the sensors used in the test.)

5 Ask students to read the article about crash test dummies and check their answers to 4. Then ask students to read the three statements at the bottom of the page. Tell students to look back at the article and find the three types of sensors these sentences describe and write their names in the gaps.

> **1** Motion
> **2** Acceleration
> **3** Load

Vocabulary

6 Ask students to look at the diagrams. First, they should match the diagrams to the names of the forces (a). Then they should match them to the description of the names of the forces (b).

> 1 (a) compression (b) squeezing or pressing together
> 2 (a) tension (b) stretching or pulling apart
> 3 (a) bending (b) squeezing one side + stretching the other side
> 4 (a) shear (b) sliding in opposite directions
> 5 (a) torsion (b) twisting

Language

Noun + noun combinations

Go through the Language box with the class on noun + noun combinations. Explain that in English nouns can often act as adjectives and come before the noun they are describing. Point out that more than two nouns can be put together.

7 Ask students to read through the phrases first. Then tell them to look back at the article in 5 and match them with noun + noun combinations in the article.

> 1 tension forces
> 2 motion sensors
> 3 side chest deflection
> 4 front impact crashes
> 5 a front impact crash test dummy

Extra activity

Ask students to look back at the article in 5 and underline all the examples of noun + noun combinations that they can find.

---

8 Ask students to expand the noun phrases. Go through the example with the class. Remind them of the work they did on (used) for + verb ing in Unit 5.1 and defining relative clauses in Unit 5.3. Point out that they can change the words and add extra information.

> 1 a meter which measures/for measuring the flow of gas (along a pipe).
> 2 a dial which shows/for showing the engine speed.
> 3 a gauge which measures/for measuring tyre pressure.
> 4 an indicator which shows/for showing bass volume.
> 5 a sensor which detects/for detecting air pressure.
> 6 a port which allows/for allowing fuel to enter into the engine.

9 Ask students to make full sentence definitions for each of the phrases in 8. Go through the example with the class to show them what to do.

> *Possible answers:*
> 1 A gas flow meter is a meter which measures the flow of gas along a pipe.
> 2 An engine speed dial is a dial for showing the engine speed.
> 3 A tyre pressure gauge is a gauge for measuring tyre pressure.
> 4 A bass volume indicator is an indicator which shows the bass volume.
> 5 An air pressure sensor is a sensor which detects air pressure.
> 6 A fuel inlet port is a port for allowing fuel to enter into the engine.

Task

10 If students work in the same industry or technical field, put them in small groups. Focus students' attention on the examples in the table, showing what sensors are used in the civil engineering and construction industry. Ask students to make a similar table for the sensors that they use in their industry.

11 Students now take it in turns to explain the sensors they listed in their table to the class.

3 Positioning

Start here

1 Put students in pairs. Ask them to look at the pictures of the systems and choose from the words the most important thing that each one calculates.

> 1 depth
> 2 distance
> 3 height
> 4 location
> 5 speed

Reading

2 Explain that this is a web page from a website giving the answers to FAQ (frequently asked questions) about the Global Positioning System. Ask them what they know about this system.

Ask students to look at the footnotes at the end of the web page. Tell them that these explain the terms which have been numbered in the text. However, the footnotes are in the wrong order. Tell them to find where the footnotes should go in the text and write the correct number next to its footnote.

> **4** in other words, *when it was sent*
> **2** that is, *how far away they are*
> **1** or, *exactly where you are*
> **3** i.e., *exactly where they (the satellites) are*

3 Ask students to look back at the text and choose the correct calculation.

> c) $D = (T_2 - T_1) * c$

> **Extra activity**
>
> Revise the mathematical terms before doing this exercise. Write the following on the board and ask students to match the symbols with the words.
>
> | | | | |
> |---|---|---|---|
> | **1** = | | **a** | multiplied by |
> | **2** – | | **b** | equals |
> | **3** × | | **c** | divided by |
> | **4** ÷ | | **d** | minus (subtract x from y) |
>
> Then choose individual students to read out the calculations in 3.

4 Ask students to look at the words in 1–6 from the text. These words are all discourse markers, which help develop ideas and link them to one another. They are very useful in technical writing and in presentations to make information clear. Ask students to choose the correct meaning for each of the words.

Point out that *In addition*, *For instance* and *However* (at the beginning of a sentence) are always followed by a comma.

> 1 in other words
> 2 for example
> 3 For example
> 4 and
> 5 But
> 6 in other words

Language

Direct and indirect questions

Go through the Language box with the class.

Point out the structure of the noun phrases which use noun + preposition + noun, e.g. *the depth of the river*.

Tell students that in direct questions, you invert the word order, e.g. *What is their position? Where are you?,* and that in indirect questions, you don't invert the order, e.g. *I need to know what their position is. Please tell me where you are*. Note that in indirect questions you don't use a question mark.

I need to know	What is their position?
	what their position is.
Please tell me	Where are you?
	where you are.

5 Ask students to read the sentences and point out that they all use indirect questions. Tell them that they should replace the phrases in italics with the nouns in the box and any other necessary words. Go through the example with the class first.

1 Please find out the location of the ship, and her speed.
2 Before you touch the liquid, you should check its temperature/the temperature of it.
3 I want to find out the distance of the plane, and its altitude.
4 Could you please tell me the depth of the river below the bridge.
5 I also need to know the width, the length and the height of the bridge.

6 Tell students that this time all the words in italics are noun phrases. Ask students to read the sentences and replace these phrases using the words in brackets to make indirect questions. Go through the example with the class first.

1 how high the plane is above sea level
2 where the ships are
3 how far a vehicle is, how fast the vehicle is
4 how fast the sound signal is, how far the plane is

Task

7 Put students in groups. First, brainstorm an everyday application which uses GPS. They can choose from the applications listed at the bottom of the page, or another application that interests them.

Tell students that they must prepare a short presentation, showing how the GPS system works in the application. Remind them of the work they did on discourse markers, and to use examples to make their points clear.

Finally, students take it in turns to give their presentations to the rest of the class.

After each group finishes giving their presentation, you could ask the students who were listening what they thought of the presentation, and if they thought that the group had explained the application clearly, and if not, how the presentation could be improved.

Contents

1 | Properties

Starter: identify the forces on a collapsing bridge.

Scanning task: find more about the bridge.

Read text on three destructive tests. Task 1: match with diagrams. Task 2: divide paragraphs into *objective, procedure, result*.

Word list: *bending, breaking point, clamp, compression, compressive, deform (= change shape), impact-resistance, shearing, tension, tensile, torsion, yield point*

Language: stating objectives: *The aim of … is to find out/ discover if/ whether …* Practice. Transform questions into objectives: *Does it break? → The purpose of the test is to discover if it breaks.*

Vocabulary: (1) syllable stress changes *ductile/ ductility* etc. (2) sort into noun/ adjective columns.

Group task: work out how to test strength of bike part. Write a test description. Explain the test to the class.

Word list: *aim/purpose/objective, compressive/ compression, deformation, elastic/elasticity, find out/ discover, flexible/flexibility, plastic/plasticity, rigid/rigidity, tensile/tension*

2 | Resistance

Starter: discuss and report ways to make buildings earthquake resistant.

Listen to a presentation. Tasks (1) delete notes not mentioned (2) tick 'signpost phrases' heard (3) label diagrams.

Language: signpost phrases: stating objectives, starting/ ending a topic (e.g. *let's move on to, in conclusion*) and referring to a visual (e.g. *as you can see in Figure 1*)

Word list: *brace, conclusion, damper, deck (= floor), earthquake, isolate, joint, presentation, problem, resistant, solution, strengthen, truss*

Read texts about structures mentioned in the talk. Task: match with six diagrams.

Language: ability/ inability in properties: *can* + active/ passive, affixes-*able* and –*ible, un-/in-/non-*, hyphenated forms: -*proof*, -*resistant*. Task: underline examples in text.

Practice: re-phrase sentences: *it is water-resistant/ it resists water/ it can resist water*

Word list: *combustible, cross brace, diagonal, frame, heat-resistant, horizontal deck, horizontal truss, rigid joint, shear wall, single brace, slab, portable, vertical, waterproof*

3 | Results

Test knowledge of safe electrical circuits (in diagram) in group and then present ideas to class.

Read captions and match them to the diagrams. Each caption describes result of the circuit (electric shock or no shock).

Language: ways of expressing cause and result: *as a result, therefore, and so, as, because, since*

Practise using these phrases.

Word list: *earthed, hot wire, in contact, neutral wire, (electric) shock*

Vocabulary: verbs ending in -*en* expressing causation: *strengthen* etc. Practise changing phrases to verbs: *to make it stronger → to strengthen it*.

Discuss in groups the 'rivet theory' of why the Titanic sank, based on a detailed diagram.

Write an individual account of the 'rivet theory', based on notes and the diagram.

Word list: *flatten, harden/soften, hull, iron, lengthen/ shorten, lighten/darken, plate, rivet, sharpen, slag, straighten, strengthen/weaken, tighten/loosen, widen*

Briefing

This unit looks at physical or electrical forces.

Section 1 deals with the **properties** (characteristics) of materials used in structures that can **withstand** (or **resist**) extreme natural forces. It looks at the forces acting on the Tacoma Narrows Bridge, which collapsed during a storm in the 1940s. Although the wind speed was relatively low (about 65 km/h) it was enough to create a powerful torsional (twisting) force on the bridge deck. Three **destructive tests** of materials are described in the reading text. The **tensile strength test** finds out the strength of a material when it is subjected to tension. If the material does not deform or break when it is pulled apart with a specified force, it is **strong in tension**/ it has good **tensile strength**. The **compressive strength test** measures how far a material can resist compression. The **impact-resistance test** measures how strong the material is when struck, for example with a hammer, with a specified force. Materials are tested with increasing force until they either break (at the **breaking point**) or deform (at the **yield point**). The Vocabulary activity introduces more words describing properties: a **rigid** material resists bending; a **flexible** material can bend slightly without breaking or deforming permanently; an **elastic** material changes its shape when a force is applied, and then returns to its original shape when the force is removed; a **plastic** material deforms permanently when a force is applied.

Section 2 deals with ways of making a building **resistant** to **earthquakes**. Basic units in buildings include **columns** (which are vertical), **beams** (horizontal) and **braces** (diagonal). A brace is placed at the junction of a column and beam to form a strong triangular connection. A particularly strong structure (in bridges and buildings) is the **truss**: this is a beam which is not solid but made up of a series of triangular structures. Six methods of strengthening a building to make it **earthquake-resistant** are covered in the unit: (1) adding a single diagonal brace; (2) adding two braces crossing each other; (3) adding a solid horizontal steel or concrete deck between floors; (4) adding a horizontal truss to the roof; (5) making rigid connections between columns and beams; and (6) adding a shear wall, which is a vertical steel or concrete wall (without windows) that can resist shear forces.

Section 3 deals with causes of electric shocks. Electricity flows where there is a closed **circuit** made of conductive material. Copper wire, the earth and the human body are all **conductors** of electricity. For electrons to flow through a conductor, there must be a **voltage** (or **electromotive force**) caused by one **terminal** of the **power source** having a different **electric charge** from the other terminal. A high voltage across the power source and the **load** (or **appliance**) means that there is a powerful electromotive force causing the electrons to flow round the circuit from one terminal, through the appliance, and back to the other terminal. In the six circuit diagrams, the person gets a shock if his body completes a path from one terminal to the other. The earth acts as a conductor only if the circuit has **two** points of contact with the earth (whether a fixed earth, a tree or a person's feet). In the third scenario, the system is **unearthed**, so the person can touch any wire (even a live wire) without being shocked. But this is dangerous, because an accidental earthing (such as a tree touching a wire) would complete a circuit through the person touching the live wire. This is why all electrical circuits are deliberately **earthed**: in earthed circuits, it is always safe to touch a neutral wire. The unit ends with information about a theory that the sinking of the *Titanic* was made more rapid by a failure of rivets. (more information below).

Tacoma Narrows Bridge disaster: http://britton.disted. camosun.bc.ca/tacoma/tacoma.html

Properties and materials testing: http://www. bsieducation.org/Education/14-19/default.shtml

Earthquake resistant buildings: http://www.ideers.bris. ac.uk/earth/earth_home.html

Safe electrical circuits: http://www.allaboutcircuits. com/vol_1/chpt_3/3.html

The 'rivets' theory of the Titanic: http://www. timesonline.co.uk/tol/news/uk/article640365.ece

---

Teacher's notes

1 | Properties

Start here

1 Ask students to look at the photo of the bridge. Explain that there was a storm when the photo was taken, and a short time after, the bridge collapsed. Ask students to look at the words in the box describing different forces and label the bridge with the forces acting on it.

a	tension
b	tension
c	shearing
d	torsion
e	compression

Scanning

2 Go through the instructions and questions for the task with students. Then ask them to turn to pages 118–119 and find the information about the bridge. Remind them to find the answers to the questions as quickly as they can, and not to look at every word in the text. Ask students to put up their hand when they've finished, so that you know who the winner is, and ask them to answer the questions.

Then ask students if they know about any other bridges that have collapsed. Ask them to tell the class.

The Tacoma Narrows Bridge.
It collapsed in 1940.
The winds were about 65 km/h.

Reading

3 Ask students to look at the diagrams of three different tests. Then ask them to read the description about the tests and write the figure number in the gaps.

Fig. 2
Fig. 3
Fig. 1

4 Ask students to look back at the descriptions of the tests in 3 and to divide each paragraph into the three different sections: *Objective*, *Procedure* and *Result*. To make sure that they understand what to do, go through the example with the class and ask them to find the phrases in the description, and refer them to the Language box on the next page to help them. Tell them that organising their written work into paragraphs under headings will make it clearer for the reader.

Paragraph 1:
Objective. The purpose of the tensile strength test …
Procedure. The material is secured …
Result. This measurement shows you the tensile strength of the material.
Paragraph 2:
Objective. The aim of the impact-resistance test …
Procedure. The bottom of the material is placed …
Result. This indicates the impact resistance of the material.
Paragraph 3:
Objective. The objective of the compressive strength test …
Procedure. The material is secured …
Result. This indicates the compressive strength of the material.

Language

Describing the objective of a process

Go through the Language box with students. Explain that you can use this sentence pattern to state the objective of a process.

5 Ask students to change the questions into statements about objectives. Tell them that they should use each word or phrase in the box at least once. Go through the example with the class and refer them back to the Language box to help them. Tell them that they can compare their sentences with a partner before you check with the class.

> *Possible answers:*
> 1 The purpose of the test is to discover if this metal deforms easily when it is hammered.
> 2 The aim of the test is find out if this material is elastic or plastic when it is stretched.
> 3 The objective of the investigation is to test if this metal breaks when you strike it with a force of 10,000 newtons.
> 4 The aim of the test is to discover whether this plastic will withstand deformation when it is heated to 120°C.
> 5 The purpose of this investigation is to find out whether these three types of ceramic melt when they are heated to over 500°C.
> 6 The objective of this investigation is to discover if this concrete beam will crack when it is compressed under a weight of 5 tonnes.

Vocabulary

6 Ask students to underline the stressed syllable in the nouns and adjectives. Do not confirm answers at this stage.

7 ▶ 🎧 24

Students listen to the recording and check their answers to 6.

> (See answers underlined in the audio script below.)

▶ 🎧 24

1	ten<u>sile</u>	ten<u>sion</u>
2	com<u>pressive</u>	com<u>pression</u>
3	<u>rigid</u>	ri<u>gidity</u>
4	flexi<u>bility</u>	<u>flexible</u>
5	elas<u>ticity</u>	e<u>lastic</u>
6	<u>plastic</u>	plas<u>ticity</u>

8 Ask students to copy the table. They then add the words from 6 to the table.

noun	adjective
tension	tensile
compression	compressive
rigidity	rigid
flexibility	flexible
elasticity	elastic
plasticity	plastic

Task

9 Put students in groups. Ask them to look at the diagram of the tests on parts of a bicycle and choose one of them. They then discuss in their groups how they would conduct this test. Tell them to make brief notes on their discussion.

10 Students now work on their own. Tell them to use their notes from 9 and write a description of the test. Point out that they should organise the description under the three headings listed and refer them back to the text in 2 to help them.

> *Model answers:*
> **1 Test on wheel**
> **Objective**
> The aim of this test is to discover if the wheel can resist a bending force from the side.
> **Procedure**
> The wheel is supported and clamped in position. A load is then applied to the wheel rim, on the side of the drive sprocket. The load is at right angles to the wheel. The yield point and/or the breaking point is measured.
> **Result**
> This measurement indicates the strength, rigidity and toughness of the wheel.
>
> **2 Test on saddle**
> **Objective**
> The purpose of the test is to discover if the saddle can resist a bending force from below.
> **Procedure**
> The saddle is placed in a clamp. A force of 400 newtons is applied in turn under the rear and nose of the saddle. The yield point and/or the breaking point is measured.
> **Result**
> This measurement shows how rigid and tough the saddle is.
>
> **3 Test on frame**
> **Objective**
> The objective of this test is to find out whether the frame can withstand a sudden impact against the ground.
> **Procedure**
> The frame is attached at the rear axle. The frame is able to rotate freely at the rear axle. A weight of 70 kg is fixed to the saddle pillar. The frame is dropped forwards onto a block. Any deformation of the frame is measured.
> **Result**
> This measurement shows the compressive strength and impact resistance of the frame.

11 Students explain their group's test to the rest of the class.

2 Resistance

Start here

1 Focus students' attention on the photo and ask them what they think has happened. (A building has collapsed in an earthquake.)

Put students into small groups and ask them to discuss the two questions on buildings and earthquakes.

Listening

2 ▶ 💿 25

Tell students that they're going to listen to a talk about earthquakes. Ask them to look at the speaker's notes and read the list of topics. Tell them that they should tick the topics they hear the speaker talk about. If a topic isn't mentioned, they should leave it blank.

After you've played the recording, students can compare their answers with a partner. Play the recording one more time for students to check.

> **Earthquake-resistant buildings**
> **1 Introduction: what causes earthquakes?** ✓
> **2 The problem for buildings** ✓
> **3 Some solutions**
>   3.1 Strengthening buildings ✓
>   3.2 Isolating buildings
>   3.3 Adding Dampers

▶ 💿 25

Good afternoon everyone, and welcome. The aim of my talk today is to discuss the problem of earthquakes, the damage they cause buildings, and some solutions to this problem.

I'd like to begin by talking about what causes earthquakes. As you know, the tectonic plates on the Earth's surface have been moving for millions of years, and they're still moving. Sometimes this movement causes the surface to break. This break or fracture in the Earth's crust is called a fault. When the rock breaks, there is a sudden release of energy. Shock waves spread out through and around the Earth in all directions, starting from the focus, or epicentre, of the earthquake. At the Earth's surface the ground vibrates as the waves pass through it. This is what we call an earthquake.

And that brings me to the problem which earthquakes cause for buildings. The problem for buildings is that, during an earthquake, the ground moves in all directions. It moves horizontally. It moves up and down. It rotates and it twists. All these movements affect buildings. But horizontal movement is the most damaging for a building. As you can see in the photograph, if a building moves too much from side to side the structure can collapse.

So, now let's move on to talk about some solutions to this problem. There are three main solutions. The first one is strengthening buildings. We do this by adding some materials, or structure, to the building to make it stronger and help it to resist the sideways movement.

3 Go through the explanation and table of signpost phrases with the class. Tell students that these are all useful phrases they could use when giving a presentation.

Ask students to listen to the talk once again and tick the phrases in the table that they hear.

Giving the purpose of the talk	Starting a new topic	Referring to visual
the aim of my talk today is to	I'd like to begin by that brings me to lets move on to	as you can see in the photo or photograph

4 ▶ 💿 26

Ask students to look at the diagrams of the different structures and find a horizontal, vertical and diagonal line, a triangle and a 90 degree angle.

Tell students that they're going to listen to the next part of the talk and that they should label the structures the speaker talks about. Check their answers and then play the recording a second time.

> **D** Fig. 1
> **C** Fig. 2
> **F** Fig. 3

▶ 💿 26

So, now let's move on to talk about some solutions to this problem. There are three main solutions. The first one is strengthening buildings. We do this by adding some materials or structure to the building to make it stronger and help it to resist the sideways movement.

So, let's have a very quick look at ways to strengthen a building and help it to resist an earthquake. And there are in fact six ways of strengthening a building.

The first method is the single diagonal, or brace. You have a vertical column and a horizontal beam. Then you put a diagonal brace between them at 45 degrees. This strengthens the connection between the beam and the column, as you can see in Figure 1. …

OK? So, let's move on to the second method. This is where you use two diagonals, as shown in Figure 2. The two braces cross each other. This is a much stronger way to connect a beam and a column …

Right. Now I'd like to move on to a third method of strengthening a building. This is called a horizontal deck. As Figure 3 shows, this is a flat, horizontal plate of rigid material, usually concrete. It strengthens the vertical columns and walls.

Is that clear? Fine. So, that brings me to the fourth method of strengthening buildings … a horizontal truss…

Reading

5 Explain that the text shows the key to the diagrams in 4. Point out the names of the structures (*single brace*, etc). Then ask students to read the key and write the correct diagram leters of the structures in the spaces provided.

Structure 1: D
Structure 2: C
Structure 3: F
Structure 4: E
Structure 5: A
Structure 6: B

Language

Ability and inability

Go through the Language box with the class. Point out that both *can* and *able to* are used in active sentences, but *be able to* isn't used in passive sentences. You can only use *can* in the passive. Then go through the list of suffixes and prefixes which can be used to express ability when talking about properties.

6 Ask students to look back at the text in 5 and underline examples for expressing ability and inability that are mentioned in the Language box.

The single diagonal is able to resist both tension and compression.
… they must be able to resist tension, but they need not be compression-resistant.
This is a flat unbendable steel plate or concrete slab.
It forms a rigid, unmoveable structure for the roof.
The angle cannot be changed.
The column and beam must be made of strong but flexible materials.
They can be bent slightly, but the connection is unmoveable.
This is a vertical steel plate of concrete slab that can resist sideways shear forces.

7 Ask students to rewrite the sentences, using *can* or *cannot* and the correct form of the words in brackets.

1 This plastic can resist heat and cannot be bent.
2 A cross-brace can withstand tension in two directions.
3 These sunglasses cannot be scratched, but can be broken.
4 The emergency generator can be moved by forklift but it cannot be carried by hand.

Extra activity

Write the information below on the board or OHP. Ask students to discuss the information about how this method of earthquake-proofing a building works. Tell them that this is the second method that the speaker in the recording mentions in his talk.

Tell students to make notes on their discussion. They then work on their own and write a description on how this system works.

Isolation Systems – fact sheet

• purpose: to prevent building from vibrating too much during an earthquake
• isolation systems use special bearings
• properties: bearings are not rigid in the horizontal direction
• method: the bearings are placed between the foundation and the bottom of the building
• operation: during an earthquake, bearings move sideways, but building doesn't move

3 Results

Start here

1 Ask students to look at the circuit diagrams. Tell them to decide if the people would get an electric shock in each of the situations and to put a tick next to them if they would get a shock.

> 1 unshocked
> 2 shocked
> 3 unshocked
> 4 both shocked
> 5 shocked
> 6 top: unshocked; bottom: shocked

2 Put students in small groups. Ask them to discuss the reasons why people would get or wouldn't get an electric shock in the situations in 1.

When they've finished, tell them to explain their group's decision to the class. Don't confirm their answers at this stage, as they'll be reading about the diagrams in the following exercise.

Reading

3 Explain that the text gives the answers to 1 on why people do or don't get electric shocks. Tell them that each of the captions matches one of the diagrams. Ask them to read the captions and write the figure number of the diagrams they describe. They can then compare their answers with a partner before you check with the class.

> A Fig 2
> B Fig 5
> C Fig 4
> D Fig 1
> E Fig 3
> F Fig 6

Language

Cause and result

Go through the Language box with the class. Tell students that these words are expressions to show the cause or result of something. The expressions help develop ideas and link them to one another, either to show that something results from what was said before, or to explain a cause of something that was mentioned before. Point out that you can change the order of the clauses for *as*, *because* and *since* without changing the meaning.

Tell students that they will find more information on these expressions on page 107.

4 Ask students to read the sentences and replace the words in italics with the words in brackets, making the appropriate changes to the punctuation and word order.

> 1 Ben touched an earthed live wire, and as a result he got a shock.
> 2 Ron was safe because he touched an earthed neutral wire.
> 3 Bill touched an unearthed wire, and so he didn't get a shock.
> 4 Bob got a shock because he touched a live wire when a tree touched a neutral wire.
> 5 Pete was safe, since he touched a live wire when a tree touched it.
> 6 Tom and Del touched an unearthed wire, and therefore they got a shock

---

Extra activity

Students rewrite each of the sentences they underlined in the text, using a different linking word or phrase, and using different punctuation or reversing the order of the clauses. Give them a couple of examples first to show them what to do.

1 As Ben touched the earthed live wire, he got a shock.

2 Ron touched the earthed neutral wire. Therefore he was safe.

Vocabulary

Go through the information about the causative verbs with the class. Explain that these verbs end with the suffix *-en* to express the idea of cause. Point out the doubling of the final consonant in *flatten*. Note that you form the causative verbs *lengthen* and *strengthen* from nouns (i.e. not ~~longen~~ and ~~strongen~~), and the other verbs from adjectives.

5 Ask students to read the sentences and replace the phrases in italics using verbs from the Vocabulary box above in the correct tense.

> 1 The torsion forces in the storm must have weakened the bridge.
> 2 The purpose of adding carbon to steel is to strengthen it.
> 3 Long ago, humans used stones to sharpen and straighten their knife blades.
> 4 In forging, metal is heated to soften it. Then it is put in water to harden it again.
> 5 Hot weather lengthens railway lines and cold weather shortens them.
> 6 If the race has loosened the bike saddle, you should tighten it with a spanner.

Task

6 Put students into small groups. First, ask students to discuss all they know about the ship the *Titanic* for a couple of minutes, then tell the class what they know.

Remind students on the work they did on modal verbs in the past for certainty and possibility (*may/might/could* + past participle) in Unit 7 Section 1. Remind them that *must* is used when you are certain of the fact, and *may* and *might* if something possibly happened. Remind them also that the negative of *must* is *can't* not ~~mustn't~~ in this context.

Ask students to look at the diagram and read the note. Tell them to discuss what happened to the *Titanic* according to the rivet theory in their groups. They should then discuss whether they agree with it or not. If they don't agree, they should give their own opinion on what they think made the *Titanic* sink so quickly. Tell them to come to a consensus and make notes on their group's decision on what they think could have caused the ship to sink. Encourage them to use models of certainty and possibility.

7 Groups take it in turns to explain their understanding of the rivet theory to the class and say what their group thought about the theory. They can then tell the class about any other ideas they had on why the ship sank so quickly.

8 Students write an explanation of why the *Titanic* sank so quickly from their discussion in 7, using the notes given and the information on the diagram. Tell them to use modal verbs for certainty and possibility and the causative verbs they studied in the lesson.

> *Sample answer:*
> The iceberg hit the hull causing bending forces on the plates which must have led to shear forces on the rivets.
> The rivet head broke which may have weakened the other rivets.
> The extra load could have made the good rivets break, and as a result, water entered the ship.
> Because water filled five or six compartments, the ship sank quickly.
> Since the *Titanic* sank so quickly, the *Carparthia* was too late and so couldn't rescue the passengers.

Review Unit E

Answer key

1 *Sample answers:*

1 Less than one twentieth of the students are studying software engineering.
2 Exactly one twentieth of the students are studying electronics.
3 Nearly a quarter of the students are studying electrical engineering.
4 Just under one tenth of the students are studying automotive engineering.
5 More than one tenth of the students are studying chemical engineering.
6 Almost a fifth of the students are studying design.
7 Approximately one third of the students are studying construction.

2 1 g 2 f 3 a 4 b 5 d 6 c 7 e

3

1 The odometer measures how far the cyclist has travelled.
2 The altimeter tells the pilot how high the plane is above sea level.
3 The lidar equipment told the police how fast the car went.
4 You should use these scales to check how heavy the boxer is.
5 The radar system indicated how far the planes were from the tower.
6 The GPS system will tell you exactly where the motorboats are.
7 I used a sound level meter to find out how loud the guitars were last night.

4

1 Please make sure that the brakes are adjusted correctly.
2 Check that the saddle is tight and at the correct height.
3 Make sure that there is no lubricant on the wheel trims.
4 Ensure that the wheel spokes are all at the same tension.

5

1	to discover	6	is held
2	deforms	7	is attached
3	breaks	8	is increased
4	is bent	9	is measured
5	is secured	10	shows

6 1 f 2 e 3 i 4 b 5 g 6 a 7 h 8 c 9 d

7

1 We need to bring some diggers here to make the trench deeper.
2 Last year's small earthquakes have made the foundations weaker.
3 The only way to make the walls stronger is to add braces between them.
4 You have to make the metal softer before you can hammer it into shape.

9 *Model answer:*

Frame test: The aim of the test is to find out whether the car frame can withstand the impact of a heavy weight on the roof. A plate which weighs 50% more than the weight of the car is dropped onto one edge of the roof. The car passes the test if the roof doesn't bend more than 12.5 cm.

Drop test: The purpose of this test is to discover whether the car frame can resist the impact when it is dropped upside down on the ground. The car is suspended upside down from steel cables 1.5 metres above the ground. Then the car is dropped on one edge of the roof. The car passes the test if the roof doesn't bend more than 12.5 cm.

Roll test: The objective of this test is to find out if a test dummy is thrown from the car when it rolls over onto its roof. The car is placed at an angle of 23 degrees on the side of a truck. The truck moves at 30 mph and then stops suddenly. The car falls off the truck and rolls over on its sides and roof. The car passes the test if the dummy stays inside the car.

10 *Model answer:*

Test results on the Sunburst XJ22: The car passed the frame test, because the roof bent 3.2 cm, which is below the maximum of 12.5 cm. However, it failed the drop test, since the roof bent 12.8 cm when it was dropped on the ground. This is more than the maximum of 12.5 cm. It also failed the roll test, because when the car rolled over onto its roof, the test dummy was thrown 2.2 m from the car.

Recommendations: The frame must be strengthened to prevent it from bending, and to stop the doors from opening in a roll.

Project

12 & 13 At the end of every Review Unit is a project. Students can do their research on the internet or in a library, and in their own language if they wish. They must then write their results in English.

Quick test answer key

Part 1: Vocabulary and grammar

1
1 almost
2 exactly
3 just over
4 approximately

2
1 A barometer
2 A tachometer
3 An odometer
4 An altimeter
5 Scales

3
1 scratch-proof
2 compression-resistant
3 flexibility
4 combustible
5 breakable

4
1 ~~Compression~~ Shearing
2 ~~Torsion~~ Tension
3 ~~column~~ beam
4 ~~damper~~ brace
5 ~~non-unearthed~~ unearthed

5
1 Make sure that the screws are tight.
2 Check that the cable can reach the computer easily.
3 Make sure that the gas has been switched off.
4 Please ensure that you've washed your hands in the disinfectant.
5 Check that the materials have been tested.

6
1 A business meeting which you have online.
2 A team who rescue people on a mountain.
3 A dummy which tests a vehicle in a crash.
4 A radio with headphones which is powered by solar energy.
5 A sensor which prevents a collision.

7
1 the depth of this reservoir
2 how high the dam is
3 the height of your vehicle
4 the speed you are travelling
5 how wide the screen is
6 how long the Channel Tunnel is

8
1 can't/aren't able to
2 can be
3 can/is able to
4 can't be
5 can't/'m not able to
6 can be

9
1 because
2 Therefore
3 since
4 as a result

10
1 The aim of the test is ~~for checking~~ to check the tension forces on the neck of the dummy.
2 A strain gauge is used ~~for to measure~~ to measure the deformation of the bridge.
3 Sensors are located in parts of the robot's body, ~~that is~~ for example/for instance in its chest.
4 The odameter can measure how far ~~can I travel~~ I can travel.
5 The purpose of the test is to discover ~~does the material break~~ if/whether the material breaks when it is pulled apart.

Part 2: Reading and writing

Reading

1 The main purpose of the material is to provide freedom of movement and to protect parts of the body from injury in an accident.
2 It's soft and flexible.
3 The molecules in the material lock together and harden. This absorbs the shock and acts as a protective shield.
4 The material gives you the same level of protection as a bicycle helmet, it's comfortable to wear, light, breathable and washable.
5 They can be used in clothing for motorcyclists, shoes for skateboarders and gloves for goalkeepers.

Writing

GPS is used in many applications, <u>for instance</u> in earthquake research. <u>Because</u> it can record highly accurate measurements, movements of a millimetre in the Earth's crust, <u>that is</u> its outer layer, can be taken. GPS helps scientists understand the mechanics of earthquakes. <u>In addition</u>, it can predict damage and danger to buildings. Emergency services can respond quickly, <u>as</u> the system provides data to show the tilt or strain of an earthquake on a building.

Review Unit E Quick test

Total _____ /65

Part 1: Vocabulary and grammar

1 Complete the gaps with the words from the box.

almost   approximately   exactly   just over

1 61% of the workers … _____ two-thirds
2 50% of the workers … _____ a half
3 77% of the workers … _____ three-quarters
4 33% of the workers … _____ a third

(4 marks)

2 Match the instrument to what it measures.

An altimeter   A barometer   An odometer   Scales   A tachometer

1 _____ measures pressure in kilopascals.
2 _____ measures speed in kilometres per hour.
3 _____ measures distance in kilometres for cyclist.
4 _____ measures height above sea level in metres.
5 _____ measure weight in kilograms.

(5 marks)

3 Write words with these suffixes: *ity*, *able/ible*, *-proof* and *-resistant*.
1 Something that doesn't scratch is _____.
2 Something that withstands compression is _____.
3 An object has this when it can be bent without damage. _____.
4 Something that can be burnt is _____.
5 Something that can be broken is _____.

(5 marks)

4 One word in each sentence is incorrect. Correct the word.
1 Compression is when two objects slide in the opposite direction.
2 Torsion is when something is pulled apart or stretched.
3 A column is a horizontal structure which spans a room.
4 A damper is a device which holds a structure together.
5 The person doesn't get a shock because he touches a live wire in the non-earthed system.

(5 marks)

5 Rewrite the questions as statements, using the words given + *that*.
1 Are the screws tight?
Make sure _____
2 Can the cable reach the computer easily?
Check _____
3 Has the gas been switched off?
Make sure _____
4 Have you washed your hands in the disinfectant?
Please ensure _____
5 Have the materials been tested?
Check _____

(5 marks)

6 Write full sentences explaining these noun phrases.
1 online business meeting

_____
2 a mountain rescue team

_____
3 vehicle crash test dummy

_____
4 solar headphone radio

_____
5 a collision avoidance sensor

_____

(5 marks)

7 Rewrite these questions, using the words in brackets.
1 How deep is this reservoir?
Please tell me _____
(the depth)
2 How high is the dam?
I'd like to know _____
(high)
3 How heavy is your vehicle?
I need to know _____
(the height)
4 How fast are you travelling?
Could you tell me _____
(the speed)
5 How wide is the screen?
Would you mind telling me _____. (wide)
6 How long is the Channel Tunnel?
Please tell me _____. (long)

(6 marks)

8 Complete the sentences in the active or passive. Use *can/can't* or *able to*.

1 These glasses aren't impact-resistant.

These glasses _____ resist impact.

2 Rubber is flexible.

Rubber _____ bent.

3 Ceramic is heat-resistant.

Ceramic _____ resist heat.

4 You can't scratch a diamond.

A diamond _____ scratched.

5 The speaker is inaudible.

I _____ hear the speaker.

6 This material is waterproof.

This material _____ put in water.

(6 marks)

9 Underline the correct word in these sentences.

1 I was late **because/as a result** there was a lot of traffic.

2 The connection is rigid. **Therefore/As** it won't move in an earthquake.

3 You won't get an electric shock **since/therefore** it's a neutral wire in an earthed system.

4 We did a crash test on the vehicle and **as a result/ since** we're going to improve the design of the car.

(4 marks)

10 Correct these sentences.

1 The aim of the test is for checking the tension forces on the neck of the dummy.

2 A strain gauge is used for to measure the deformation of the bridge.

3 Sensors are located in parts of the robot's body, that is in its chest.

4 The odometer can measure how far can I travel.

5 The purpose of the test is to discover does the material break when it is pulled apart.

(5 marks)

Part 2: Reading and writing

Reading

Read the text and answer the questions.

D3o is a new protective material used in sportswear. The sports clothing looks like normal sportswear, but this material can provide freedom of movement, and in addition, can protect the body from injury in an accident. The orange material is made from 'intelligent molecules'. The material is designed to feel soft and flexible when in use, but when the material is compressed on impact in an accident, the material immediately locks together and hardens. As a result, it absorbs the shock and acts as a protective shield. Once the impact is over, the molecules unlock and the material becomes soft and flexible again.

The material has been tested for impact absorption, tensile strength, flexibility, tear strength and breathability. The results show that d3o can give you the same level of protection as a bicycle helmet. In addition, it is comfortable to wear, light and breathable. It is also washable.

D3o can be made into many types of protective sportswear, for example, pads for motorcyclists to protect their elbows and knees, soles of shoes for skateboarders to protect them when they land from jumps, and gloves for goalkeepers in football when they punch balls away from the goal.

1 What is the main purpose of d3o?

_____

2 What are the properties of the material?

_____

3 What happens to the material when it is compressed in an accident?

_____

4 What was the purpose of the tests?

_____

5 What sportswear can the material be made into?

_____

(5 marks)

Writing

Read the notes about GPS and earthquakes. Rewrite the notes as a paragraph in your notebook, using the phrases in the box and any other words.

as	Because	for instance	In addition	that is

GPS and earthquakes

- GPS used in many applications – earthquake research

- Record highly accurate measurements – movements of a millimetre in the Earth's crust (outer layer) can be taken

- GPS helps scientists understand mechanics of earthquakes + predict damage and danger to buildings

- Emergency services can respond quickly. The system provides data to show the tilt or strain of an earthquake on a building.

(5 marks)

Contents

1 | Working robots

Photos of different robots: say what they do.

Scanning task: search for more information about robots.

Listen to engineers answering questions about the robots. (1) Match speakers with photos. (2) Complete a robot user survey form.

Word list: *improve, improvement, modify, robot, strength, survey, weakness*

Listen again and focus on language: *its main strength/ advantage/ weakness/ disadvantage is that; I suggest that you should …*

Tell class about strengths/ weakness/ suggested improvements in common items.

Interview each other and ask about robots (factsheets at back of book). Complete a form. Write a report from the form.

Write a report on the robot, based on completed form.

Word list: *console, inspect, safety wire, scaffolding, track* (vb), *vacuum, voice-activated*

2 | Eco-friendly planes

Starter: forces acting on a plane.

Read descriptions of six new aircraft designs. Match these with diagrams.

Word list: *brace* (vb), *cone, diagonal, drag* (= friction), *expel, fuel consumption, fuselage, lift* (= upwards push), *structure, strut, taper, thrust, turbine, weight, wing tip*

Read design brief for a new plane, and decide (with partner) which design fulfils the design brief.

Group task. Read group's design brief for an improved product, and produce a design (draw a diagram and write a short description). Then present the design to the class.

Listen to other designs and tell them (a) whether they meet the brief (b) their advantages/ disadvantages.

Word list: *carbon emission, design brief, global warming, noise level, noise pollution, non-renewable energy, pressure-resistant, wingspan*

3 | Free-flying sails

Listen to a presentation about a traction kite for cargo boats. Task: put speaker's notes into the correct order.

Word list: *capsule, cargo ship, client ship, helium, non-renewable, oval, supertanker, traction*

Fill in gaps in list of signpost phrases and questions (the questions are used as signpost phrases).

Listen to presentation again and check answers.

Practise using signpost phrases/ questions giving short talk (based on sets of notes).

Word list: *built-in, click wheel, docking port, earphone jack, media player, multi-functional, multi-touch, polymer, scroll, touchscreen, USB port*

Briefing

This unit deals with design in modern technology.

Section 1 looks at robot design. Two robots are highlighted in the listening activity. The **SnakeBot** (or 'snake' robot) is a type of robot that moves like a snake. This is being developed in a NASA project to explore the surface of Mars. SnakeBots are able to slide and dig underneath the soil for geological surveying, or carry tools for astronauts on space walks. The main body of a SnakeBot consists of about 30 modules linked together in a chain, and controlled by a central computer in the 'head' of the SnakeBot, which receives data from sensors all over the body. These modules are connected by a central spine and works together to make a twisting movement. **Search-and-rescue** robots such as the one described in the listening exercise are still at an experimental stage. They look like small tanks with treads, and they can be directed by an emergency worker (using a joystick and computer) into small holes in the rubble of a disaster such as an earthquake to search for survivors. Cameras and other sensors can be fitted to them to send data to the surface. In serious disasters, dogs trained for search and rescue are not always able to climb across debris, and the dusty air often weakens the dogs' keen sense of smell. The **robotic building inspector** in the Task can climb up a wall and record information about the building using a video camera. It clings to vertical surfaces by means of a rotor blade which creates a vacuum between itself and the wall. Two wheels drive the robot forwards, and another wheel helps it to turn. Sensors tell the robot whether it is upside down, flat or sideways. The **robotic surgeon** in the Task is used by doctors to perform delicate surgery. The surgeon controls the movements of the 'hands' and 'fingers' of the robot from a console with a screen showing images from the camera on the robot.

Section 2 introduces the idea of a **design brief**. This is a document which contains the main **requirements** or **criteria** which must be met when designing a new product. Design briefs often begin by stating the **need** for a new design, and what is wrong (the **problem**) with existing designs. The unit looks at new designs for aircraft that will need less fuel by reducing their **drag** and **weight**. The four forces acting on a plane are **thrust** (or forwards movement, provided by the engine), **lift** (or upwards movement, caused by the shape and angle of the wings), **drag** (or backwards pull, caused by friction of the **fuselage** and **wing** against the air) and **weight** (or downwards movement caused by **gravity**). The four new designs for future planes are intended to reduce drag (through an improved shape of fuselage and wings) and weight (by using lighter materials). This would mean an increase in thrust (and speed) using less fuel. One of the planes in the reading text uses **struts**, which act like diagonal braces connecting the wing to the fuselage. This allows the wings to be longer and lighter, which reduces drag and weight.

Section 3 looks at an example of a **traction kite**, a huge sail designed to pull **cargo ships** (when the wind is in the right direction) thereby making huge savings in the cost of fuel. The type of kite shown here can be powered independently by a three-man crew in a **capsule** suspended from the sail. It can be **steered** to a client ship and attached to it by a cable. When the journey is finished (or the winds change) the traction kite can be unfastened and steered towards another client ship. The transcript for the listening activity contains full information about this, and general information about traction kites can be found on the website below.

SnakeBots: http://electronics.howstuffworks.com/snakebot.html/printable

Search-and-rescue robots: http://www.msnbc.msn.com/id/9131498/

Robots in surgery: http://www.fda.gov/Fdac/features/2002/302_bots.html

Eco-friendly plane designs: http://www.newscientist.com/article/mg19325921.600.html

Traction kites: http://www.kiteship.com/index.php

Teacher's notes

1 | Working robots

Start here

1 Put students in pairs. Ask them to read the questions and brainstorm their ideas with their partner.

Scanning

2 Go through the instructions with students. Then ask them to turn to pages 118–119 and find the text on robots. Remind them to read the text as quickly as they can and look for the answers to the questions. Ask students to put up their hand when they've finished, to find out who the winner is and check their answers.

> Approximately 33%.
> Japan.
> They've covered over 15 km on Mars.

Listening

3 Ask students to look at the pictures of the four robots and ask them what they think these robots do.

4 ▶ 💿 27

Tell students that they're going to listen to two interviews with participants at an Industrial Robot Convention. Ask students to identify the two robots that they're talking about from the pictures. Then play the recording.

> 1) Snakebot and 3) RescueRobot

▶ 💿 27

[I = Interviewer; P1 = Participant 1; P2 = Participant 2]

1

I: Good morning. Welcome to the Industrial Robot Convention. I hope you're enjoying it. I'm doing a survey to find out how people use robots, and what improvements can be made. Would you mind if I ask you some questions?

P1: Sure, go ahead.

I: First of all, would you mind telling me what you do, and where you work?

P1: Yes, I'm a construction engineer, and I specialise in building work on high rise buildings and skyscrapers.

I: And what kind of robot do you use in your work?

P1: I use the SnakeBot.

I: What do you think of it? Does it help your work?

P1: Yes, if I forget to take a tool to the top of a building, I press a joystick and the SnakeBot brings it to me.

I: So, what are the advantages of the SnakeBot?

P1: Well, its main strength is that it can twist around things like girders, pipes and scaffolding. In addition, it is strong enough to carry small loads like spanners and hammers, and bring them up to me at the top of a building.

I: Excellent. So, would you say that it has any drawbacks, or disadvantages?

P1: Yes, its main weakness is that you have to control every movement with a joystick. It's a bit time-wasting, because

I can't do my building work and push the joystick at the same time.

I: So, in the future, how would you suggest that it could be improved?

P1: Well, I would suggest that you should design a voice-activated SnakeBot. Then I can shout to make it climb up to me.

2

I: Hello. Welcome to the Industrial Robot Convention. I'm doing a survey to find out how people use robots, and what improvements can be made. Would you mind if I ask you some questions?

P2: I'm a bit busy. Oh all right, go on, ask away.

I: Thanks. Well, first of all, what do you do, and where do you work?

P2: I'm an emergency response worker. I search for people, and try to rescue them from under collapsed buildings, after a major disaster, such as an earthquake or explosion.

I: And which robot do you use in your work?

P2: I use the Rescue Robot.

I: What do you think of it. Does it help your work?

P2: Yes, it helps me to locate people buried under collapsed buildings.

I: So, what would you say are its main strengths?

P2: Well, I would say it has two important advantages. First of all, it can access areas which are potentially dangerous for humans to go into. It can easily move over and under things, and it can get into spaces which are too small for me to climb into. In addition to this, its camera and microphone are more sensitive than human eyes and ears.

I: So, do you think it has any drawbacks or weaknesses?

P2: Well, one thing I've noticed is that the robots are too big and heavy to climb over very large piles of rubble.

I: So, looking into the future, how do you suggest we could modify or improve it?

P2: Well, I think you need to find a way to make smaller, lighter versions of it.

I: I see. Well thanks very much indeed for sparing me your time.

P2: Don't mention it.

5 Tell students that they're going to listen to the recording again and complete the form. Ask students to check what information they have to listen out for in the form before playing the recording.

Robot user survey form	
Occupation: Robot name:	Construction engineer SnakeBot
Function of robot	Brings tools to top of buildings
Strength(s)	1 Can twist around girders, pipes and scaffolding 2 Strong – can carry small loads, e.g. spanners and hammers
Weakness(es)	Have to control every movement with a joystick – time consuming
Suggested improvement(s)	Design a voice-activated robot

Occupation:	Emergency response worker
Robot name:	Rescue Robot
Function of robot	Locates people buried under collapsed buildings
Strength(s)	1 Access areas too dangerous for humans. Moves over and under things, gets into very small spaces 2 Has a camera and microphone – more sensitive than human eyes and ears
Weakness(es)	Too big and heavy to climb over very large piles of rubble
Suggested improvement(s)	Make a smaller, lighter version of it

Listening

6 ▶ 🔊 **28**

Ask students to listen to the first part of the interview again. As they listen they should complete the transcript of the interview with the words in the box.

1	advantages	**5**	weakness	**9**	could
2	strength	**6**	that	**10**	would
3	drawbacks	**7**	would	**11**	that
4	disadvantages	**8**	suggest	**12**	should

▶ 🔊 **28**

[I = Interviewer; P1 = Participant 1]
I: So what are the advantages of the SnakeBot?
P1: Well, its main strength is that it can twist around things like girders, pipes and scaffolding.
I: Excellent. So, would you say that it has any drawbacks, or disadvantages?
P1: Yes, its main weakness is that you have to control every movement with a joystick.
I: So, in the future, how would you suggest that it could be improved?
P1: Well, I would suggest that you should design a voice-activated SnakeBot.

Speaking

7 Focus students' attention on the list of products. Tell them that people often experience problems with these products. Tell them to discuss the strengths and weaknesses of these products and/or any other products they have with problems with, and to suggest improvements.

8 Put students in A and B pairs. Tell them that they're going to interview their partner about a robot. Ask them to look at the form for the information they'll need to ask their partner about in order to complete it.

Then ask students to read their instructions and turn to their notes at the back of the book (pages 113 and 116). They take it in turns to ask about their partner's robot and make notes about it in the form on page 85.

Student A
Robot user survey

Occupation of user	Safety Inspector
Name of robot	Robo Inspector
Function of robot	Inspects buildings
Frequency of use	60% of inspections
Specifications of robot	Weighs 1kg, has three wheels
How it works	Creates strong vacuum – can adhere to hard surfaces
Strength(s)	Can move quickly across ceilings and climb brick walls Can inspect surfaces too difficult for humans to climb
Weakness(es)	Can't use more than one at the same time as they crash into each other
Suggested improvement(s)	Supply with sensors so that they can work in teams

Student B
Robot user survey

Occupation of user	Hospital surgeon
Name of robot	Robo Surgeon
Function of robot	Used in hospital operations
Frequency of use	Once or twice a month
Specifications of robot	Four arms
How it works	Controlled from a console by surgeon
Strength(s)	Arms and fingers move more precisely than humans; can operate in spaces too small for surgeons; wrists can move 360°
Weakness(es)	Camera only on one arm. Can see only in one direction
Suggested improvement(s)	The fourth arm should have two cameras

Writing

9 Students use the information on the form they completed to write a short report about their partner's robot.

Students could write the report for homework if you are short of time.

2 | Eco-friendly planes

Start here

1 Focus students' attention on the diagram and tell them that it shows forces which act on planes. Ask them to label the diagram with the words: *thrust*, *weight*, *drag* and *lift*. They can compare their answers with a partner before you check with the class.

Ask students to explain the role of the *engine*, *gravity*, *friction* and *shape of wing* in these forces.

> **1** lift
> **2** drag
> **3** thrust
> **4** weight
> engine – the engine produces thrust which pushes the plane forwards.
> gravity – weight is caused by gravity. It pulls the plane downwards.
> friction – the friction of the fuselage and wing against the air causes the plane to drag or pull backwards.
> shape of wing – lift is mainly influenced by the shape of the wing. The forces under and over the wing lift the plane upwards.

Reading

2 Ask students what new types of plane are being developed at the moment. Tell them to talk about any new technical developments they know about in plane design.

Ask students to look at the diagrams of the four designs for future passenger planes. Ask them what effects they think the four forces will have on these types of planes.

Tell them to read the article and identify the plane design for each description by writing the number of the design in the gaps.

> Design B
> Design A
> Design D
> Design C

3 Focus students' attention on the text. Tell them that it's the design brief for future passenger planes in the article in 2. Point out that the brief is organised into three sections: the need for the design, the problem with current designs and what is required in the new design, and what the designers must include if they want their design to be accepted. Ask students to read the brief and then underline the things that are required. Point out the use of the modal verb + passive *have to be* and *must be* to express necessity.

Put students in pairs. Ask them to look back at the designs and their descriptions in the article. Tell them to discuss with their partner which of the designs they think best followed the guidelines in the brief, and which of the designs is the worst and didn't follow the guidelines in the brief.

> Design A is best
> Though it is open to discussion, Design C is probably the worst, as the brief says that a cylindrical body is essential for safety.

Task

4 Put students in four small groups. In large classes, divide the class into two and put the two halves of the class into groups of four. In small classes, you could have two groups only and use two of the design briefs.

Tell students that they're going to follow a design brief for an improved product. Ask them to read their design brief on the relevant pages at the back of the book. Tell them that they should discuss in their groups the design of the product and draw a diagram of it and write a description for it. Point out the requirements that they need to follow in their drawings and description.

5 Students take it in turns to present their new design to the class.

6 Ask students to listen to the presentations by the other groups. When each group has finished their presentations, they should discuss in their groups whether the design met the brief and give their reasons why or why not. Students then tell the group giving the presentations what the advantages and disadvantages of their design are.

> **Extra activity**
> You could set the following activity for homework.
> Students write a design brief for a future energy-efficient product, or a future product in their own technical field.

3 Free-flying sails

Start here

1 Ask students to look at the diagram of the traction kite and read the information about it. Then discuss the question with the class.

Listening

2 ▶ 🔘 29

Tell students that they're going to listen to a designer giving a presentation about the traction kite. Focus their attention on the index card notes. Tell them that these are cards that the presenter made for the presentation as a reminder of what to say. Explain that the cards are not in the correct order, and that they should listen to the recording and number the index card notes in the correct order.

Allow students a couple of minutes to look at the information on the cards before you play the recording. Students can then compare their answers with a partner. Play the recording a second time for them to check the order.

The correct order of the index card notes is:
J, H, C, I, A, E, K, G, L, F, D, B

▶ 🔘 29

Good morning everyone, and thanks for coming.

The aim of this short presentation is to tell you about our new traction kite for cargo ships and supertankers.

I'd like to start by asking a question. Why do we need a traction kite?

Well, as we all know, cargo ships and supertankers weigh tens of thousands of tons. And the diesel oil that drives these ships is non-renewable and very expensive. We need to use less oil. So, we need to use wind energy. We need to use sails to harness that energy.

So what is the problem with other designs for sails?

Other designs use a fixed and permanent mast and sail. But this is very expensive for the ship owners, as they need to buy a new boat, or fix a mast and sail to their boats.

And that brings me to our design brief.

Our brief was to design a traction kite which is strong enough to pull a large cargo ship through the water. It must be detachable – that means it can be removed from the ship.

Now let's move on to materials. What is the traction kite made of? And what are the properties of the materials?

Well, the kite is made of a special polyester. This material is tough but flexible and lightweight. It has very high tensile strength and low friction.

Right, so now let's look at the main parts of the traction kite, and their function.

As you can see in the diagram, the kite has two very large sails. These are attached to a large oval balloon. The balloon is filled with helium. A small capsule is suspended from the balloon. This capsule contains a three-man crew and computers. There are sensors on the wings. These sensors detect air pressure and air speed, and send data to the computers. The computers control the speed and direction of the kite. The kite is connected to the client ship using a strong cable.

So how large is this kite? And how high does it fly? Let's look at some dimensions.

Well, it's a giant kite. The wingspan is 120 metres from wing tip to wing tip. The area of the sail is 5,000 square metres. And it flies about 300 metres above sea level.

All right, now let's turn to the operation of the kite. How does it work?

The kite crew steer the kite to a client ship. They drop the cable to the ship, and the ship's crew attach the cable to the ship. The kite then catches the wind, and pulls the ship along with about 6,000 horsepower. When the wind direction changes, or the wind drops, the kite is untied from the ship and travels to another client ship.

And finally, I'd like to mention some of the advantages of the traction kite.

The kite uses wind power, which is a renewable source. Ships which use the traction kite can use 35% less fuel on a voyage. Carbon emissions are also reduced. And the system is less expensive for the ship owners. They don't have to buy new ships with sails. They simply pay to use the kite sail when they need it.

3 Remind students that signpost phrases tell the listener where the speaker is in the talk. You could tell students to look back at 3 on page 76 at the examples of signpost phrases.

Explain that the speaker introduces each section of the presentation with a signpost phrase or question. Focus students' attention on the table showing headings and the words the speaker uses in the presentation. Ask students to complete the signpost phrases and questions with the words in the box. Point out that they can use the words once only.

They could then compare their answers with a partner. Do not confirm their answers yet as they'll be checking them in the following exercise.

4 Students listen to the presentation again and check their answers to 3.

1	aim	**7**	let's
2	start	**8**	look
3	need	**9**	turn
4	problem	**10**	finally
5	brings	**11**	mention
6	move		

Speaking

5 Tell students that they're going to prepare a short presentation, using the notes on the MP3 player and the ephone. Tell them to use the signpost phrases or questions from 3 when they want to tell the listeners that they are moving on to the next point.

Extra activity

You could set the following exercise for homework.

If students did the Extra activity at the end of the previous lesson, they could use the same structure and signpost phrases and questions in 3 to write a short presentation for the future energy-efficient product, or the future product in their own technical field they described in their design brief.

Contents

1 Zero emission

Discuss how zero-emission cars work and help the environment.

Study diagram of a fuel cell car, and discuss how it works.

Jigsaw reading: in pairs, read about two technologies (fuel cells and capacitors) and tell each other about them.

Pairs link up into groups to discuss how the two technologies are combined in a zero-emission car.

Write questions to ask the inventor of the car (based on notes).

Word list: *capacitor, hydrogen fuel cell, idling, storage tank, ultra-capacitor, zero-emission*

Read press release about the car, and find answers to own questions.

Write correct figure numbers in text (from diagrams).

Roleplay interview between journalist and car inventor.

Language: reduced relative clause: *the energy (which is) released during braking.* Practise adding *which is/are* to reduced relatives.

Word list: *compressed, cruise, fossil fuel, recover (energy), torque*

2 Technological change

Decide on most important tools in history. Explain to class. Compare with survey list.

Read text describing top ten tools in survey. Task: mark the inventions on a timeline to show date of invention.

Word list: *abacus, align, ancestor, balance scales, craft (vb), flint, mass-produced, pyramid, scythe, sharpen, straighten*

Vocabulary: simple machines: eg *rack and pinion.*

Complete a gapped text about changes in oil drilling requiring past/ present/ active/ passive verbs.

Group task: explain how industrial process have changed over time.

Word list: *cam, crank and rod, derrick, drill bit, fibre-optic cable, gear, laser, lens, lever, percussion drilling, pulley and belt, rack and pinion, ratchet and pawl, rotary drilling, screw, tripod, wedge, wheel and axle*

3 Vehicle safety

Brainstorm car safety features.

Explain how safety systems (pictures) work.

Listen to an interview about one of the systems. Identify the system.

Listen again. Delete unasked questions from notes.

Listen again and write main points of interview in gapped notes.

Word list: *cruise control, laser, obstacle, protection, radar, sensor*

Listen to another interview about engineer's bio-data. Task: correct mistakes in written bio-data.

Roleplay similar interviews.

Find out about each other's car safety system (factsheets at end of book).

Write a press release on one of the car safety systems.

Choose another factsheet from end of book, read it up, add own ideas, and explain to the group.

Word list: *air bag (in car), career, degree, design company, diploma*

Briefing

This unit looks at technological innovation and change.

Section 1 deals with **zero-emission** cars, which do not emit **greenhouse gases** such as carbon dioxide as **exhaust**. One technology which achieves this is the **hydrogen fuel cell**. Water (H_2O) is composed of hydrogen and oxygen. If hydrogen and oxygen molecules are chemically combined to make water, electricity is released. This electricity can be used to power an electric motor in a car, and the only exhaust from the fuel cell will be water vapour. In the past electric cars (powered by large batteries which had to be recharged frequently) were not popular because they lacked speed and acceleration. This problem is beginning to be solved by the use of **ultra-capacitors** (very powerful capacitors). A **capacitor** is a device that can discharge its complete store of electricity in a short burst of high energy, for example in a camera flash. Ultra-capacitors produce the high-energy surge of electricity which is needed for fast acceleration, supplementing the more steady current from the hydrogen fuel cell which sustains the car's cruising speed. The zero-emission car in the reading text combines the two technologies of hydrogen fuel cells and ultra-capacitors. The ultra-capacitors are recharged by absorbing energy from the motion of the car during braking and slowing down.

Section 2 looks at the history of tools. A survey by a magazine (see the website below) asked 3000 technologists to rank tools in order of importance throughout history. The tools were limited to hand-held (or easily carried) tools such as chisels or knives. The lathe mentioned in the answers was a simple hand operated version. Simple machines such as **levers**, **wedges**, **pulleys** and so on were also excluded. The Vocabulary activity deals with the simple machines excluded from the survey: a **crank and rod** (a wheel with a pivoting arm attached near its edge) forms the basis of the crankshaft in an engine; the **cam and follower** are also used in car engines (where the followers are the inlet and exhaust valves). A **ratchet** is a toothed gear wheel that can move in only one direction, and a **pawl** is a small pivoted wedge that prevents the ratchet from moving backwards. A **rack and pinion** are like two interlocking gear wheels, except that the rack is straight, not circular. This simple machine converts rotary into linear motion, and linear into rotary. Laser drilling is a new technology in the oil industry. The rock is cut by a **laser beam** instead of by a rotating drill bit at the end of a long pipe or **drill string**.

Section 3 looks at car safety systems. Smart Adaptive Cruise Control uses a **laser sensor** fitted to the front of your car. It sends a laser beam to the vehicle in front. The beam is reflected back to the sensor, which then calculates the distance of your car from the vehicle in front and automatically activates the brakes or accelerator very slightly until the correct distance is maintained. The Side Impact Protection System is a development of the **air bag system** (**ABS**). Most cars today have an air bag which inflates rapidly in a crash, and cushions the impact on the driver or passenger. The side impact system uses air bags at the sides of the car. It also has sensors which detect the location of the impact, and activate a mechanism that moves the seat away from the impact. The third system, the Rear Obstacle Warning System, has sensors fixed to the rear of the car which activate warning alarms if the car is about to reverse into something. There is also a video camera in the rear window to show the driver the situation.

Eco-cars (zero-emission cars): http://kron1.eng.ox.ac.uk/pages/research/life-car.php

Hydrogen fuel cells: http://www.hydrogenhighway.ca/code/navigate.asp?Id=220

Capacitors: http://electronics.howstuffworks.com/capacitor.htm/printable

Top 20 tools: http://www.forbes.com/2006/03/15/technology-tools-history_cx_de_0315intro.html

Simple machines: http://www.mos.org/sln/Leonardo/InventorsToolbox.html

Oil drilling: http://www.howstuffworks.com/oil-drilling.htm/printable

Laser drilling: http://www.ne.anl.gov/facilities/lal/laser_drilling.html

Car safety systems: http://www.edmunds.com/reviews/list/top10/114984/article.html

Teacher's notes

1 | Zero emission

Start here

1 Put students in pairs. Ask students to look at the diagram of the car. Tell them that it is a zero-emission car. Ask students to discuss the questions with their partner, referring to the diagram of the car.

2 Ask students to work with the same partner. Tell them to look at the four diagrams of the power system for the car and discuss how they think the car works.

Task

3 Put students in pairs. Ask them to look at the large diagram of the car again and explain that it combines two different technologies: fuel cells and capacitors to invent a new power system. Tell them that they're going to read about these technologies. Let the pairs decide who is going to read about which system and ask them to turn to the relevant pages at the back of the book.

Students read their fact sheet and look at the diagram to find out how their system works.

4 Ask students to take it in turns to explain to their partner how the technology for their system works. Tell the student listening to ask questions to clarify any information that they don't understand.

5 Tell students to join up with another pair to work in groups of four. Ask them to decide how the inventors combined the two technologies they've just read about to produce the car in 2.

6 Students then explain their groups' ideas to the class. Tell them to draw diagrams on the board to illustrate their ideas if they want.

Writing

7 Tell students to imagine that they're TV journalists and that they're going to interview one of the inventors of the Hydro-X car. Focus their attention on the reporter's notes at the bottom of the page. Tell them to use these notes to write questions to ask the inventor about the car.

Model answers:

1 What type of new car is needed? Why do we need this type of car to protect the environment?

2 What are the problems with petrol and diesel cars? What are the problems with other cars, such as hydrogen fuel cell ones?

3 What is the maximum speed of the new Hydro-X car? What is the range of the car? What is the acceleration like? What emissions does it have?

4 What technology is the Hydro-X based on?

5 What are the advantages of the new Hydro-X?

6 What is the power output of the fuel cell in kW? Where is the fuel cell located and why is it located there?

7 Where is the motor located and what is its output in kW?

8 What is the function/purpose of the control unit?

9 What is the function/purpose of the ultra-capacitor? Where is it located and why is it located there?

10 Where are the hydrogen storage tanks located? What is the capacity of the tanks in L/kg? How are they connected to the fuel cell?

11 Why is an air pump needed?

12 How does the Hydro-X work? How does it start, cruise, brake and idle?

Reading

8 Ask students to read the press release on the Hydro-X car, and ask them to find and underline the answers to the questions that they've just written.

Model answers:

1 A hydrogen fuel cell car. It's needed to protect the environment and reduce the amount of emissions of greenhouse gasses into the atmosphere.
2 Petrol and diesel cars consume too much fossil fuel and emit too much greenhouse gas. Hydrogen fuel cell cars are too heavy and have low acceleration.
3 The new Hydro-X car can cruise at high speeds of 160 km/h. It has a range of 480 km. It can accelerate quickly. It's only emission is water vapour.
4 The hydrogen fuel cell and the ultra-capacitor.
5 The fuel cell is smaller and lighter than the ones used in other vehicles. It's also more powerful than other vehicles because of the ultra-capacitors.
6 The fuel cell provides a maximum output of 93 kW. It's located under the floor to provide more space.
7 The motor is mounted between the front wheels. Its output is 90 kW.
8 The control unit controls the electrical systems.
9 The ultra-capacitor provides immediate high-output power during startup and acceleration. It's located at an angle behind the rear seat. It's located there to increase the luggage space.
10 The hydrogen storage tanks are located under the rear seat. The tanks have a capacity of 168.3 L/kg. They are connected to the fuel cell by special pipes.
11 The air pump is needed to supply the fuel cell with oxygen.
12 Starting: power comes from both the ultra-capacitor and the fuel cell to provide acceleration.
Cruising: power comes from the fuel cell, but not from the capacitor.
Braking: the ultra-capacitor absorbs the energy released during deceleration and braking and stores it with power from the fuel cell.
Idling: when the car is idling, there is no power from the fuel cell.

9 Ask students to look at the final paragraph of the press release. Tell them that the figure numbers are missing in them and that these numbers refer to the diagrams in 2. Ask students to look at the diagrams and write the correct figure number in the text.

1 Acceleration – Fig 3	3 Deceleration – Fig 2
2 Steady speed – Fig 4	4 Stopped – Fig 1

Speaking

10 Put students in pairs. Ask them to decide who wants to be the journalist and who wants to be the inventor. They then roleplay an interview between them, using the questions and answers from 7 and 8.

Language

Reduced relative clauses

Go through the Language box on reduced relative clauses with the class. Explain that when the relative clause is in the passive (underlined in the example below), you can omit the relative pronoun. The meaning of the sentence remains the same.

The ultra-capacitor recovers the energy (which + is) released during deceleration.

Tell students that they'll find more information on reduced relative clauses in the Grammar summary on page 103.

11 Ask students to read the sentences and find and underline the reduced relative clauses.

1 The Hydro-X fuel cell is lighter than the ones used in other vehicles.
2 The fuel cell, positioned under the floor, provides an output of 93 kW.
3 The motor, located between the front wheels, provides a powerful torque.
4 The fuel tanks, placed under the rear seat, are filled with hydrogen.
5 The ultra-capacitor absorbs the energy released during braking.
6 The electricity needed to operate the lights comes from the ultra-capacitor.

12 Ask students to insert *which is* or *which are* where possible in the sentences in 11 and also in the text in 8.

1 The Hydro-X fuel cell is lighter than the ones which are used in other vehicles.
2 The fuel cell, which is positioned under the floor, provides an output of 93 kW.
3 The motor, which is located between the front wheels, provides a powerful torque.
4 The fuel tanks, which are placed under the rear seat, are filled with hydrogen.
5 The ultra-capacitor absorbs the energy which is released during braking.
6 The electricity which is needed to operate the lights comes from the ultra-capacitor.

(from the text in 8)

1 The fuel cell, which is positioned under the floor …
2 The motor, which is mounted between the front wheels …
3 The control unit, which is located over the motor …
4 The ultra-capacitor, which is set at an angle …
5 … and recovers energy which is generated during braking.
6 The hydrogen storage tanks, which are placed …
7 The air pump, which is mounted directly on the …
8 The ultra-capacitor absorbs the energy which is released during deceleration …

Start here

1 Put students in pairs. Ask them to decide on the ten most important tools in the history of mankind. Point out the list of conditions about their choice of tools which they need to follow when making their decision. Then tell them to make a list and put them in order of importance.

2 Students explain their list to the class and give reasons for their choice.

> **Alternative activity**
>
> Students could join up with another pair to form groups of four. They compare their list and discuss and agree between them on a new list for the ten most important tools and write this list down.
>
> They then join up with another group and discuss and draw up a new list between them. Continue this way until the whole class is involved in discussing and agreeing on one list for the ten most important tools in the history of mankind.

3 Tell students to turn to page 111 and compare their list to the one shown there. If their list is different, ask them to give reasons for their choices of tools.

Reading

4 Tell students that they're going to read an article about the history of tools. Focus their attention on the timeline and explain that they have to mark the inventions on the timeline. Tell them to read the note and then check they understand by asking them what century they're living in, and when a couple of famous historical events took place.

Give students a time limit of three to four minutes to read the article and mark the inventions on the timeline. When they've finished, they could compare their timelines with a partner before you check with the class. Then ask students if they're surprised about any of the information they have read.

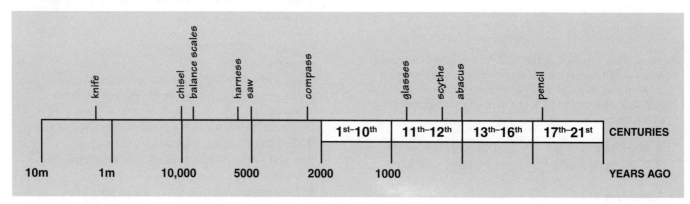

Vocabulary

5 Ask students to look at the pictures of the machines and tell them to match the pictures with the words for them in the box.

When they've finished, they can check their answers on page 114.

```
1   wheel and axle
2   pulley and belt
3   wedge
4   screw
5   lever
6   gear
7   rack and pinion
8   cam and follower
9   crank and rod
10  ratchet and pawl
```

6 Ask students to look back at the pictures and tell the class which of the machines they use in their industry or technical field.

Language

7 Tell students that this exercise is a general revision of active and passive structures in the present or past. Ask students to read the article on the history of oil drilling and complete it with the correct form of the verbs in the brackets.

```
1   were dug
2   was suspended
3   was pulled up
4   was dropped
5   was broken
6   are dug
7   is suspended
8   is rotated
9   is broken
10  cuts
11  is used
12  is split
13  carries
14  focus
15  cuts
16  is reduced
17  are completed
```

Task

8 Ask students to work in small groups. Tell them to choose an industry or work process they know about, and discuss how the work was done in the past, and compare it with how the work is done now. Tell them to make brief notes on their discussion.

Students can then choose one of their group to explain their ideas to the class.

> **Extra activity**
>
> You could set the following activity for homework. Students write up their description, using the text in 7 as a model.

3 Vehicle safety

Start here

1 Ask students to make a list of car safety systems which are installed in new cars. They then compare the systems they listed with a partner.

2 Ask students to look at the three diagrams showing car safety systems. They work with the same partner and discuss how they think these systems work. Tell them that they'll find out information about these systems in the lesson.

Listening

3 ▶ 🎧 30

Tell students that they're going to listen to an expert talking about one of the car safety systems in the pictures. Ask them to listen to the recording and decide which one the expert is talking about.

> The smart adaptive cruise control.

▶ 🎧 30

[P = Presenter; M = Michela Rossi]

P: Hello and welcome to the show. This week, we're looking at new car safety systems, and in the studio we have an expert on car safety, Michela Rossi. Welcome, Michela. So, let's talk first of all about the new cruise control safety system for cars. First of all, what's the full name of the system?

M: Hello Jane, and thanks for having me on the programme. Well, it's called the Smart Adaptive Cruise Control, or SACC.

P: And what's it for? What does it do exactly?

M: Well, it's a safety system, which maintains a safe distance between your car and the vehicle in front of you.

P: Why do you think we need this new system?

M: Well, you see, the statistics show that many road accidents are caused when the vehicle in front suddenly stops.

P: So, you expect this invention will prevent some of those accidents from happening?

M: Yes, that's right.

P: And what technology or principle is this invention based on?

M: It makes use of laser technology, and the principle of radar. And of course it uses sensor technology. So, you could say it's based on three technologies: lasers, radar and sensors.

P: So, the main component is a laser sensor?

M: That's right. A laser sensor and a computer which is connected to the braking and acceleration systems.

P: Where is the sensor located?

M: The sensor's mounted on the front of the vehicle. It's built into the windscreen, at the top.

P: So, tell me about its operation. How does it work?

M: Well, first of all you key in the distance you want to maintain between your car and the vehicle in front. So, if it's raining, for instance, you can key in a shorter distance. Then the system works automatically. If your car moves too close to the one in front, the sensor activates the brakes. And if your car moves too far behind, the sensor activates the

accelerator a little. But you can over-ride the system by touching the brakes or acceleration pedal yourself.

P: Let's go through that step by step. You key in a distance between you and the car in front.

M: Right.

P: Then it works automatically.

M: That's right. If your car moves too close to the one in front, the sensor activates the brakes.

P: And if your car moves too far behind, the sensor activates the accelerator.

M: That's right. But you can over-ride the system. You can press the brakes or acceleration pedal yourself.

P: Well, that sounds like a great invention. Just to sum up for us, could you tell us very briefly, what are the benefits or advantages of this new invention?

M: Well, I expect it will reduce the chances of a serious accident. It's automatic, and it thinks much faster than the driver.

P: Michela Rossi, thank you very much for talking to us.

M: You're welcome.

4 Focus students' attention on the checklist. Explain that it's a checklist of questions that the journalist wants to ask the expert. Ask students to listen to the interview again and delete the questions the journalist does not ask.

> (See answers to 5 below.)

5 Ask students to listen to the interview again and note down the main points that the expert gives in answer to the journalists questions.

> **Questions about cruise control system**
> - name of invention: The Smart Adaptive Cruise Control, or SACC
> - ~~name of inventor~~
> - function or purpose: safety system – to maintain a safe distance between your car and the vehicle in front of you
> - need: prevent accidents caused when the vehicle in front suddenly stops.
> - technology/principle: uses laser, radar and sensors
> - main parts/features: a laser sensor and a computer
> - location of parts: the laser sensor is mounted on the front of the vehicle. It's built into the windscreen, at the top. The computer is connected to the braking and acceleration systems
> - operation/how it works: you key in the distance you want to maintain between your car and the vehicle in front. Then the system works automatically. If your car moves too close to the one in front, the sensor activates the brakes. If your car moves too far behind, the sensor activates the accelerator a little. You can over-ride the system by touching the brakes or acceleration pedal yourself.
> - advantages: reduces the chances of a serious road accident. It's automatic and it thinks faster than a driver.
> - ~~disadvantages~~

Listening

6 ▶ 🔊 31

Tell students that the journalist is now interviewing the same expert about her career as a car safety engineer. Ask them to read the biodata about her. Then tell students that there are some mistakes in Michela's biodata. Tell them to listen to the recording and correct the mistakes.

> She's designed or invented six new products (not ~~four~~).
> She's now working on a new type of rear camera for cars (not ~~a new type of air bag~~).

▶ 🔊 31

[P = Presenter; M = Michela Rossi]

P: Good morning, and welcome to the programme. Today I'm interviewing Michela Rossi, a young engineer who works for Central Motors. We'll be talking about her, and about her career in automotive technology. Good morning, Michela. And you are very young, aren't you? How old are you, exactly?

M: Good morning, Jane. Well, since you ask, I'm 24. Is that too young to be an engineer?

P: No, no, not at all. The younger the better. And how long have you worked for Central Motors?

M: I've been here for about four years now.

P: I see. So what's your job title? Inventor?

M: No, no. I'm a design engineer. I work in a team of designers and inventors.

P: And how many things have you invented?

M: I think, with the team, I've designed or invented five, no, six new products since I joined Central Motors.

P: That's fantastic. So, what qualifications do you have?

M: I have a technician's diploma from Toulouse Technical Institute and an engineering degree from the Polytechnic University of Turin.

P: Great. So, Michela, let's talk a little about your future intentions. Are you planning to invent anything else in the near future?

M: Yes, I am. In fact I'll be working on a new type of rear camera for cars. The camera will see obstructions and will warn the driver.

P: I see. And after that. What are your long-term plans for your career?

M: Ah, who knows? I'll continue working here in Central Motors for several years, I hope. Then I may start my own design company.

P: Well, Michela, it's been very interesting talking to you. And good luck with your career.

M: Thanks very much.

Speaking

7 Put students in pairs. Ask them to roleplay an interview between a journalist and a car safety engineer. Tell them to decide who's going to be the journalist and who's going to be the engineer and read their roles. Ask Student A to read the information for their roles and prepare a checklist of questions to ask the engineer. Student B reads the information for their role and writes notes using one of the bio-data factsheets on page 117, or alternatively they can use information about themselves.

8 Put students in pairs. Tell them that they're going to read about the other two car safety systems in the diagrams on page 94. Ask them to turn to their factsheets at the back of the book and read about their system. They then take it in turns to ask and answer questions about their systems, referring to the factsheet and the diagram of that system.

Writing

9 Ask students to write a press release on their car safety system. Tell them to look at the press release on page 91 to help them and to use the headings that are given.

Students could write the press release for homework if you are short of time.

Task

10 Put students in groups of three. If necessary, have one or two groups of two. Ask them to choose one of the car safety systems on page 113, 115 or 116. Ask them to read the factsheet and add notes expressing their own ideas and opinions about the system.

They then explain their system to the rest of the group and answer their questions about it.

Answer key

1

Q 6	How many years have you worked in your job?
Q 8	When did you purchase the robot?
Q 10	Are you using it now/today?
Q 11	What is the main function/purpose of the robot?
Q 12	What can the robot do?
Q 13	Where is the robot used?
Q 16	How does it work/do you operate the robot?
Q 17	What are the advantages/strengths of your robot?
Q 18	What are the disadvantages/weaknesses of your robot?/Does it have any design flaws?
Q 19	How can it be improved?

3   **1** b   **2** e   **3** a   **4** f   **5** c   **6** d

6
1 were created
2 are used
3 was made
4 are installed
5 was invented
6 are designed
7 are controlled
8 were introduced

7 *Model answers:*

Purpose
The main aim of the space elevator is to carry people and cargo into space.

Main components
The space elevator consists of a robot climber, a counterweight and a cable. It does not use rockets for propulsion.

Location and dimensions
The cable is 100,000 km long. One end is attached to a platform in the sea, and the other end is fixed to the counterweight, which floats in space in zero gravity.

Materials and properties
The cable is very light and strong, because it is made of carbon nanotubes, which are lightweight but strong in tension. They can also be manufactured cheaply.

Operation
The counterweight floats in zero gravity. Meanwhile, as the earth rotates, the platform moves away from the counterweight and the cable is pulled and tightened between the platform and the counterweight. The robot climber then moves up the cable at 200 km/h, and escapes the gravity of the earth.

Advantages
The main advantages of the space elevator are, firstly, that the cable is cheap to manufacture and, secondly, that rockets are not needed for propelling the robot into space.

Problems
The main disadvantage of the space elevator is the radiation belt, which is located around the Earth at an altitude of 1,000 to 20,000 km. This belt is dangerous for the cargo and people in the robot climber.

8   Smart Adaptive Cruise Control is a car safety system, <u>which was</u> invented by a team of engineers at Central Motors. It can be found in all new cars, <u>that are</u> manufactured by Central Motors. It is an automatic impact-prevention system <u>that is</u> designed to maintain a safe distance between your car and the vehicle in front. It uses a laser sensor, <u>which is</u> mounted on the front of the vehicle in the upper part of the windscreen.

Project

10 & 11   At the end of every Review Unit is a project. Students can do their research on the internet or in a library, and in their own language if they wish. They must then write their results in English.

Quick test answer key

Part 1: Vocabulary & grammar

1 1 e   2 c   3 d   4 f   5 b   6 a

2
1 scaffolding
2 girder
3 mast
4 pulley
5 wedge

3
1 disadvantage
2 weakness
3 accelerate
4 non-renewable

4
1 weakness
2 accelerate
3 advantage
4 non-renewable

5
1 suggest
2 requirement
3 steer
4 pulley
5 fuselage
6 emission

6
2 The oil rig I worked on was located in the North Sea.
3 The motor, located between the front wheels, provides high output.
4 Cromoly is an alloy made from ceramic and steel.
5 The robot I use can climb to the top of high-rise buildings.
6 They visited the building destroyed in the earthquake.
(Sentences 1 and 7 are correct.)

7
1 were sent; needs
2 pulled; is put
3 dug; is done
4 were used; warn

8
1 does he do
2 is Jim working
3 you'll choose
4 has she worked
5 did they test
6 do you want to be
7 Does the car have

Part 2: Reading and writing

Reading

1 They were made from redwood trees.
2 They were heavy, long and they weren't very buoyant.
3 They're made from fibreglass and polyurethane foam.
4 They are made from petrochemicals which aren't environmentally friendly.
5 The boards are made from plant-based materials: balsa wood, hemp and resins from oil producing plants. They need to be made lighter than they are now.

Writing

Model answers:

Robots	
Function	(1) Increase productivity in factories
Advantage(s)	(2) They can work in dangerous environments. For example, they can work with poisonous chemicals and in high temperatures. (3) They can work continuously: they don't get tired and they don't get bored.
Weakness	(4) They can't move around quickly.
Suggested improvements	(5) Improve the speed of robot by making lighter robot.

Hydrogen fuel cell cars	
Function	(1) Vehicle that is environmentally friendly
Advantage(s)	(2) It runs on water: its only emission is water vapour. (3) Hydrogen is a renewable energy.
Weakness	(4) Difficult to refill the car with hydrogen since there aren't many hydrogen fuel stations.
Suggested improvements	(5) Make the cars cheaper. The cars will then become more popular and more fuel stations will be built.

Satellite navigation systems	
Function	(1) Gives car drivers directions
Advantage(s)	(2) If you are the only person in the car, you don't need to stop the car to ask another person for directions or to look at a road map. (3) You won't get lost.
Weakness	(4) Can send wide vehicles down roads that are too narrow.
Suggested improvements	(5) System to warn vehicles about the width of roads.

Review Unit F Quick test

Total _____/55

Part 1: Vocabulary and grammar

1 Match the words with their definitions.

1	cruising	a)	pushes the plane forwards
2	drag	b)	pushes the plane upwards
3	gravity	c)	pulls the plane backwards
4	idling	d)	pulls the plane downwards
5	lift	e)	moving at a steady speed
6	thrust	f)	not moving

(6 marks)

2 Match the word in the box to the definition.

> girder   mast   pulley   scaffolding   wedge

1 long metal structure which is put against a building. Painters and builders work on it.

2 long, heavy piece of steel that is used to support bridges and large buildings

3 tall pole for the sail of a ship

4 a device which has a wheel and a rope and is used to lift heavy things

5 a piece of wood with one thick end and one pointed end that you use to separate two things.

(5 marks)

3 Write the opposite of these words.

1 advantage _____

2 strength _____

3 brake _____

4 renewable _____

(4 marks)

4 Complete the sentences, using any of the words from 3.

1 The robot's only _____ is that it isn't able to climb over rocks.

2 The car can _____ from 0–100 kph in under five seconds.

3 The main _____ of this new design is that the product is cheap to make.

4 _____ sources of energy, for example fossil fuel, pollute the atmosphere and cannot be replaced.

(4 marks)

5 Underline the words in these sentences.

1 Can you **mention/suggest** how I can make the robot move faster?

2 The main **improvement/requirement** for the new laptop computer is that it needs to be light.

3 The crew **steer/drive** the kite to the ship.

4 A **pinion/pulley** is used to lift the rocks to the top.

5 You can find the pilots, the passengers and the cargo in the **cockpit/fuselage** of a plane.

6 The new car will cut vehicle **emissions/gas** by 20% and improve air quality.

(6 marks)

6 You can use reduced relative clauses in five of these sentences. Find the sentences and rewrite them using reduced relative clauses.

1 The Hydro-X is a car that runs on hydrogen fuel.

_____

2 The oil rig which I worked on was located in the North Sea.

_____

3 The motor, which is located between the front wheels, provides high output.

_____

4 Cromoly is an alloy which is made from ceramic and steel.

_____

5 The robot which I use can climb to the top of high-rise buildings.

_____

6 They visited the building which was destroyed in the earthquake.

_____

7 Cars emit greenhouse gases that go into the atmosphere.

_____

(5 marks)

7 Complete the text using the passive form in the past or present of the verbs in brackets.

1 In the 19th century, children, as well as adults, _____ _ to work down the mines. (send)

Nowadays, the industry _____ miners to be highly skilled and well trained. (need)

2 In the past, children _____ carts filled with coal from the coal face to the main road. (pull)

Nowadays, the coal _____ on conveyer belts from the coal face to a preparation plant. (put)

3 In the past, miners _____ coal from the mines using a hand pick. (dig)

Nowadays, mining _____ using hydraulic loading shovels. (do)

4 In the past, canary birds _____ to detect poisonous gases in mines. (use)

Nowadays, electronic detectors _____ miners about poisonous gasses. (warn)

(8 marks)

8 **Complete the sentences in the correct form and use any other words that are necessary.**

1 What _____? (he / do)

He's an electrician.

2 Where _____ at the moment? (Jim / work)

In Japan.

3 Which design do you think _____ for the new plane? (you / choose)

The first one.

4 How long _____ for the company? (she / work)

About four years.

5 When _____ the equipment? (they / test)

A week ago.

6 What _____ in the future? (you / want / be)

An astronaut.

7 _____ a Smart Adaptive Cruise Control System? (the car/have)

(7 marks)

Part 2: Reading and writing

Reading

Read the text and answer the questions.

The earliest surfboards come from Hawaii and date back to the 18th century. Many changes have since been made to the design of the surfboard, which affect its size, weight, shape and the materials used.

Early surfboards were made from wood from redwood trees. This wood is tough, durable, but very heavy – 31kg to 91kg. The boards were shaped by hand, they were three to six metres long and they weren't very buoyant.

Early in the 20th century, the boards were shortened to two to three metres. They were made from balsa wood, which is much lighter than redwood, and they coated with a waterproof varnish. The boards were cut out in the centre to make them hollow and therefore reduce their weight.

The first fin was placed at the rear of the surfboard in 1935. This helped the surfer to go in a straight line and to keep the board stable.

Fibreglass started to be used for surfboards in the late 1940s. This meant that strong, light, waterproof boards could be made. At first, balsa wood was still used in the central part of the board, and they were still shaped by hand. The boards were then coated with a thin fibreglass skin. The development of polyurethane foam in surfboards began at this time, and balsa wood was replaced with this foam.

Most modern surfboards are still made in the same way, using lightweight fibreglass and foam. However, the main drawback with these surfboards is that the materials mainly come from petrochemicals and are not environmentally friendly. New eco-friendly boards are now being developed made from plant-based materials. The boards are once more constructed from balsa wood, but this time they are coated with a composite layer of hemp cloth and resins from an oil producing plant to make them waterproof. Improvements on the design need to be made, as they aren't light enough.

1 What were the earliest surfboards made from?

_____

2 Describe the problems with them.

_____

3 What are surfboards today made from?

_____

4 Describe the problems with these surfboards.

_____

5 Describe the new developments in surfboard design. What needs to be improved?

_____

(5 marks)

Writing

Choose from the following: *robots, hydrogen fuel cells* or *satellite navigation systems*. Write this as the heading in the form. Then write notes in the form. In the notes, you should compare: robots with human workers, hydrogen fuel cell cars with petrol cars, satellite navigation systems with printed road maps.

Function	(1)
Advantage(s)	(2)
	(3)
Weakness	(4)
Suggested improvements	(5)

(5 marks)

Word list

Unit 1

accelerator (noun) **3 Method exercise 4**
activate (verb) **3 Method exercise 1**
adjust (verb) **1 Teamwork exercise 2**
ahead (adverb) **3 Method exercise 8**
air pressure (noun) **1 Teamwork exercise 2**
almost done (time phrase) **2 Training exercise 4**
away (adverb) **1 Teamwork exercise 2**
blanket (noun) **1 Teamwork exercise 2**
break (verb) **3 Method exercise 1**
camera (noun) **3 Method exercise 8**
chest (noun) **3 Method exercise 8**
cockpit (noun) **1 Teamwork exercise 2**
cord (noun) **3 Method exercise 2**
detect (verb) **3 Method exercise 8**
device (noun) **3 Method exercise 1**
dial (noun) **3 Method exercise 4**
driver (noun) **1 Teamwork exercise 2**
emergency stop (noun) **3 Method exercise 4**
fault (noun) **2 Training exercise 4**
fire suit (noun) **1 Teamwork exercise 2**
flap (noun) **1 Teamwork exercise 2**
forward (adverb) **1 Teamwork exercise 2**
front (noun) **1 Teamwork exercise 2**
fuel (noun) **1 Teamwork exercise 2**
gear lever (noun) **1 Teamwork exercise 2**
handset (noun) **3 Method exercise 2**
hang on (time phrase) **2 Training exercise 4**
hose (noun) **1 Teamwork exercise 2**
immediately (time phrase) **1 Teamwork exercise 2**
insert (verb) **3 Method exercise 4**
just a minute (time phrase) **2 Training exercise 4**
kick (verb) **3 Method exercise 1**
laser beam (noun) **3 Method exercise 1**
lift up (phrasal verb) **2 Training exercise 2**
locate (verb) **3 Method exercise 8**
lower (verb) **1 Teamwork exercise 1**
mechanic (noun) **1 Teamwork exercise 1**
nearly finished (time phrase) **2 Training exercise 4**
nozzle (noun) **1 Teamwork exercise 2**
one minute (time phrase) **2 Training exercise 4**
outboard motor (noun) **3 Method exercise 1**

passenger (noun) **3 Method exercise 2**
pick up (phrasal verb) **2 Training exercise 2**
pit lane (noun) **1 Teamwork exercise 2**
pit-stop crew (noun) **1 Teamwork exercise 1**
plaster hole (noun) **2 Training exercise 4**
pull out (phrasal verb) **1 Teamwork exercise 2**
pump (verb) **1 Teamwork exercise 2**
push in (phrasal verb) **1 Teamwork exercise 2**
put down (phrasal verb) **2 Training exercise 2**
put on (phrasal verb) **1 Teamwork exercise 2**
put together (phrasal verb) **2 Training exercise 4**
raise (verb) **1 Teamwork exercise 2**
receiver (noun) **3 Method exercise 8**
rear (noun) **1 Teamwork exercise 2**
repair (verb) **2 Training exercise 4**
replace (verb) **2 Training exercise 4**
robot (noun) **3 Method exercise 7**
sensor (noun) **3 Method exercise 4**
service (verb) **1 Teamwork exercise 2**
sideways (adverb) **3 Method exercise 8**
signal (verb) **1 Teamwork exercise 2**
socket (noun) **1 Teamwork exercise 2**
spill (verb) **1 Teamwork exercise 2**
strip off (phrasal verb) **2 Training exercise 4**
surface (noun) **3 Method exercise 8**
switch off (phrasal verb) **1 Teamwork exercise 2**
switch on (phrasal verb) **1 Teamwork exercise 2**
take apart (phrasal verb) **2 Training exercise 4**
take away (phrasal verb) **1 Teamwork exercise 2**
take off (phrasal verb) **1 Teamwork exercise 2**
take out (phrasal verb) **2 Training exercise 4**
technology (noun) **3 Method exercise 8**
test (verb) **2 Training exercise 4**
ticket machine (noun) **3 Method exercise 1**
touch (verb) **3 Method exercise 1**
trainee (noun) **2 Training exercise 1**
turn off (phrasal verb) **2 Training exercise 1**
turn on (phrasal verb) **2 Training exercise 1**
tyre (noun) **1 Teamwork exercise 1**
upright (adverb) **3 Method exercise 8**
visor (noun) **1 Teamwork exercise 2**

water heater (noun) **3 Method exercise 1**
water valve (noun) **3 Method exercise 1**
wheel-gun (noun) **1 Teamwork exercise 2**
wheel-jack (noun) **1 Teamwork exercise 2**
wireless (noun) **3 Method exercise 8**

Unit 2

accident rate (noun) **2 Plans exercise 8**

activity (noun) **3 New job exercise 2**

appreciate (verb) **2 Plans exercise 8**

attach (verb) **2 Plans exercise 8**

attend (verb) **1 Routines exercise 3**

available (adjective) **2 Plans exercise 8**

aware (adjective) **2 Plans exercise 8**

blowout preventer (noun) **1 Routines exercise 4**

business (noun) **3 New job exercise 2**

casualty (noun) **2 Plans exercise 10**

catalogue (noun) **2 Plans exercise 5**

conference (noun) **1 Routines exercise 3**

confirm (verb) **2 Plans exercise 8**

control room (noun) **1 Routines exercise 4**

crane operator (noun) **1 Routines exercise 5**

CV (noun) **3 New job exercise 5**

deck (noun) **1 Routines exercise 4**

derrick (noun) **1 Routines exercise 5**

diploma (noun) **3 New job exercise 2**

driller (noun) **1 Routines exercise 5**

electrician (noun) **1 Routines exercise 3**

electron (noun) **3 New job exercise 6**

electronic (adjective) **3 New job exercise 6**

electronics (noun) **3 New job exercise 2**

emergency escape (noun) **2 Plans exercise 9**

employment (noun) **3 New job exercise 2**

engineer (noun) **1 Routines exercise 5**

engineering (noun) **3 New job exercise 6**

equipment (noun) **1 Routines exercise 4**

experience (noun) **3 New job exercise 2**

fantastic (adjective) **1 Routines exercise 3**

grateful (adjective) **2 Plans exercise 8**

heat-resistant (adjective) **2 Plans exercise 10**

heat shield (noun) **2 Plans exercise 10**

hesitate (verb) **2 Plans exercise 8**

inspect (verb) **1 Routines exercise 4**

intend (verb) **2 Plans exercise 4**

introduce (verb) **2 Plans exercise 8**

job title (noun) **1 Routines exercise 8**

ladder (noun) **2 Plans exercise 10**

maintain (verb) **1 Routines exercise 6**

maintenance (noun) **1 Routines exercise 4**

mechanical (adjective) **3 New job exercise 6**

mechanics (noun) **3 New job exercise 6**

mechanism (noun) **3 New job exercise 6**

occupation (noun) **3 New job exercise 2**

oil platform (noun) **1 Routines exercise 1**

off duty (adverb) **1 Routines exercise 2**

offshore (adverb) **1 Routines exercise 1**

on duty (adverb) **1 Routines exercise 2**

on leave (adverb) **1 Routines exercise 2**

onshore (adverb) **1 Routines exercise 2**

operate (verb) **1 Routines exercise 4**

participant (noun) **2 Plans exercise 3**

plan (verb) **2 Plans exercise 4**

position (noun) **3 New job exercise 2**

qualification (noun) **3 New job exercise 2**

repair (verb) **1 Routines exercise 4**

report (verb) **1 Routines exercise 4**

request (verb) **2 Plans exercise 8**

responsibility (noun) **3 New job exercise 2**

rig (noun) **1 Routines exercise 3**

roustabout (noun) **1 Routines exercise 5**

run (= conduct) (verb) **2 Plans exercise 5**

safety drill (noun) **1 Routines exercise 4**

safety officer (noun) **2 Plans exercise 1**

sector (noun) **3 New job exercise 2**

sick leave (noun) **2 Plans exercise 8**

site manager (noun) **2 Plans exercise 7**

supervise (verb) **1 Routines exercise 3**

supervisor (noun) **1 Routines exercise 5**

technical (adjective) **3 New job exercise 6**

technologist (noun) **3 New job exercise 6**

technology (noun) **3 New job exercise 2**

train (verb) **1 Routines exercise 4**

underwater (adjective) **1 Routines exercise 4**

Unit 3

4x4 (noun) **3 Equipment exercise 6**

acceleration (noun) **3 Equipment exercise 3**

best (superlative) **3 Equipment exercise 2**

better (comparative) **1 Limits exercise 4**

board (verb) **1 Limits exercise 4**

cab (noun) **3 Equipment exercise 6**

cancel (verb) **2 Products exercise 2**

catalogue (noun) **2 Products exercise 2**

classic (adjective) **2 Products exercise 2**

clearance (noun) **3 Equipment exercise 6**

coal-fired (adjective) **3 Equipment exercise 4**

coin (noun) **1 Limits exercise 5**

combination (noun) **1 Limits exercise 4**

complain (verb) **2 Products exercise 2**

consumption (noun) **3 Equipment exercise 3**

cruising speed (noun) **1 Limits exercise 6**

diesel (noun) **3 Equipment exercise 4**

dimension (noun) **1 Limits exercise 4**

farther (comparative) **1 Limits exercise 4**

farthest (superlative) **3 Equipment exercise 3**

fleet (noun) **3 Equipment exercise 2**

further (comparative) **1 Limits exercise 4**

furthest (superlative) **3 Equipment exercise 3**

hire (noun) **3 Equipment exercise 2**

idle speed (noun) **3 Equipment exercise 3**

least (superlative) **3 Equipment exercise 3**

less (comparative) **1 Limits exercise 4**

luggage (noun) **1 Limits exercise 4**

mode (noun) **1 Limits exercise 7**

more (comparative) **1 Limits exercise 4**

most (superlative) **2 Products exercise 1**

nanometre (noun) **3 Equipment exercise 1**

nanotube (noun) **3 Equipment exercise 2**

normal (adjective) **1 Limits exercise 6**

nuclear power (noun) **3 Equipment exercise 4**

performance (noun) **3 Equipment exercise 2**

petrol (noun) **1 Limits exercise 6**

portable (adjective) **2 Products exercise 9**

purchase (noun) **3 Equipment exercise 2**

rapid (adjective) **3 Equipment exercise 3**

rechargeable (adjective) **2 Products exercise 9**

recommendation (noun) **1 Limits exercise 7**

roof rack (noun) **1 Limits exercise 2**

standard (adjective) **1 Limits exercise 4**

storage capacity (noun) **2 Products exercise 1**

strength (noun) **1 Limits exercise 6**

tender (noun) **3 Equipment exercise 2**

tow (verb) **3 Equipment exercise 6**

transistor (noun) **3 Equipment exercise 1**

trailer (noun) **1 Limits exercise 4**

unleaded (adjective) **1 Limits exercise 6**

van (noun) **1 Limits exercise 2**

vehicle (noun) **1 Limits exercise 2**

weakness (noun) **1 Limits exercise 6**

wheelbase (noun) **3 Equipment exercise 6**

wingspan (noun) **1 Limits exercise 6**

world record (noun) **3 Equipment exercise 1**

worse (comparative) **1 Limits exercise 4**

worst (superlative) **3 Equipment exercise 3**

Unit 4

air conditioning (noun) **2 Manufacturing exercise 4**

assembly line (noun) **2 Manufacturing exercise 4**

belt (noun) **1 Infrastructure exercise 1**

body shop (noun) **2 Manufacturing exercise 4**

bonnet (noun) **2 Manufacturing exercise 4**

bumper (noun) **2 Manufacturing exercise 4**

chassis (noun) **2 Manufacturing exercise 1**

chassis line (noun) **2 Manufacturing exercise 4**

chute (noun) **1 Infrastructure exercise 3**

communications satellite (noun) **3 Communications exercise 1**

component (noun) **1 Infrastructure exercise 7**

convert (verb) **3 Communications exercise 3**

conveyor belt (noun) **1 Infrastructure exercise 1**

cutter (noun) **1 Infrastructure exercise 1**

cutter face (noun) **1 Infrastructure exercise 1**

deliver (verb) **2 Manufacturing exercise 4**

digital TV card (noun) **3 Communications exercise 3**

display (verb) **3 Communications exercise 5**

drill (noun) **1 Infrastructure exercise 1**

drill (verb) **1 Infrastructure exercise 3**

drive shaft (noun) **2 Manufacturing exercise 1**

extract (verb) **3 Communications exercise 3**

feed horn (noun) **3 Communications exercise 3**

finally (adverb) **1 Infrastructure exercise 6**

first (adverb) **1 Infrastructure exercise 6**

frequency (noun) **3 Communications exercise 1**

grip (verb) **1 Infrastructure exercise 3**

high frequency (noun) **3 Communications exercise 3**

hydraulic cylinder (noun) **1 Infrastructure exercise 1**

laser guide (noun) **2 Manufacturing exercise 4**

lastly (adverb) **2 Manufacturing exercise 4**

low frequency (noun) **3 Communications exercise 7**

manpower (noun) **1 Infrastructure exercise 2**

meanwhile (adverb) **2 Manufacturing exercise 4**

next (adverb) **1 Infrastructure exercise 6**

now (adverb) **1 Infrastructure exercise 6**

oil drain plug (noun) **1 Infrastructure exercise 6**

oil filler cap (noun) **1 Infrastructure exercise 6**

orbit (noun) **3 Communications exercise 3**

paint shop (noun) **2 Manufacturing exercise 4**

panel (noun) **2 Manufacturing exercise 3**

propeller (noun) **1 Infrastructure exercise 8**

process (verb) **1 Infrastructure exercise 6**

reflect (verb) **3 Communications exercise 3**

rightside up (adverb) **2 Manufacturing exercise 4**

roller (noun) **2 Manufacturing exercise 2**

rust (noun) **1 Infrastructure exercise 8**

rusty (adjective) **1 Infrastructure exercise 8**

satellite dish (noun) **3 Communications exercise 1**

scoop (noun) **1 Infrastructure exercise 3**

simultaneously (adverb) **2 Manufacturing exercise 4**

steel shoe (noun) **1 Infrastructure exercise 1**

strengthen (verb) **1 Infrastructure exercise 3**

supply (verb) **1 Infrastructure exercise 3**

suspension (noun) **2 Manufacturing exercise 4**

then (adverb) **1 Infrastructure exercise 3**

tooth/teeth (noun) **1 Infrastructure exercise 3**

transmission (noun) **2 Manufacturing exercise 1**

transport (verb) **2 Manufacturing exercise 4**

trim line (noun) **2 Manufacturing exercise 4**

PC monitor (noun) **3 Communications exercise 3**

transmit (verb) **3 Communications exercise 3**

TV station (noun) **3 Communications exercise 3**

upside down (adverb) **2 Manufacturing exercise 4**

weld (verb) **2 Manufacturing exercise 3**

Unit 5

absorb (verb) **1 Uses exercise 2**
adjuster (noun) **3 Definitions exercise 1**
alarm pod (noun) **3 Definitions exercise 5**
appearance (noun) **2 Appearance exercise 2**
assistance (noun) **1 Uses exercise 2**
audible (adjective) **3 Definitions exercise 5**
basically (adverb) **2 Appearance exercise 9**
bass amplifier (noun) **2 Appearance exercise 9**
bend (noun) **2 Appearance exercise 10**
booster car seat (noun) **3 Definitions exercise 1**
bridge (boat) (noun) **2 Appearance exercise 3**
calculate (verb) **1 Uses exercise 7**
calculator (noun) **1 Uses exercise 7**
capsule (noun) **2 Appearance exercise 9**
carburettor (noun) **1 Uses exercise 5**
chain (noun) **2 Appearance exercise 3**
chisel (noun) **2 Appearance exercise 3**
circle (noun) **2 Appearance exercise 3**
circular (adjective) **2 Appearance exercise 3**
clamp (noun) **2 Appearance exercise 10**
conduct (verb) **1 Uses exercise 8**
conductor (noun) **1 Uses exercise 8**
cone (noun) **2 Appearance exercise 5**
conical (adjective) **2 Appearance exercise 9**
consist (verb) **2 Appearance exercise 3**
contain (verb) **1 Uses exercise 8**
container (noun) **1 Uses exercise 8**
cube (noun) **2 Appearance exercise 5**
cubic (adjective) **2 Appearance exercise 9**
cylinder (noun) **2 Appearance exercise 5**
cylindrical (adjective) **2 Appearance exercise 6**
dashboard (noun) **3 Definitions exercise 5**
design (verb) **1 Uses exercise 2**
digital-sonar (adjective) **3 Definitions exercise 5**
dolphin (noun) **1 Uses exercise 2**
dome (noun) **2 Appearance exercise 3**
dome-shaped (adjective) **2 Appearance exercise 3**
download (verb) **3 Definitions exercise 1**
entrepreneur (noun) **3 Definitions exercise 1**
generate (verb) **1 Uses exercise 8**
generator (noun) **1 Uses exercise 8**
helm unit (noun) **3 Definitions exercise 5**
H-shaped (adjective) **2 Appearance exercise 3**
hemisphere (noun) **2 Appearance exercise 5**
hemispherical (adjective) **2 Appearance exercise 6**
hull (noun) **2 Appearance exercise 3**

hydrophone (noun) **3 Definitions exercise 5**
invent (verb) **3 Definitions exercise 1**
inventor (noun) **1 Uses exercise 4**
jump lead (noun) **1 Uses exercise 2**
junction (noun) **2 Appearance exercise 10**
ladder (noun) **2 Appearance exercise 3**
link (noun) **2 Appearance exercise 3**
moisture (noun) **1 Uses exercise 2**
navigate (verb) **3 Definitions exercise 5**
ocean liner (noun) **2 Appearance exercise 3**
onion (noun) **2 Appearance exercise 2**
overboard (adjective) **3 Definitions exercise 1**
profit (noun) **3 Definitions exercise 1**
propel (verb) **1 Uses exercise 8**
propeller (noun) **1 Uses exercise 5**
protractor (noun) **2 Appearance exercise 9**
receive (verb) **1 Uses exercise 7**
receiver (noun) **1 Uses exercise 7**
rectangle (noun) **2 Appearance exercise 5**
rectangular (adjective) **2 Appearance exercise 3**
relay (verb) **3 Definitions exercise 5**
semi-circle (noun) **2 Appearance exercise 5**
semi-circular (adjective) **2 Appearance exercise 6**
skewer (noun) **2 Appearance exercise 3**
skyscraper (noun) **2 Appearance exercise 3**
soup bowl (noun) **2 Appearance exercise 3**
sphere (noun) **2 Appearance exercise 5**
spherical (adjective) **2 Appearance exercise 3**
square (noun) **2 Appearance exercise 5**
square (adjective) **2 Appearance exercise 3**
stabilise (verb) **1 Uses exercise 8**
stabiliser (noun) **1 Uses exercise 8**
submerge (verb) **3 Definitions exercise 5**
surfboard (noun) **2 Appearance exercise**
tag (noun) **1 Uses exercise 2**
torque wrench (noun) **3 Definitions exercise 3**
transducer (noun) **3 Definitions exercise 5**
transmit (verb) **1 Uses exercise 7**
transmitter (noun) **1 Uses exercise 7**
triangle (noun) **2 Appearance exercise 5**
triangular (adjective) **2 Appearance exercise 9**
tripod (noun) **2 Appearance exercise 3**
via (preposition) **3 Definitions exercise 5**
visible (adjective) **3 Definitions exercise 5**
aisle (noun) **1 Safety exercise 2**

Unit 6

anchor (noun) **2 Emergency exercise 1**
artificial respiration (noun) **2 Emergency exercise 2**
attend to (verb) **1 Safety exercise 7**
attract (verb) **2 Emergency exercise 2**
authorise (verb) **1 Safety exercise 7**
available (adjective) **2 Emergency exercise 3**
belongings (noun) **1 Safety exercise 7**
blockage (noun) **1 Safety exercise 2**
buoyant (adjective) **2 Emergency exercise 2**
calm (adjective) **1 Safety exercise 7**
cardio-pulmonary resuscitation (noun) **1 Safety exercise 7**
casualty (noun) **2 Emergency exercise 2**
chain (verb) **1 Safety exercise 2**
chemical spill (noun) **1 Safety exercise 7**
crate (noun) **1 Safety exercise 1**
crossroads (noun) **3 Directions exercise 2**
evacuation (noun) **1 Safety exercise 7**
first aid (noun) **1 Safety exercise 7**
fork (noun) **1 Safety exercise 1**
freezer (noun) **1 Safety exercise 5**
flyover (noun) **3 Directions exercise 1**
gantry (noun) **3 Directions exercise 1**
hand truck (noun) **1 Safety exercise 1**
handle (verb) **1 Safety exercise 5**
inflate (verb) **2 Emergency exercise 3**
injure (verb) **2 Emergency exercise 1**
lake (noun) **3 Directions exercise 3**
level (adjective) **1 Safety exercise 2**
liquid (noun) **1 Safety exercise 4**

locate (verb) **2 Emergency exercise 2**
motorway (noun) **3 Directions exercise 1**
oxygen (noun) **2 Emergency exercise 2**
overload (verb) **1 Safety exercise 2**
pallet (noun) **1 Safety exercise 1**
procedure (noun) **1 Safety exercise 2**
pulse (noun) **1 Safety exercise 7**
purchase (verb) **2 Emergency exercise 4**
ramp (noun) **1 Safety exercise 1**
recommend (verb) **2 Emergency exercise 4**
recovery position (noun) **1 Safety exercise 7**
roundabout (noun) **3 Directions exercise 1**
scuba diver (noun) **2 Emergency exercise 1**
seabed (noun) **2 Emergency exercise 1**
secure (verb) **2 Emergency exercise 7**
shelf (noun) **1 Safety exercise 1**
shipwreck (noun) **2 Emergency exercise 1**
sketch map (noun) **3 Directions exercise 6**
slip road (noun) **3 Directions exercise 1**
stack (verb) **1 Safety exercise 2**
strap (verb) **1 Safety exercise 2**
suggest (verb) **2 Emergency exercise 4**
traffic lights (noun) **3 Directions exercise 2**
turning (noun) **3 Directions exercise 2**
tow (verb) **2 Emergency exercise 2**
underpass (noun) **3 Directions exercise 1**
warehouse (noun) **1 Safety exercise 1**
wet suit (noun) **1 Safety exercise 3**

Unit 7

admit (verb) **3 Dealing with complaints exercise 4**

apologise (verb) **3 Dealing with complaints exercise 7**

appoint (verb) **2 Reporting to clients exercise 9**

attachment (noun) **1 Technical support exercise 2**

beam (noun) **2 Reporting to clients exercise 6**

browser (noun) **1 Technical support exercise 3**

code (noun) **1 Technical support exercise 3**

connection (noun) **1 Technical support exercise 2**

connectivity (noun) **1 Technical support exercise 2**

CCTV camera (noun) **2 Reporting to clients exercise 2**

clarification (noun) **2 Reporting to clients exercise 5**

client (noun) **2 Reporting to clients exercise 5**

compress (verb) **1 Technical support exercise 7**

contractor (noun) **2 Reporting to clients exercise 5**

corner (noun) **3 Dealing with complaints exercise 6**

crush (verb) **3 Dealing with complaints exercise 6**

deal (with) (verb) **3 Dealing with complaints exercise 2**

destroy (verb) **3 Dealing with complaints exercise 10**

detail (noun) **3 Dealing with complaints exercise 3**

diagnosis (noun) **1 Technical support exercise 3**

disconnect (verb) **1 Technical support exercise 7**

edge (noun) **3 Dealing with complaints exercise 8**

evidence (noun) **3 Dealing with complaints 4**

expand (verb) **2 Reporting to clients exercise 6**

fault (noun) **3 Dealing with complaints 4**

firewall (noun) **1 Technical support exercise 3**

freeze (verb) **1 Technical support exercise**

friendly (adjective) **3 Dealing with complaints exercise 4**

front (noun) **3 Dealing with complaints exercise 6**

gesture (noun) **3 Dealing with complaints exercise 7**

goodwill (noun) **3 Dealing with complaints exercise 7**

helpful (adjective) **3 Dealing with complaints exercise 4**

however (adverb) **3 Dealing with complaints 7**

image (noun) **1 Technical support exercise 2**

impractical (adjective) **2 Reporting to clients exercise 6**

in addition (phrase) **3 Dealing with complaints exercise 7**

inconvenience (noun) **3 Dealing with complaints exercise 7**

interfere (with) (verb) **1 Technical support exercise 3**

IP address (noun) **1 Technical support exercise 3**

in stock (phrase) **3 Dealing with complaints exercise 7**

jam (verb) **3 Dealing with complaints exercise 10**

log (into) (verb) **1 Technical support exercise 2**

loose (adjective) **1 Technical support exercise 7**

monitor (noun: screen for a computer or TV) **1 Technical support exercise 2**

monitor (verb: to check something at regular intervals) **2 Reporting to clients exercise 2**

offer (verb) **3 Dealing with complaints exercise 3**

parachute (noun) **2 Reporting to clients exercise 2**

password (noun) **1 Technical support exercise 2**

polite (adjective) **3 Dealing with complaints exercise 4**

pop-up (noun) **1 Technical support exercise 3**

purchase (noun) **3 Dealing with complaints exercise 4**

query (noun) **3 Dealing with complaints exercise 7**

rear (noun) **3 Dealing with complaints exercise 6**

reboot (verb) **1 Technical support exercise 3**

reconnect (verb) **1 Technical support exercise 7**

record (verb) **3 Dealing with complaints exercise 4**

reduce (verb) **3 Dealing with complaints exercise 3**

reduction (noun) **3 Dealing with complaints exercise 5**

refund (noun) **3 Dealing with complaints exercise 5**

refund (verb) **3 Dealing with complaints exercise 3**

reject (verb) **1 Technical support exercise 2**

repair (noun) **3 Dealing with complaints exercise 5**

repair (verb) **3 Dealing with complaints exercise 3**

replace (verb) **3 Dealing with complaints exercise 3**

replacement (noun) **3 Dealing with complaints exercise 5**

resolution setting (noun) **1 Technical support exercise 3**

security level (noun) **1 Technical support exercise 3**

skyscraper (noun) **2 Reporting to clients exercise 2**

smoke detector (noun) **2 Reporting to clients exercise 6**

solution (noun) **1 Technical support exercise 1**

split (verb) **3 Dealing with complaints exercise 6**

structural (adjective) **2 Reporting to clients exercise 6**

summarise (verb) **3 Dealing with complaints exercise 4**

surface (noun) **3 Dealing with complaints exercise 7**

sympathy (noun) **3 Dealing with complaints exercise 4**

twist (verb) **3 Dealing with complaints exercise 6**

uncheck (verb) **1 Technical support exercise 3**

unfortunately (adverb) **3 Dealing with complaints exercise 7**

walkway (noun) **2 Reporting to clients exercise 6**

wireless (noun) **1 Technical support exercise 2**

Unit 8

absorb (verb) **3 Cooling and heating exercise 1**

anti-clockwise (adverb) **1 Wave power exercise 5**

benefit (noun) **1 Wave power exercise 6**

buoy (noun) **1 Wave power exercise 8**

cam (noun) **2 Engines exercise 1**

clockwise (adverb) **1 Wave power exercise 5**

coil (noun) **3 Cooling and heating exercise 3**

compress (verb) **2 Engines exercise 5**

compression (noun) **2 Engines exercise 5**

compressor (noun) **3 Cooling and heating exercise 3**

condense (verb) **3 Cooling and heating exercise 1**

condenser (noun) **3 Cooling and heating exercise 1**

crankshaft (noun) **2 Engines exercise 1**

cycle (noun) **3 Cooling and heating exercise 2**

cylinder (noun) **2 Engines exercise 1**

decompress (verb) **3 Cooling and heating exercise 1**

displaced (adjective) **3 Cooling and heating exercise 1**

energy resource (noun) **1 Wave power exercise 7**

evaporate (verb) **3 Cooling and heating exercise 1**

evaporator (noun) **3 Cooling and heating exercise 1**

exhaust (noun) **2 Engines exercise 1**

expand (verb) **2 Engines exercise 5**

expansion (noun) **3 Cooling and heating exercise 1**

explosion (noun) **2 Engines exercise 5**

extract (verb) **3 Cooling and heating exercise 3**

fluid (noun) **3 Cooling and heating exercise 1**

force (noun) **2 Engines exercise 7**

fossil fuel (noun) **1 Wave power exercise 7**

geothermal (adjective) **3 Cooling and heating exercise 7**

high pressure (noun) **2 Engines exercise 8**

hydrogen (noun) **2 Engines exercise 9**

ignite (verb) **2 Engines exercise 5**

ignition (noun) **2 Engines exercise 5**

inlet (noun) **2 Engines exercise 5**

intake (noun) **2 Engines exercise 1**

internal-combustion engine (noun) **2 Engines exercise 1**

linear (adjective) **1 Wave power exercise 3**

melt (verb) **3 Cooling and heating exercise 2**

operate (verb) **3 Cooling and heating exercise 5**

operation (noun) **1 Wave power exercise 5**

oscillate (verb) **1 Wave power exercise 5**

oscillating (adjective) **1 Wave power exercise 3**

pendulum (noun) **1 Wave power exercise 3**

piston (noun) **1 Wave power exercise 2**

port (noun) **2 Engines exercise 1**

principle (noun) **3 Cooling and heating exercise 1**

rapidly (adverb) **2 Engines exercise 8**

reaction (noun) **3 Cooling and heating exercise 3**

reciprocate (verb) **1 Wave power exercise 5**

reciprocating (adjective) **1 Wave power exercise 3**

reduce (verb) **3 Cooling and heating exercise 3**

refrigerant (noun) **3 Cooling and heating exercise 5**

refrigeration (noun) **3 Cooling and heating exercise 2**

reverse (verb) **3 Cooling and heating exercise 3**

rotary (adjective) **1 Wave power exercise 3**

simultaneously (adverb) **2 Engines exercise 5**

solidify (verb) **3 Cooling and heating exercise 2**

spark plug (noun) **2 Engines exercise 1**

stroke (noun) **2 Engines exercise 5**

top dead centre (TDC) (adverb) **2 Engines exercise 5**

torsion (noun) **2 Engines exercise 5**

transfer (verb) **3 Cooling and heating exercise 3**

vacuum (noun) **2 Engines exercise 8**

valve (noun) **2 Engines exercise 1**

upthrust (noun) **3 Cooling and heating exercise 1**

Unit 9

accelerometer (noun) **2 Sensors exercise 5**

altimeter (noun) **1 Sports data exercise 2**

altitude (noun) **1 Sports data exercise 2**

almost (adverb) **1 Sports data exercise 2**

apply (verb) **1 Sports data exercise 2**

approach (verb) **3 Positioning exercise 6**

approximately (adverb) **1 Sports data exercise 1**

atmospheric (adjective) **1 Sports data exercise 2**

barometer (noun) **1 Sports data exercise 2**

bass volume (noun) **2 Sensors exercise 8**

bending (noun) **2 Sensors exercise 5**

blog (noun) **1 Sports data exercise 2**

burst (noun) **3 Positioning exercise 6**

chain (noun) **1 Sports data exercise 2**

chest (noun) **2 Sensors exercise 5**

compete (noun) **1 Sports data exercise 2**

compete (verb) **1 Sports data exercise 2**

convert (verb) **2 Sensors exercise 3**

cyclist (noun) **1 Sports data exercise 1**

data (noun) **1 Sports data exercise 2**

deflection (noun) **2 Sensors exercise 5**

deformation (noun) **2 Sensors exercise 10**

detect (verb) **2 Sensors exercise 3**

dial (noun) **2 Sensors exercise 8**

dummy (noun) **2 Sensors exercise 5**

ensure (verb) **1 Sports data exercise 2**

environment (noun) **2 Sensors exercise 3**

exactly (adverb) **3 Positioning exercise 2**

filter (noun) **1 Sports data exercise 9**

for example (phrases) **3 Positioning exercise 4**

for instance (phrases) **3 Positioning exercise 2**

gauge (noun) **2 Sensors exercise 8**

Global Positioning System (GPS) (noun) **3 Positioning exercise 2**

heart rate monitor (noun) **1 Sports data exercise 4**

heart beat (noun) **1 Sports data exercise 4**

impact (noun) **2 Sensors exercise 5**

in addition (phrases) **2 Sensors exercise 5**

in other words (phrases) **3 Positioning exercise 2**

just over (adverb) **1 Sports data exercise 7**

just under (adverb) **1 Sports data exercise 7**

kilopascal (noun) **1 Sports data exercise 4**

latitude (noun) **3 Positioning exercise 2**

lidar system (noun) **3 Positioning exercise 6**

load (noun) **2 Sensors exercise 5**

longitude (noun) **3 Positioning exercise 2**

lubricant (noun) **1 Sports data exercise 2**

lubricate (verb) **1 Sports data exercise 9**

more than (adverb) **1 Sports data exercise 7**

multiply (verb) **3 Positioning exercise 2**

nautical mile (noun) **3 Positioning exercise 2**

nearly (adverb) **1 Sports data exercise 7**

odometer (noun) **1 Sports data exercise 2**

orbit (verb) **3 Positioning exercise 2**

ping (noun) **3 Positioning exercise 6**

pinger (noun) **3 Positioning exercise 6**

power output (noun) **1 Sports data exercise 4**

precise (adjective) **3 Positioning exercise 2**

quick-release (adjective) **1 Sports data exercise 2**

radar system (noun) **3 Positioning exercise 6**

reflect (verb) **3 Positioning exercise 6**

rib (noun) **2 Sensors exercise 5**

saddle (noun) **1 Sports data exercise 2**

satellite (noun) **3 Positioning exercise 2**

scales (noun) **1 Sports data exercise 4**

sea level (noun) **3 Positioning exercise 5**

sensor (noun) **2 Sensors exercise 1**

shear (noun) **2 Sensors exercise 5**

slip (verb) **1 Sports data exercise 2**

stop watch (noun) **1 Sports data exercise 4**

strain (noun) **2 Sensors exercise 10**

squeeze (verb) **2 Sensors exercise**

subtract (verb) **3 Positioning exercise 2**

such as (phrases) **3 Positioning exercise 2**

tachometer (noun) **1 Sports data exercise 2**

tension (noun) **2 Sensors exercise 5**

that is (phrases) **3 Positioning exercise 2**

torsion (noun) **2 Sensors exercise 6**

transmission (noun) **3 Positioning exercise 2**

wear (noun) **1 Sports data exercise 2**

wheel rim (noun) **1 Sports data exercise 2**

wirelessly (adverb) **1 Sports data exercise 2**

worn (adjective) **1 Sports data exercise 2**

Unit 10

aim (noun) **1 Properties exercise 3**
and so (phrase) **3 Results exercise 3**
apart (adverb) **1 Properties exercise 3**
as (phrase) **3 Results exercise 3**
as a result (phrase) **3 Results exercise 3**
because (phrase) **3 Results exercise 3**
bending (noun) **1 Properties exercise 1**
bio-gas (noun) **3 Results exercise 5**
breakable (adjective) **2 Resistance exercise 5**
carbon (noun) **3 Results exercise 5**
carbon emission (noun) **3 Results exercise 5**
combustible (adjective) **2 Resistance exercise 5**
compression (noun) **1 Properties exercise 1**
compressive (adjective) **1 Properties exercise 6**
compressive strength (noun) **1 Properties exercise 3**
cross brace (noun) **2 Resistance exercise 5**
damper (noun) **2 Resistance exercise 2**
damping (noun) **2 Resistance exercise 10**
darken (verb) **3 Results exercise 5**
deform (verb) **1 Properties exercise 3**
deformation (noun) **1 Properties exercise 5**
destructive (adjective) **1 Properties exercise 3**
earth (noun: wire that connects electrical equipment to the ground) **3 Results exercise 3**
earthed (adjective) **3 Results exercise 3**
earthquake (noun) **2 Resistance exercise 1**
elastic (adjective) **1 Properties exercise 5**
elasticity (noun) **1 Properties exercise 6**
fail (verb) **3 Results exercise 5**
flatten (verb) **3 Results exercise 5**
flexibility (noun) **1 Properties exercise 6**
forge (verb) **3 Results exercise**
graph (noun) **2 Resistance exercise 3**
hammer (verb) **1 Properties exercise 3**
harden (verb) **3 Results exercise 5**
high-rise building (noun) **2 Resistance exercise 1**
hull plate (noun) **3 Results exercise 8**
hydrogen (noun) **3 Results exercise 5**
iceberg (noun) **3 Results exercise 8**
impact (noun) **1 Properties exercise 3**
impact-resistance (noun) **1 Properties exercise 3**
inaudible (adjective) **2 Resistance exercise 5**
indicate (verb) **1 Properties exercise 3**
install (verb) **3 Results exercise 5**
investigation (noun) **1 Properties exercise 5**
isolate (verb) **2 Resistance exercise 2**
isolation (noun) **2 Resistance exercise 10**

joint (noun) **2 Resistance exercise 5**
lengthen (verb) **3 Results exercise 5**
lighten (verb) **3 Results exercise 5**
live (adjective) **3 Results exercise 3**
load (noun) **1 Properties exercise 3**
moveable (adjective) **2 Resistance exercise 7**
neutral (adjective) **3 Results exercise 3**
newton (noun) **1 Properties exercise 5**
non-combustible (adjective) **2 Resistance exercise 5**
non-portable (adjective) **2 Resistance exercise 5**
objective (noun) **1 Properties exercise 3**
perishable (adjective) **2 Resistance exercise**
plastic (adjective) **1 Properties exercise 5**
plasticity (noun) **1 Properties exercise 6**
procedure (noun) **1 Properties exercise 4**
resist (verb) **1 Properties exercise 5**
resistant (adjective) **2 Resistance exercise 1**
Richter scale (noun) **3 Results exercise 5**
rigidity (noun) **1 Properties exercise 6**
rivet (noun) **3 Results exercise 6**
rivet head (noun) **3 Results exercise 6**
scratchproof (adjective) **2 Resistance exercise 7**
sharpen (verb) **3 Results exercise 5**
shear wall (noun) **2 Resistance exercise 5**
shearing (noun) **1 Properties exercise 1**
shock (noun) **3 Results exercise 1**
shorten (verb) **3 Results exercise 5**
since (phrase) **3 Results exercise 3**
single brace (noun) **2 Resistance exercise 5**
slag (noun) **3 Results exercise 6**
soften (verb) **3 Results exercise 5**
specified (adjective) **1 Properties exercise 3**
straighten (verb) **3 Results exercise 5**
strengthen (verb) **2 Resistance exercise 2**
tensile (adjective) **1 Properties exercise 6**
tensile strength (noun) **1 Properties exercise 3**
tension (noun) **1 Properties exercise 1**
therefore (phrase) **3 Results exercise 3**
torsion (noun) **1 Properties exercise 1**
truss (noun) **2 Resistance exercise 5**
unbreakable (adjective) **2 Resistance exercise 5**
unmoveable (adjective) **2 Resistance exercise 5**
waterproof (adjective) **2 Resistance exercise 5**
weaken (verb) **3 Results exercise 5**
widen (verb) **3 Results exercise 5**
withstand (verb) **1 Properties exercise 5**
yield point (noun) **1 Properties exercise 3**

Word list

advantage (noun) **1 Working robots exercise 6**
ambitious (adjective) **1 Working robots exercise**
arguably (adverb) **2 Eco-friendly planes exercise**
atmosphere (noun) **2 Eco-friendly planes exercise 3**
automatic (adjective) **1 Working robots exercise**
balloon (noun) **3 Free-flying sails exercise 2**
bookmark (noun) **3 Free-flying sails exercise 5**
bow (noun) **3 Free-flying sails exercise**
capsule (noun) **3 Free-flying sails exercise 2**
cargo (noun) **3 Free-flying sails exercise 2**
click wheel (noun) **3 Free-flying sails exercise 5**
client ship (noun) **3 Free-flying sails exercise 2**
combine (verb) **2 Eco-friendly planes exercise 2**
compact (adjective) **1 Working robots exercise**
conduct (verb) **1 Working robots exercise 8**
consume (verb) **2 Eco-friendly planes exercise 2**
consumption (noun) **2 Eco-friendly planes exercise 2**
convention (noun) **1 Working robots exercise 4**
cruise control (noun) **3 Free-flying sails exercise**
current (adjective) **2 Eco-friendly planes exercise 3**
curved (adjective) **2 Eco-friendly planes exercise 2**
data (noun) **3 Free-flying sails exercise 2**
design brief (noun) **2 Eco-friendly planes exercise 3**
diesel oil (noun) **3 Free-flying sails exercise 2**
disadvantage (noun) **1 Working robots exercise 6**
drag (noun) **2 Eco-friendly planes exercise 1**
drawback (noun) **1 Working robots exercise 6**
eco-friendly (adjective) **2 Eco-friendly planes exercise 2**
emit (verb) **2 Eco-friendly planes exercise 3**
environment (noun) **2 Eco-friendly planes exercise 2**
environmental (adjective) **2 Eco-friendly planes exercise 3**
expel (verb) **2 Eco-friendly planes exercise 2**
frequency (noun) **1 Working robots exercise 8**
friction (noun) **2 Eco-friendly planes exercise 1**
fuselage (noun) **2 Eco-friendly planes exercise 2**
girder (noun) **1 Working robots exercise 6**
gravity (noun) **2 Eco-friendly planes exercise 1**
greenhouse gas (noun) **2 Eco-friendly planes exercise 3**
helium (noun) **3 Free-flying sails exercise 2**
horse power (hp) (noun) **3 Free-flying sails exercise 2**
improve (verb) **1 Working robots exercise 6**
industrial (adjective) **1 Working robots exercise 4**
issue (noun) **2 Eco-friendly planes exercise 3**
jack (noun) **3 Free-flying sails exercise 5**
jet turbine (noun) **2 Eco-friendly planes exercise 2**
lampshade (noun) **2 Eco-friendly planes exercise 2**
leather (adjective) **3 Free-flying sails exercise 5**

lift (noun) **2 Eco-friendly planes exercise 1**
living quarters (noun) **3 Free-flying sails exercise**
majority (noun) **1 Working robots exercise 2**
mast (noun) **3 Free-flying sails exercise 2**
maximise (verb) **3 Free-flying sails exercise**
mention (verb) **3 Free-flying sails exercise 3**
mooring bit (noun) **3 Free-flying sails exercise**
multi-functional (adjective) **3 Free-flying sails exercise 5**
multi-touch (adjective) **3 Free-flying sails exercise 5**
navigational (adjective) **1 Working robots exercise**
noise level (noun) **2 Eco-friendly planes exercise 3**
noisy (adjective) **1 Working robots exercise**
non-renewable (adjective) **2 Eco-friendly planes exercise 3**
participant (noun) **1 Working robots exercise 4**
perform (verb) **2 Eco-friendly planes exercise 2**
permanently (adverb) **3 Free-flying sails exercise 2**
pollution (noun) **2 Eco-friendly planes exercise 3**
polymer (noun) **3 Free-flying sails exercise 5**
pressure-resistant (adjective) **2 Eco-friendly planes exercise 3**
propose (verb) **3 Free-flying sails exercise**
QWERTY keyboard (noun) **3 Free-flying sails exercise 5**
reduce (verb) **2 Eco-friendly planes exercise 2**
resource (noun) **2 Eco-friendly planes exercise 3**
routing (noun) **3 Free-flying sails exercise**
scroll (verb) **3 Free-flying sails exercise 5**
smoothly (adverb) **2 Eco-friendly planes exercise 2**
stability (noun) **3 Free-flying sails exercise**
stainless steel (noun) **3 Free-flying sails exercise 5**
strut (noun) **2 Eco-friendly planes exercise 2**
suggest (verb) **1 Working robots exercise 5**
supertanker (noun) **3 Free-flying sails exercise 2**
survey (noun) **1 Working robots exercise 5**
taper (verb) **2 Eco-friendly planes exercise 2**
technically (adverb) **2 Eco-friendly planes exercise**
technology (noun) 2 **Eco-friendly planes exercise 2**
thrust (noun) 2 **Eco-friendly planes exercise 1**
touchscreen (noun) 3 **Free-flying sails exercise 5**
traction kite (noun) 3 **Free-flying sails exercise 2**
trigger (verb) 2 **Eco-friendly planes exercise**
trimming (noun) 3 **Free-flying sails exercise**
TV remote (noun) **1 Working robots exercise 7**
untie (verb) **3 Free-flying sails exercise 2**
upwards (adverb) **2 Eco-friendly planes exercise 2**
USB connector (noun) **3 Free-flying sails exercise 5**
USB port (noun) **3 Free-flying sails exercise 5**
voice-activated (adjective) **1 Working robots exercise 6**

voicemail (noun) **3 Free-flying sails exercise 5**

weakness (noun) **1 Working robots exercise 5**

wingspan (noun) **2 Eco-friendly planes exercise 3**

wingtip (noun) **2 Eco-friendly planes exercise 2**

Unit 12

abacus (noun) **2 Technological change exercise 4**

accelerate (verb) **1 Zero emission exercise 8**

accurate (adjective) **2 Technological change exercise 4**

air conditioner (noun) **1 Zero emission exercise 8**

align (noun) **2 Technological change exercise 4**

ancestor (noun) **2 Technological change exercise 4**

automotive (adjective) **3 Vehicle safety exercise 6**

axe (noun) **2 Technological change exercise 4**

balance scales (noun) **2 Technological change exercise 4**

bead (noun) **2 Technological change exercise 4**

calculation (noun) **2 Technological change exercise 4**

cam and follower (noun) **2 Technological change exercise 5**

capacitor (noun) **1 Zero emission exercise 3**

career (noun) **3 Vehicle safety exercise 6**

cart (noun) **2 Technological change exercise 4**

compass (noun) **2 Technological change exercise 4**

compressed (adjective) **1 Zero emission exercise 8**

copper (noun) **2 Technological change exercise 4**

craft (verb) **2 Technological change exercise 4**

craftsman (noun) **2 Technological change exercise 4**

crank and rod (noun) **2 Technological change exercise 5**

cruise (verb) **1 Zero emission exercise 8**

deceleration (noun) **1 Zero emission exercise 8**

derrick (noun) **2 Technological change exercise 7**

diploma (noun) **3 Vehicle safety exercise 6**

drill bit (noun) **2 Technological change exercise 7**

drill string (noun) **2 Technological change exercise 7**

fact sheet (noun) **3 Vehicle safety exercise 7**

fibre-optic cable (noun) **2 Technological change exercise 7**

flint (noun) **2 Technological change exercise 4**

focus (verb) **2 Technological change exercise 7**

fossil fuel (noun) **1 Zero emission exercise 8**

fuel cell (noun) **1 Zero emission exercise 3**

gain (verb) **3 Vehicle safety exercise 6**

gear (noun) **2 Technological change exercise 5**

harness (noun) **2 Technological change exercise 4**

harvest (verb) **2 Technological change exercise 4**

hydraulic jack (noun) **2 Technological change exercise 1**

idle (verb) **1 Zero emission exercise 7**

irrigation (noun) **2 Technological change exercise 8**

invention (noun) **3 Vehicle safety exercise 4**

inventor (noun) **3 Vehicle safety exercise 4**

journalist (noun) **3 Vehicle safety exercise 3**

laser (noun) **2 Technological change exercise 7**

lens (noun) **2 Technological change exercise 4**

lever (noun) **2 Technological change exercise 1**

lightweight (adjective) **1 Zero emission exercise 8**

luggage space (noun) **1 Zero emission exercise 8**

magnetic (adjective) **2 Technological change exercise 4**

magnetic pole (noun) **2 Technological change exercise 4**

mallet (noun) **2 Technological change exercise 4**

manufacture (noun) **2 Technological change exercise 4**

mass-produced (adjective) **2 Technological change exercise 4**

mathematical (adjective) **2 Technological change exercise 4**

methane (noun) **1 Zero emission exercise 8**

mining (noun) **2 Technological change exercise 8**

navigate (verb) **2 Technological change exercise 4**

nitrous oxide (noun) **1 Zero emission exercise 8**

output (noun) **1 Zero emission exercise 7**

pan (noun) **2 Technological change exercise 4**

pencil (noun) **2 Technological change exercise 4**

percussion drilling (noun) **2 Technological change exercise 7**

position (verb) **1 Zero emission exercise 8**

press release (noun) **1 Zero emission exercise 8**

principle (noun) **3 Vehicle safety exercise 4**

productive (adjective) **2 Technological change exercise 4**

pulley (noun) **2 Technological change exercise 1**

pulley and belt (noun) **2 Technological change exercise 1**

pyramid (noun) **2 Technological change exercise 4**

rack and pinion (noun) **2 Technological change exercise 5**

ratchet and pawl (noun) **2 Technological change exercise 5**

recover (verb) **1 Zero emission exercise 8**

release (verb) **1 Zero emission exercise 8**

rotary (adjective) **2 Technological change exercise 7**

rotation (noun) **2 Technological change exercise 7**

screw (noun) **2 Technological change exercise 5**

scythe (noun) **2 Technological change exercise 4**

spectacles (noun) **2 Technological change exercise 4**

split (verb) **2 Technological change exercise 7**

startup (noun) **1 Zero emission exercise 8**

tame (verb) **2 Technological change exercise 4**

torque (noun) **1 Zero emission exercise 8**

tripod (noun) **2 Technological change exercise 7**

ultra-capacitor (noun) **1 Zero emission exercise 7**

wedge (noun) **2 Technological change exercise 5**

wheel and axle (noun) **2 Technological change exercise 5**

windmill (noun) **2 Technological change exercise 1**

zero-emission (noun) **1 Zero emission exercise 1**